WIRED CITIZENSHIP

Wired Citizenship examines the evolving patterns of youth learning and activism in the Middle East and North Africa (MENA). In today's digital age, in which formal schooling often competes with the peer-driven outlets provided by social media, youth all over the globe have forged new models of civic engagement, rewriting the script of what it means to live in a democratic society. As a result, state-society relationships have shifted—never more clearly than in the MENA region, where recent uprisings were spurred by the mobilization of tech-savvy and politicized youth.

Combining original research with a thorough exploration of theories of democracy, communications, and critical pedagogy, this edited collection describes how youth are performing citizenship, innovating systems of learning, and re-imagining the practices of activism in the information age. Recent case studies illustrate the context-specific effects of these revolutionary new forms of learning and social engagement in the MENA region.

Linda Herrera is Associate Professor of Education Policy, Organization and Leadership at the University of Illinois at Urbana-Champaign, USA.

Critical Youth Studies

Series Editor: Greg Dimitriadis

WIRED CITIZENSHIP

Youth Learning and Activism in the Middle East

Edited by Linda Herrera
with Rehab Sakr

Routledge
Taylor & Francis Group

NEW YORK AND LONDON

First published 2014
by Routledge
711 Third Avenue, New York, NY 10017

and by Routledge
2 Park Square, Milton Park, Abingdon, Oxon, OX14 4RN

Routledge is an imprint of the Taylor & Francis Group, an informa business

© 2014 Taylor & Francis

Library of Congress Cataloging-in-Publication Data

Wired citizenship : youth learning and activism in the Middle East /
    edited by Linda Herrera.
        pages cm. — (Critical youth studies)
    Includes bibliographical references and index.
    1. Citizenship—Middle East.   2. Citizenship—Africa, North.
3. Youth—Political activity—Middle East.   4. Youth—Political activity—
Africa, North.   5. Revolutions—Middle East.   6. Revolutions—Africa,
North.   7. Democracy—Middle East.   8. Democracy—Africa, North.
I. Herrera, Linda.
    JQ1758.A92W58 2014
    322.40835′0956—dc23
    2013034869

ISBN: 978-0-415-85393-4 (hbk)
ISBN: 978-0-415-85394-1 (pbk)
ISBN: 978-0-203-74757-5 (ebk)

Typeset in Bembo
by Apex CoVantage, LLC

Printed and bound in the United States of America by Publishers Graphics,
LLC on sustainably sourced paper.

To all people engaged in the noble struggle for human dignity

CONTENTS

SERIES EDITOR INTRODUCTION

Greg Dimitriadis

When *Time Magazine* named "The Protester" the 2011 Person of the Year (*Time Magazine*, 2011), it put a fine point on the global tumult and transition that had marked the previous year. As is well known by now, the Tunisian fruit seller Mohamed Bouazizi set himself on fire in late December 2010 in frustration at his own inability to earn a decent wage and live a life of dignity. His protest highlighted the government's corruption, and the lack of democratic opportunities, and transparency. Soon, the Arab uprisings unfurled, as popular protest spread from Tunisia to Egypt, Libya, Algeria, and Syria, toppling several long-standing autocratic governments.

While taking to the streets to protest injustice was nothing new, the role that social media played in these revolutions was seemingly unique. Many media outlets took to calling the Egyptian revolution a "Facebook Revolution," as they had called the 2009 protests in Iran a "Twitter Revolution." A debate soon developed around the role that social media had, in fact, played in these struggles. In an article entitled "Small change: Why the revolution will not be tweeted," Malcolm Gladwell debunked what he saw as overblown claims that social media had played a pivotal role in these protests by citing a much longer line of social activism. Discussing the civil rights struggle in the US, he wrote, "The events in the early sixties became a civil-rights way that engulfed the South for the rest of the decade—and it happened without e-mail, texting, Facebook or Twitter." Perhaps more ominously, Evgeny Morozov argued in *The net delusion: The dark side of internet freedom* that regimes like that in Iran have used social media to track potential protesters and work towards new forms of social control.

All of this makes Linda Herrera and Rehab Sakr's *Wired Citizenship* such a profoundly important and timely collection of articles. Herrera and Sakr do not uncritically project their hopes, dreams, and fears onto these youth or the media they employ. Rather, they and their contributors unpack in very specific ways the unique affordances of social media and youth as well as the unique issues and challenges they often face. For each chapter that highlights the power of social media to contest unfair social arrangements (as in Egypt), another highlights how such media can solidify them (as in the case of racist groups in Cyprus). Taken together, the volume contests the long-standing dispositions of many scholars in the West to uncritically fantasize about the Middle East and North Africa, a point most obviously underscored by Edward Said's magisterial *Orientalism* of 1978. These scholars—several of whom have lived and worked throughout the region—create a much more nuanced picture of life on the ground through their studies of media.

The implications of this volume have particular importance for educators. As a generation of sociologists of education has made clear, schools play a large role in reproducing ideas about what knowledge is most valuable. Schools have historically played a critical role in reproducing so-called "official knowledge," often by way of high stakes testing (Apple, 2011). Social media is an arena, however, where notions of "what is most valuable" can be struggled over. Technologies like Facebook and Twitter are playing new roles in generating different social formations and promoting social change. Information can now circulate around the world instantaneously and in ways that cannot always be controlled or contained by governments and nation states.

The rapid, worldwide proliferation of new technologies and media forms has opened up important questions about the status of culture and knowledge today— and the ways access to new knowledge through new technologies is disrupting social stratification. New and emergent cultures are developing around the world, blurring the line between "consumer" and "producer" as never before. More and more information is now available across more and more kinds of media platforms, in ways unimaginable even a generation ago. While education has never been more important, core ideas about culture and knowledge and expertise and authority are now being challenged in different ways. The stakes for educators can scarcely be higher—a point made in one way or another on every page of this critically important volume.

References

Apple, M. (1996). *Official knowledge*. New York: Routledge.

Gladwell, M. (2010). Small change: Why the revolution will not be tweeted. *The New Yorker*. Retrieved from www.newyorker.com/reporting/2010/10/04/101004fa_fact_gladwell

Morozov, E. (2011). *The net delusion: The dark side of internet freedom*. New York: Public Affairs.

Said, E. (1979). *Orientalism*. New York: Vintage.

Time Magazine. (December, 2011). 2011 Person of the year: The protester. New York.

FOREWORD

This volume began as Workshop #1 of the 13th Mediterranean Research Meeting of the Robert Schumann Center for Advanced Studies at the European University Institute by the title, "Youth and Citizenship in a Digital Era." During the three days of our lively and often impassioned discussions at Montecatini Terme, we knew that we had valuable and unique material from a highly engaged community of scholars that we should share with a wider audience, hence the conception of this volume.

A feature that makes this volume so unique is that these scholars have not developed their expertise from a distance, but rather through a deep commitment and understanding of the countries and communities under study. Much of the research was conducted for master's and doctoral dissertations for various academic departments including anthropology, sociology, political science, international relations, education policy, and linguistics. The contributors speak the local languages of the countries under study, whether Arabic, Turkish, Persian, French, Pashto, or Greek. Through entering into the life worlds of children and youth, by spending time in their virtual spaces, classrooms, communities, and streets, the authors show how young people are innovating modes of learning, socializing, and doing politics. They also speak to the formidable and daunting challenges youth face as they try to reimagine a new order.

On another point, though we did not initially set out to feature the work of junior female scholars (all the contributors are women with the exception of our dear colleague Amro Ali), this book stands as a testament to the critical, cutting edge, and artful scholarship of women from, and working in, the Middle East, North Africa, southern Europe, and West Asia.

A number of people have shared in the conversations around these chapters and helped the volume come to fruition. Many thanks go to colleagues who have provided valuable comments on the original papers at the workshop: Peter Mayo, Hisham Soliman, Sonali Pahwa, Shimaa El-Sayed Hatab, Alessio Surian, and Hasan Hüseyin Aksoy. Many thanks also go to Maddy Hamlin and Catherine Bernard at Routledge and Helen Eldakrouri for their care in seeing this volume to fruition in a relatively short period of time. We dedicate this book to the young people whose voices, struggles, and dreams resound throughout these pages. May they help us find the way to a more just, ethical, and sustainable global order.

Linda Herrera
Champaign, Illinois

Rehab Sakr
Cairo, Egypt

1

INTRODUCTION

Wired and Revolutionary in the Middle East and North Africa

Linda Herrera and Rehab Sakr

When news surfaced during Tunisia's uprising in December 2010 that Facebook served as the headquarters of the revolution (Pollock, 2011), and that the date for Egypt's 25 January Revolution was set by the Facebook page "We are all Khaled Said" (Kulina Khaled Said) (Herrera, 2013), analysts scrambled to understand what exactly had been emerging online in virtual spaces. It soon transpired that the younger generation had been experiencing novel forms of "wired citizenship" and in the process had been reimagining the very terms of the social contract and rewriting the script of what it means to live in a democratic society.

After Tunisia's uprising the new government attempted to tap into the sensibilities of its young wired citizens by developing "e-government" and "e-citizenship" programs. It opened an online portal where citizens could report incidents of government corruption, and it set up Facebook pages to allow citizens to write their ideas for administrative reforms (Republic of Tunisia, 2012). Citizens could also go online to obtain official documents, register for school, and vote. Similar programs had already been initiated in Morocco, Turkey, and Egypt, largely funded by the United Nations Development Programme (UNDP), the World Bank, and the Organisation for Economic Co-operation and Development (OECD). These programs take a view of digital citizens as "those who use technology frequently, who use technology for political information to fulfill their civic duty, and who use technology at work for economic gain" (Mossberger, Tolbert, & McNeil, 2008, p. 2). It may come as little surprise that with minor exceptions, these programs are less than robust and the people show scant interest in being molded into the government's view of a digital citizen.

E-government is a mere instrumental means to ensure more bureaucratic efficiency, rather than a way for citizens to participate in a genuinely critical and unscripted way with their governments and each other. Citizens in the Middle

East and North Africa (MENA) do not primarily view the internet as a place to obtain services, but as a space to congregate. In contrast to "e-government," people in the region are organically developing their own model of e-democracy. They may go online to express their voice as citizens by way of criticizing the government, occupying virtual spaces, performing e-strikes and e-demonstrations (see Sakr, Chapter 11). They also go online to build right-wing nationalist communities. As Christou and Ioannidou highlight in their chapter, "At the same time as online networking is used for social justice causes on a global scale, the internet is also used by groups that mobilize transnationally in order to connect on a variety of issues, including racist ideology" (Chapter 8). Whatever the people's prerogative, their digital society is a networking society, a place where they meet in virtual spaces to communicate with each other away from the heavy hand of government interference and institutional constraints.

The societies throughout MENA, southern Europe, and western Asia provide an especially compelling vantage point from which to understand the condition of growing up in the digital age and in virtual spaces. This region constitutes a geopolitical hotspot with no dearth of youth triggered popular mobilizations. From Iran's Green Movement, which erupted in 2009 in response to a disputed presidential election, to the Arab uprisings, followed by the anti-austerity demonstrations around southern Europe in 2012, and in the following year the Taksim Square protests in Turkey, young citizens have been challenging the state and the status quo on the streets and in virtual spaces.

The internet penetration rate in the Middle East is 40%. Social media use is increasing at a rapid pace. In 2012 Facebook subscription from the MENA region grew 29% to a total of 44 million users, 77% of whom are in the 16 to 34 age group, and 35% of whom are female. The growth rates for Iraq, Libya, and Qatar are even steeper, at 81%, 86%, and 115% respectively (Socialbakers, 2012). Users of social media gain a Web 2.0 sensibility. They learn that they have a choice to be not merely the recipients of prepackaged information and ideological messages, whether from school textbooks or state media. Through practice they develop ways of being the producers, aggregators, and scrutinizers of content. Living and learning on social media fosters certain virtual citizenship values that are related to these nine core principles of social media, as elaborated by Herrera and Peters, who draw on Bradley's new definition of social media (2010):

1. *Participation: user participation taps mass collaboration.*
2. *Collective wisdom: users 'collect', share and modify user-generated content.*
3. *Transparency: each participant gets to see, "use, reuse, augment, validate, critique and evaluate each other's contributions" (Bradley, 2010) leading to collective self-improvement.*
4. *Decentralization: from "one to many" to "many to many"—interactive anytime, anyplace collaboration independently of other contributors.*
5. *Virtual community: sociality based on "conversations" that are relationship-seeking.*

6. *Design is politics: how a social media site is designed determines how people will use it.*
7. *Emergence: self-organizing social structures, expertise, work processes, content organization and information taxonomies that are not a product of any one person.*
8. *Revisability: social media can be altered, unlike industrial media.*
9. *Ownership: social media are accessible and available at little cost, unlike industrial media that government- or privately owned.*

(Herrera & Peters, 2011, p. 364)[1]

It is no coincidence that in addition to having high and growing rates of connectivity, this region, where up to 70% of the population is under 35, has also been witnessing escalating rates of youth poverty. Decades of structural adjustment, rule by corrupt oligarchies, and neoliberal economic and social policies have hit young citizens hard. Youth unemployment and underemployment rates in MENA and southern Europe are among the highest in the world at roughly 25%. That figure skyrockets in countries experiencing extreme austerity measures in the wake of economic crises, such as in Greece, where youth unemployment reached 64.9% in 2013. In places affected by military conflict and occupation like Palestine, Syria, and Iraq, youth unemployment can exceed 70%. Youth insecurity in the labor market has led the International Labour Organization to characterize this global generation as "a generation at risk" (International Labour Organization, 2013). We argue that the economic situation is much more insidious; it has led to a condition where youth are the new poor.

A major difference between the old disenfranchised and marginalized poor of laborers, peasants, and members of the urban underclasses, and new youthful poor, however, is that youth constitute a highly schooled and tech-savvy cohort. As they work out ways to live outside the system and to construct alternatives, the young devise their own methods and spaces to engage politically. To a greater extent these spaces are online and virtual. The communication tools and virtual platforms on which youth challenge the system and forge alternatives are no "weapons of the weak," to use James Scott's term (1985). These are the tools of commerce, the weapons of power, but they are also the weapons of the people. Generational fault lines are widening at ever-larger proportions as youth use connection tools and virtual spaces to pursue their own trajectories of learning, socializing, working, playing, networking, doing politics, and exercising citizenship.

We are aware that youth do not make up a monolithic and homogeneous category, and that inequality around connectivity, class, gender, region, religion, and any number of areas of difference persists. We argue, nevertheless, that it is valid to conceptualize youth as a generational cohort who carry features of a "wired generation" (Herrera, Chapter 2). Users of digital media seamlessly move between online and offline spaces. They carry virtual attitudes, values, and behaviors to their peers in schools, on streets, and in popular culture. They transform society and social relations in their wake, even among people who do not participate directly in virtual spaces.

The young citizens who have been coming of age on social media have been the instigators of mass mobilizations and revolutions. This observation may seem unremarkable; after all, "Revolutions are the empire of the young," as Simon Schama writes in his magisterial work on the French Revolution, *Citizens* (1989, p. 8). Young and determined citizens who took part in the major revolutions of the last two and a half centuries—from the American, French, Russian, Iranian, and Egyptian revolutions—share a common political genealogy. They have sought emancipation from the institutions of the ruling class, and liberation from the ideological frames by which the oligarchies perpetuate their rule and justify taking the lion's share of wealth and resources.

In the past, revolutionaries cultivated a political culture that tended to glorify violence and justify the purging of what Schama calls "uncitizens." During the many stages of the French Revolution, the youth popular culture was complicit in normalizing the reign of violence:

> While it would be grotesque to implicate the generation of 1789 in the kind of hideous atrocities perpetrated under the Terror, it would be equally naïve not to recognize that the former made the latter possible. All the newspapers, the revolutionary festivals, the painted plates; the songs and street theater; the regiments of little boys waving their right arms in the air swearing patriotic oaths in piping voices—all these features of what historians have come to designate the 'political culture of the Revolution'—were the products of the same morbid preoccupation with the just massacre and the heroic death.
>
> (Schama, 1989, p. 856)

We hypothesize that the political culture of those growing ranks of protesters who make up the backbone of the current uprisings do not seem to be valorizing a dogma of unbridled violence as in past revolutions. This does not mean that violence is absent in the revolting societies. On the contrary, violence has spiraled to devastating depths in Syria, Libya, and Egypt, to name but a few of the countries. However, if one looks closely at the "problem of evil," to borrow a phrase from Hannah Arendt (1945), it is evident that it is being perpetrated by groups from among the Old Order, namely the army, the Muslim Brotherhood, members of the ousted regimes, the police, the US military, and their proxies. The harrowing episodes of torture, killings, kidnapping, mob sexual assaults (in Egypt), bombings—including by drones in Pakistan—are meant to subdue and co-opt peoples' struggles for freedom and thwart their march towards a New Order.

Without romanticizing or homogenizing the multi-faceted culture of this revolutionary generation, it can be observed that growing numbers of youth in the MENA are pursuing a more civil, inclusive, and liberatory form of democracy. Their culture is playing out on the streets and in virtual communities. These are complex spaces where the old dogmas mix and comingle with the new. As the

chapters in this volume attest, youth who make up the political and cultural vanguard often carry both tendencies of liberation and oppression within themselves.
As Ali and El-Sharnouby astutely show in their sensitive investigative portrait of
Khaled Said, the namesake of the path-breaking Facebook page that issued the call
for Egypt's 25 January Revolution, revolutionaries can also be unaware of the ways
in which they reinforce reactionary dogmas around class and culture to the detri-
ment of their own emancipation (Chapter 6). What is certain is that large swaths
of youthful populations are struggling to realize a more just and liberatory form
of democracy, but they have a steep learning curve ahead of them. Pertinent questions to pose at this juncture are: How are concepts and practices of democracy
and citizenship changing in this digital revolutionary age? More importantly, what
do rebelling youth understand by political and social change?

Democracy in the Age of Revolution and Networks

The Algerian-born French philosopher Jacques Rancière is a figure with whom
to think about democracy during times of revolutionary hope and despair. He
came of age during the 1968 student movement, and he looked deep into the
French and American revolutions for ideas about how to achieve emancipatory
democracy. In his book provocatively titled *Hatred of democracy* (2006), Rancière
argues against the normalized conception of representative ballot box democracy
as the gold standard that a society has reached the democracy apex. Ballot box
democracy often—not always—reinforces rule by an elite oligarchy, a group that,
by virtue of their very privilege and position, harbor a deep-seated disdain of the
people's politics. Rancière goes back in history to remind us that representative
government and democracy have not always been conflated. He argues:

> The self-evidence which assimilates democracy to a representative form of
> government resulting from an election is quite recent in history. Originally
> representation was the exact contrary of democracy. None ignored this at the
> time of the French and American revolutions. The Founding Fathers and a
> number of their French emulators saw in it precisely the means for the elite
> to exercise power *de facto,* and to do so in the name of the people that repre-
> sentation is obliged to recognize but that could not exercise power without
> ruining the very principle of government. [. . .] 'Representative democracy'
> might appear today as a pleonasm. But it was initially an oxymoron.
>
> (Rancière, 2006, p. 53)

In the contemporary era participation in campaigning, party politics, and voting
are often used as barometers to gage whether a citizenry is active or passive. Even
when young voters turn out for elections in droves, as in Iran in 2009 or in post-
Mubarak Egypt in 2012, they often quickly get disillusioned by a system they
experience as being rigged or open to manipulation by powerful actors. When

young citizens disengage with the formal political system they face accusations of being apolitical, lazy, and apathetic.

The large-scale withdrawal of young people from formal institutional life can be read as their indictment against the system. Lüküslü argues in her chapter about Turkey that young people are not apathetic; rather they refuse to participate in institutions they do not trust and that do not look out for their interests. In refusing to fulfill the expectations placed on them by the state, they are in fact saying that they "reject the definition of youth as a political category destined to save or advance the state" (Chapter 5). They sometimes need to work within the system, to abide by the rules and logic of the government and its bureaucracy, but they often do this reluctantly, with an attitude Lüküslü calls "necessary conformism." This behavior "hides a real and strong discontent and can mask a profound agony. According to the logic of necessary conformism, young people are only conformist when they believe it to be necessary, but they try to escape being so whenever possible" (Chapter 5).

Sociologist Manual Castells makes a similar point about ways in which politics is leaving the sphere of formal institutions in the age of the network society. He argues, "Distrustful of political institutions, but dedicated to asserting their rights, citizens look for ways of mobilizing within and outside the political system on their own terms. *It is precisely this growing distance between belief in political institutions and desire for political action that constitutes the crisis of democracy*" (italics in original) (Castells, 2010, p. 295). We are evidently living in an age when social movements are changing form—for ill or for good—away from rigid hierarchical structures with strong charismatic leaders, towards alliances by the multitudes who are not constrained by national affiliation and borders (Hardt & Negri, 2005) and the network society (Castells, 2010).

According to Castells, the presence of inter"net" as a new technology leads necessarily to the "net"work as the main unit of social analysis. He presents two related ideas: societies are characterized by a new social structure, the network; and new information and communication technologies (ICTs) are the leading force for creating networks (2010). In *The internet galaxy* (2001), he postulates, "the network society [. . .] is made of networks in all the key dimensions of social organization and social practice" (p. xviii).

For all the plausibility of the network society, its critics fault Castells on a few fronts, starting with technological determinism. Garnham (2004), for example, sees that traditional relations of production between capital and labor still control the global capitalistic economy. Perhaps the flow of capital has changed, but social structures remain the same. Smart (2000) also rejects Castells claims by observing that in our information age, even as new digital tools dominate our activities, it is not really a novelty for technology to be ubiquitous in our lives. The changes brought about by the information-digital age have not canceled out the older, traditional forms of social relations. Both old and new forms of social relations can and do co-exist (Smart, 2000).

It is against the backdrop of a complex and contested media terrain that we try to understand how this wired revolutionary generation negotiates a complex space that is simultaneously public and private, free and restrictive, liberating and repressive. Questions that beg to be asked at this historical junction are: How can wired youth address the pressing needs of a generation that finds itself politically and economically marginalized but digitally empowered? How are the attributes and definitions of what it means to be a citizen—whether expressed in the nation state or as deterritorialized virtual citizenship—changing? What new conceptual tools and empirical understandings are needed to better engage issues of youth citizenship and struggles for democracy in the digital revolutionary age?

To address these questions this volume is organized into two sections. The first, "Virtual Learning for Critical Citizenship," deals more with the learning and citizenship culture of children and youth within discrete nation states. The second, "Internet, Geopolitics, and Redefining the Political," considers how media studies needs to be more cognizant of international politics and the exercise of power, how transnational networks influence national politics, and ways in which citizenship is becoming more globalized.

Section I: Virtual Learning for Critical Citizenship

We begin with a vignette from the streets of Cairo. It is the story of Mohamed, a 12-year-old protester from a poor neighborhood in Cairo. He was randomly interviewed in Tahrir Square in March 2013 for the YouTube channel, Free Arabs, during a demonstration against the then president Mohamed Morsi and his Muslim Brotherhood-dominated government.

The interviewer asked young Mohamed to explain why he was protesting in Tahrir Square and he answered, "I'm here today to help prevent Egypt from becoming a commodity owned by one person. And to protest how one party has taken over the constitution. We didn't get rid of a fascist regime to replace it with a fascist theocracy." Clearly impressed, the interviewer pressed him further to explain his terminology to see if he understood his own words. Without missing a beat Mohamed continued, "a fascist theocracy is when you manipulate religion and enforce extremist regulations in the name of religion even though religion doesn't command it." When asked if his ideas came from Al Azhar, the seat of Islamic learning, he replied that they did not and proceeded to explain how he forms his political opinions: "I listen to people a lot and I use my own brain. Plus I read newspapers, watch TV and search the internet." Mohamed's interview was posted to YouTube and within four months it accumulated over 3.5 million hits. His voice and ideas found their way into a much wider public conversation.

The chapters in this section grapple with emerging forms of emancipation within a context of a radically changing children and youth culture in the region. They deal with generational change in the digital age (Herrera, Chapter 2), students' decolonization of knowledge through virtual spaces (Boutieri, Chapter 3), the awakening of Egyptian children's citizenship in times of revolution (Diana, Chapter 4), ways that cyberspace serves as a platform for Turkish youth to express their discontent and suffering in ways that differ from conventional modes of resistance (Lüküslü, Chapter 5), and the need for online youth activism to refrain from idealizing youth and instead tackle their condition, their flaws, and confusion in more honest and holistic ways (Ali and El-Sharnouby, Chapter 6).

In her chapter on children in revolutionary Egypt, Diana shines a spotlight on this demographic group who are usually overlooked, presumed to be too young to really understand or make a difference. By drawing on the new social studies of childhood as the theoretical framework, her chapter situates children as social actors who have found a political voice through street mobilizations, school initiatives, and online communities. As she discovers, "The revolutionary context, combined with technological social media, has given children the opportunity to explore 'adult' aspects of life such as politics, and instill some concepts and ideas necessary to build a political consciousness and citizenship values" (Chapter 4).

Children and youth make up a rising generation that takes pride in being independent minded, discerning, and able to process and critically analyze a wealth of information to arrive at an informed opinion. These values are not remotely connected to the school-based learning where the education system continues to instill discipline and obedience to the young through an oppressive hierarchical system (Diana, Chapter 4), and where governments adopt educational polices that promote a "consumerist and entrepreneurial model of citizenship" (Boutieri, Chapter 3). By design, schools perpetuate "the order of things" as Rancière reminds us in *The ignorant schoolmaster: Five lessons in intellectual emancipation* (1991). But in times of upheaval, the system experiences deep cracks and people understand that they need to emancipate their minds from the mental frames of the Old Order.

Emancipatory learning is not a top-down process that takes place when an older master enlightens a younger learner. Rather, it flourishes when students and masters become peers in an environment where "every common person might conceive his human dignity, take the measure of his intellectual capacity, and decide how to use it" (Rancière, 1991, pp. xvii, 17). Rancière captures the spirit and principle of intellectual emancipation plainly when he writes:

> Whoever teaches without emancipating stultifies. And whoever emancipates doesn't have to worry about what the emancipated person learns. He will learn what he wants, nothing maybe. He will know he can learn because the same intelligence is at work in all the productions of the human mind, and a man can always understand another man's words.
>
> (1991, p. 18)

As chapters in this section attest, the relationship between the state, its institutions, and its young citizens is not merely on shifting ground, it is on a collision course. In growing proportions, children and youth have lost faith in the rhetoric about their being the pillars of the nation, and the hope for the future. They understand their governments as entities that exert little effort to protect, nurture, and listen to them, and that go to great lengths to contain, control, and persecute them. In the worst case scenario youth despair translates tragically to suicide. Growing numbers of students who are unable to cope with the pressure of the exams and perceived hopelessness (Chapter 5) are taking their own lives, including by self-immolations outside of the Ministry of Education, as happened in Morocco (Chapter 3). Despite these acts of desperation, most disenchanted youth are devising ways to fight the system and construct alternative spaces for congregating, learning, and deliberating.

In her subtle and insightful ethnography of the social media behavior of Moroccan students, Boutieri uses the term "on-trial" instead of "online" to allude to how Moroccan students perform an indictment of the education system. She quotes a student as saying, "The internet is a better school, I'm telling you!" Boutieri observes, "Cyberspace constitutes a central site where students raise the issue of the rudimentary nature of Moroccan decolonization in learning, and shape creative alternatives for moving forward." Their online activities constitute a form of activism, but not in the conventional sense of political movement building. She proposes a redefinition of activism to release the term "from the binds of normative political behavior and expand to encompass a plethora of endeavors to critique and request change" (Chapter 3). Christou and Ioannidou make a similar observation about how schools and virtual platforms are competing spaces for the cultivation of the self. They perceptively argue, "The virtual self is formed through a process in which the public and private spheres are not separate, but are in fact conflated in a 'space' that is at once virtual, physical, and social" (Chapter 8).

For all the ways virtual spaces can foster and create inclusive and utopian communities, they can also be the purveyors of a culture of intolerance. In their thought-provoking investigative piece on Khaled Said, Ali and El-Sharnouby show how the youth movement that grew around this figure ultimately harmed the cause of the revolution by whitewashing the life of Khaled Said. They extrapolate from the Khaled Said movement to the problem of sexual harassment. They write,

> the discourse around sexual harassment often suffers from some of the same societal denial that distorted the life of Khaled Said and made his martyrdom conditional upon him being a saint. This form of denial about "ourselves" as a society reinforces the syndrome of victim-blaming. A woman is blamed if she is harassed; she is accused of wearing "unsuitable clothing" or choosing to go to "the wrong place at the wrong time," just as a youth who takes drugs is perceived to deserve what he gets from the police.
>
> (Chapter 6)

These moments of revolutionary reflection provide the opportunity to apply Rancière's radical proposition that equality, not inequality, should be our point of departure

(1991, p. 138). Children, women, the poor, delinquents, activists, and ordinary students all contribute to, and can be transformed by, a liberatory education. The aim of a truly emancipatory education is to "raise up those who believe themselves inferior in intelligence, to make them leave the swamp where they are stagnating—not the swamp of ignorance, but the swamp of self-contempt, of contempt *in and of itself* for the reasonable creature. It is to make emancipated and emancipating men" (Rancière 1991, pp. 101–102).

Section II: Internet, Geopolitics, and Redefining the Political

The internet allows for a redefining of citizenship in a deterritorialized way and provides a space where issue-centered and diaspora communities congregate and bypass traditional sovereign boundaries. Although digital deterritorialization is considered in many studies a result of globalization, deterritorialization does not always refer to creating cross-border (regional/global) communities. In some cases, it may also refer to establishing stronger ties among communities living within national borders. The specific examples of deterritorialization we present here include the Palestinian online solidarity campaigns around prisoner hunger strikes (Nabulsi, Chapter 7), the diasporic identity politics of a Greek right-wing group in Cyprus (Christou & Ioannidou, Chapter 8), the pan-Arab community of independent artists (Cornet, Chapter 9), the global proponents for girls' education in Pakistan who rose out of an age of internet and drones (Rahman, Chapter 10), the network of Muslim Brotherhood media activists online (Sakr, Chapter 11), and communities living in surveillance societies in Iran and beyond (Bajoghli, Chapter 12).

We approach this section cognizant of the fact that digital technology does not necessarily change social structures, social values, and social relations, or at least change them in ways that threaten structures of power. This is to say that traditional social relations can also be reinforced though digital media as powerful actors learn to influence and infiltrate the new communication spaces. Studies of Egyptian virtual spaces reveal that Web 2.0 applications are not used for horizontal networking and for breaking hierarches alone, but are also manipulated by powerful organized groups like the military, the Muslim Brotherhood, and the US State Department to reinforce hierarchies and spread the messages and ideology of power (Herrera, 2014; Herrera and Lotfy, 2012; Sakr, Chapter 11). This is not to mention the immense capacity governments have for surveillance over their citizens who use digital media, something Iranians learned to devastating effect during the Green Movement. Bajoghli sagely cautions, "The very qualities that make new media so attractive to people seeking change from below also make them an ideal means of surveillance and manipulation from above" (Chapter 12).

In her compelling chapter about the young blogger and advocate for girls' education in Pakistan, Malala Yousafzai, Fauzia Rahman takes the questions about internet and emancipation in another direction. She asks pertinent questions about how in reality policies around digital citizenship can help young people to overcome the immense obstacles of war, poverty, and oppression. Can blogging and online organizing lead to advancing girls' education in a region like Pakistan's Swat Valley that is under the devastating scourge of both the Taliban and the US drone war (Chapter 10)?

These observations from Egypt, Iran, and Pakistan demonstrate the importance of testing theories about communications, social media, and democratization through a framework that incorporates geopolitics and attention to people living far from the centers where the technologies were created. Evaluating network society and technological innovation through a prism of the people and politics of the wider MENA region allows us to unpack some of the ideological biases embedded in the theories and to better understand the unintended results of technology. The tools of technology have hidden features that are outside prediction. The same technology can have entirely different outcomes in different places, depending on how people use it and apply it. As Christou and Ioannidou put forward in their cogent exposé of a right-wing nationalist group that propagates racism through its online portals, it is imperative to gain "an understanding of *how* globalizing forces such as the internet produce subjectivities" (Chapter 8).

We keep in mind the MENA prism as we return to the prevailing ideas about networks, digital media, and democracy. At the risk of oversimplification, the literature has been polarized along two ideological trajectories that can be categorized as "mainstream" and "critical." The more prevalent "mainstream" approach reinforces a standard narrative of democracy as tied to liberal conceptions of political participation, rights, the public sphere, and voting. Such analyses rise from a decidedly North American vantage point and are rooted in an ideological position—whether acknowledged or not—in favor of the perpetuation of the existing economic and political order. This strand of thought also supports, in overt and subtle ways, American power.

This mainstream track is represented in the writings of the so-called "techno optimists" or "techno utopians" of which Clay Shirky is a leading figure. He does not suggest that there exists a simple causal relationship between connectivity, digital media, and democratization. His work is layered with nuance about the potentially contrary effects and outcomes of communications technologies. However, when it comes to analyzing how people in authoritarian societies outside the global North use digital media to try to emancipate themselves from a repressive and exploitative system, his analysis becomes decontextualized to fit conceptual frames about liberal democracy and, we argue, American power.

For instance, in an influential article he wrote for *Foreign Affairs* by the title, "The political power of social media," Shirky is critical of the instrumentalist ways the US State Department pursues its policy of Internet Freedom. He offers an alternative "environmental view," which he explains as follows:

> Despite this basic truth—that communicative freedom is good for political freedom—the instrumental mode of Internet statecraft is still problematic. It

is difficult for outsiders to understand the local conditions of dissent. External support runs the risk of tainting even peaceful opposition as being directed by foreign elements. [. . .]. The more promising way to think about social media is as long-term tools that can strengthen civil society and the public sphere. In contrast to the instrumental view of Internet freedom, this can be called the "environmental" view. According to this conception, positive changes in the life of a country, including pro-democratic regime change, follow, rather than precede, the development of a strong public sphere.

There are two strands by which we will show political bias in Shirky's position, the first having to do with his use of public sphere. Embedded within his language are unexamined presumptions about the nature of democracy as being grounded in normative conceptions of civil society and the public sphere (Habermas, 1991), in ways that would align with American interests. He uses the notion in a generic way, as if the concept as applied to Western liberal democracies can be wholesale applied to other societies across time and place. In her chapter on Palestine, Nabulsi complicates the normative uses of public sphere and democracy in relation to Palestine. She writes, "It becomes particularly hard to talk about a single, location specific, public sphere, especially after the Oslo Accords in 1993 which gave rise to separate authorities in the West Bank and Gaza, and no representation for those in the diaspora. Thus, issues of representation, democratization and the practice of citizenship necessitate differing frameworks because of the fragmentation of people and land, as well as the transnational aspect of the Palestinian cause and movement" (Chapter 7).

The second point pertains to Shirky's affinity to the US State Department's policy position on the internet and democracy. On the surface Shirky appears to be proposing a position distinct from that of the State Department, but on closer examination he is actually reinforcing it. His use of the term "pro-democratic regime change" especially triggers to the reader that he is heavily steeped in the worldview of the US empire, which uses precisely this discourse to justify its intervention—by soft power and militarized hard power—in the lands and among the people of the region. The terms "pro-democracy" and "regime change" carry especially strong associations with the US-led war in Iraq in 2003, a war preemptively waged on the false pretext that the country harbored weapons of mass destruction.

The pro-US empire position is far more explicit in the book *The new digital age* (2013) by Google authors Eric Schmidt and Jared Cohen (formerly of the State Department). The authors continuously chastise Iran and China for not supporting a free and transparent internet, but do not problematize the growing surveillance regime in the United States with the government's own National Security Agency (NSA) (though it must be noted that the revelations about NSA came to be public knowledge after their book was published). Neither do Schmidt and Cohen attempt to explain or tackle how Google, Facebook, and other companies work in decidedly non-transparent ways with the US government, and have, for all intents and purposes, become political powerhouses in their own rights. As one author who looks at the intimate connections between the US tech industry and Washington DC notes, "The line between social media companies and intelligence agencies is becoming increasingly blurred, especially now that the government is recruiting directly from Silicon Valley" (Greig, 2013). Perhaps most confounding is how the authors conflate the corporate imperative of growing consumer markets with spreading democracy. They essentially argue that since American technology companies (like Google) supposedly transmit democratic values of openness and accountability with their products, it is preferable for their companies rather than their competitors in other countries to deliver services globally (Schmidt & Cohen, 2013, p. 112).[2]

These prevailing voices about digital media and democratization suffer from a major bias insofar as they do not attempt to take the people of the region on their own terms. Rather, they squeeze the people and their struggles into prefabricated frameworks about politics, democracy, and the current world order.

Let us take, for instance, how ingenious youth activists from Palestine have displayed high degrees of virtual astuteness as they find ways to influence the big powers. As Nabulsi documents, they "have been able to influence, if not construct, the language used by organizations like the UN and Amnesty International. This is an indicator of who is running the online media battle, and it shows that individual activists or grassroots collectives are able to influence international bodies in a bottom-up way that challenges the official Israeli propaganda machine" (Chapter 7).

Arab artists working through digital media also have much to teach us about the democratization of art and business. Arab artists have been the architects of an artistic renaissance in the MENA dating to about a decade before the Arab uprisings. Cornet shows how, through innovative and intimate use of new digital tools, art production and consumption in the region have undergone a process of genuine democratization and changed state–society relationships vis-à-vis youth citizenship. She writes, "these artists are not directly engaging in politics in the classic sense of mobilizing in the public sphere. But they are definitely developing a new cultural stratus, where freedom of expression has acquired more weight. Their political impact is difficult to ascertain since it is largely atomized" (Chapter 9). It takes patient, conscientious, and critical research to understand how people are changing society and the directions in which they want to take it.

The jury is still out as to whether recent youth-triggered and partially virtually mobilized uprisings will help the cause of increased democracy, justice, and equity, or whether they might precipitate their further demise. On a global level, the region represents a laboratory for testing the role of wired citizens in reshaping democratic thinking and practice. These diverse portraits of youth compel us to rethink traditional categories of "active" versus "passive" and to recognize how virtual spaces are allowing young people to congregate, interact, and dream outside adult supervision and the adult gaze.

We close with the wise words of a young Arab activist, Omar Robert Hamilton, about the people:

> The people are the great unknown. The people have spent two and a half years talking about little else other than politics. So is it too much to ask for commentators, writing in English, to stop telling us "how democracy works?" Because, from where we're standing, the fire sale of Greece, the bailouts of the banks, the titanic advertising budgets of electoral candidates, the Tory Old Boy's Club government and the invisible muscle of the lobbies are just a few hints that no one's democracy is working properly. [. . .] There is not a fair and functional system anywhere in the world. At least Egypt's is in flux and her governments are trembling. And as long as the people believe they don't have to accept their reality, as long as they believe that their future has not been decided for them, then something new is possible.
>
> (2013)

Notes

1. Social media can be distinguished from other forms of collaboration and communication. Herrera and Peters draw on Bradley's new definition of social media (2010) to make up these nine core principles. In his blog, Bradley identifies six characteristics of social media: participation, collective, transparency, independence, persistence, and emergence (2010).
2. Technology writer Evgeny Morozov provides a persuasive corrective to the idea that US tech companies are outside the sphere of power when he writes in his characteristically provocative manner, "Democratic and authoritarian states alike are now seeking 'information sovereignty' from American companies, especially those perceived as being in bed with the U.S. government. Internet search, social networking, and even email are increasingly seen as strategic industries that need to be protected from foreign control" (Morozov, 2011).

References

Arendt, H. (1945). Nightmare and flight. *Partisan Review,* 12(2). Reprinted in (1994) J. Kohn (Ed.), *Essays in understanding 1930–1954* (133–135). New York: Harcourt, Brace & Co.

Bedair, S. (2009). *Improving take up e-government services: Challenges Egypt experience 2009.* Ministry of the State of Administrative Development. Retrieved May 10, 2013 from www.oecd.org/dataoecd/25/62/36975584.pdf

Bradley. A. (2010, January 7). A new definition of social media. Blog accessed from http://blogs.gartner.com/anthony_bradley/2010/01/07/a-new-definition-of-social-media/

Castells, M. (2001). *The internet galaxy: Reflections on internet, business and society.* Oxford: Oxford University Press.

Castells, M. (2010). *The rise of network society: Volume 1,* 2nd edition. Oxford: Wiley Blackwell.

Christensen, C. (2011). Discourses on technology and liberation: State aid to net activists in an era of "Twitter Revolutions." *The Communication Review,* 14(3), 233–253.

Garnham, N. (2004). Information society theory as ideology. In F. Webster (Ed.), *The Information Society Reader.* New York: Routledge.

Gellman, B. & Poitras, L. (2013, June 6). U.S., British intelligence mining data from nine U.S. internet companies in broad secret program. *Washington Post*. Retrieved from http:// wapo.st/1888aNr

Greig, A. (2013, June 23). Former Facebook security chief is now working for the NSA. *MailOnline*. Retrieved from www.dailymail.co.uk/news/article-2347047/Former-Facebook-security-chief-working-NSA.html#ixzz2c5oMWSTC

Habermas, J. (1991). *The structural transformation of the public sphere: An inquiry into a category of bourgeois society*. T. Burger & F. Lawrence (Trans.). Cambridge MA: Massachusetts Institute of Technology Press.

Hamilton, O. R. (2013, July 10). Selective memories. *Mada*. Retrieved from www.madamasr. com/content/selective-memories

Hardt, A. & Negri, A. (2005). *Multitude: War and democracy in the age of empire*. New York: Penguin.

Herrera, L. (2013). Egypt's revolution 2.0: The Facebook factor reprinted. In A. Iskandar & B. Haddad (Eds.), *Mediating the Arab uprisings* (47–53). Washington DC: Tadween Publishing.

Herrera, L. (2014). *Revolution in the age of social media: People vs. power in Egypt*. New York and London: Verso.

Herrera, L. & Lotfy, M. (2012, September 5). E-Militias of the Muslim Brotherhood: How to upload ideology on Facebook. *Jadaliyya*. Retrieved from http://bit.ly/Q7vGB3

Herrera, L. & Peters, M. (2011). The educational and political significance of the new social media: A dialogue with Linda Herrera and Michael A. Peters. *E-Learning and Digital Media*, 8(4), 364–374.

International Labour Organization (2013). *Global employment trends for youth 2013: A generation at risk*. Geneva: International Labour Office.

Kingdom of Morocco, Ministry of Industry, Trade and New Technologies. (2013). *Digital Morocco 2013*. Retrieved May 12, 2013 from www.egov.ma/SiteCollectionDocuments/ Morocco%20Digital.pdf

McMurray, D. & Ufheil-Somers, A. (Eds.). (2012). *The Arab revolt: Dispatches on militant democracy in the Middle East*. Bloomington, IN: Indiana University Press.

Morozov, E. (2011, January/February). Freedom.gov: Why Washington's support for online democracy is the worst thing ever to happen to the Internet. *Foreign Policy*. Retrieved from www.foreignpolicy.com/articles/2011/01/02/freedomgov

Mossberger, K., Tolbert, C. J. & McNeil, R. S. (2008). *Digital citizenship: The internet, society, and participation*. Cambridge MA & London: Massachusetts Institute of Technology Press.

Pollock, J. (2011, August 23). Streetbook: How Egyptian and Tunisian youth hacked the Arab Spring. *MIT Technology Review*. Retrieved from www.technologyreview.com/ featuredstory/425137/streetbook/

Rancière, J. (1991). *The ignorant schoolmaster: Five lessons in intellectual emancipation*. Stanford: Stanford University Press.

Rancière, J. (2006). *Hatred of democracy*. New York: Verso.

Republic of Tunisia, Presidency of the Government. (2012). *Tunisian e-Government report*. Retrieved May 9, 2013 from unpan1.un.org/intradoc/groups/public/documents/ un.../unpan049915.pdf

Schama, S. (1989). *Citizens: A chronicle of the French revolution*. New York: Vintage Books.

Schmidt, E. & Cohen, J. (2013). *The new digital age: Reshaping the future of people, nations and business*. New York: Alfred A. Knopf.

Scott, J. (1985). *Weapons of the weak: Everyday forms of peasant resistance*. New Haven: Yale University Press.

Shirky, C. (2009). *Here comes everybody: How change happens when people come together.* London: Penguin.

Shirky, C. (2011, January/February). The political power of social media: Technology, the public sphere and political change. *Foreign Affairs.* Retrieved from www.cc.gatech.edu/~beki/cs4001/Shirky.pdf

Smart, B. (2000). A political economy of new times? Critical reflections on the network society and the ethos of informational capitalism. *European Journal of Social Theory, 3*(1), 51–65.

Socialbakers. (2012). Facebook in the Middle East and North Africa. Retrieved from www.socialbakers.com/blog/1100-facebook-in-the-middle-east-and-north-africa-infographic

Turkish Ministry of the Interior (2009). *The central civil registration system.* Retrieved Jan 19, 2012 from www.nvi.gov.tr/English/Mernis_EN,Mernis_En.html

Webster, F. & Blom, R. (2004). *The information society reader.* London: Routledge.

SECTION I

Virtual Learning for Critical Citizenship

2

YOUTH AND CITIZENSHIP IN THE DIGITAL AGE

A View from Egypt[1]

Linda Herrera

In late December 2011 education bureaus throughout Egypt dispatched year-end exams to schools in their districts. This was no business-as-usual year. Rather, the country had experienced the most momentous prodemocracy event in more than half a century—the January 25 Revolution, which lasted 18 days and led to the fall of 30-year dictator and president Mohamed Hosni Mubarak on February 11, 2011. Students carried the spirit of revolution back to their schools and universities. They led sit-ins, demonstrations, and Facebook campaigns to expose corrupt teachers and administrators; they demanded reforms of the curriculum and exam system; they set up drives to help the families of the martyrs of the revolution. In the wake of these events, many expected the government-administered annual exams to provide an opportunity for pupils to write about some aspect of these democratic changes stirring in the country that they themselves had been so instrumental in sparking. But the Arabic exam for first-year high-school students represented a conspicuously prerevolution approach to education. The one compulsory essay on an exam from the northern province of Gharbia read as follows: "Write a letter to the Supreme Council of the Armed Forces (SCAF) thanking them for supporting the revolution. Thank SCAF also for their steadfastness in protecting the nation from all the agents despite being opposed and insulted."[2]

SCAF, the temporary caretaker government composed of 21 high-ranking military officers, had been ruling the country with an iron fist since Mubarak's fall and was the object of much civil protest. The exam question signaled that the "new" ruling regime carried the mindset of the old one. It continued to equate citizenship building with obedience to authority and treated schools as hierarchical, nonconsultative, and highly controlled institutions—as if no revolution had ever taken place.

But wired students of this generation had their own ideas about their place in the nation and had been experimenting with ways of exercising citizenship and agitating for a more democratic system. Pupils used the occasion of the exam to bite back at the system. Someone made a scan of the exam question and posted it on Facebook, where it circulated among different networks. This Facebook post generated numerous comments and lively debates about the performance of SCAF, and the pros and cons of further revolt. This incident illustrates in a small but telling way how the rifts between the pedagogic spaces of formal institutions and those of youth-driven communication spaces have been widening. The concern here is with how students and graduates learn and communicate across lines of difference and, in the process, assert their will on society and its institutions.

Wired Generation

Compared to previous generations, youth coming of age in the digital era are learning and exercising citizenship in fundamentally different ways. Around the globe, a monumental generational rupture is taking place that is being facilitated—not driven in some inevitable and teleological process—by new media and communication technologies. A body of literature on generations dating to the late 1990s draws directly on communication and information technologies for naming this generation, an affirmation of how generational change and technological change are perceived as intricately connected in this era. In addition to Millennials and Gen Y, other terms for this generational cohort include: the Net Generation (Tapscott, 1998, 2009); the E-Generation (Krause, 2007); the iGeneration (Rosen, 2010); digital natives (Palfrey & Gasser, 2008); Generation txt (Rafael, 2003; Nielsen & Webb, 2011); the Facebook, Twitter, and Google Generation (McDonald, 2010; Rideout, Foehr, & Roberts, 2010); and Generation 2.0 (Rigby, 2008). I prefer *wired generation,* for it captures how communication behavior in this high-tech era leads to a "rewiring" of users' cognitive makeup, which changes their relationship to political and social systems and their notion of themselves as citizens. As youth activist and scholar Aly El Raggal explains:

> Revolutions take place first of all in our minds. The new cognitive maps we develop lead to new outlooks on the world. It is no wonder that the new generation led the call for the revolution in Egypt because we were the only ones who succeeded in making an epistemological rupture with the system—and I mean the general system, not only the political one.
>
> (Herrera, 2011b)

The writers cited above share an understanding of this generation as possessing patterns of sociability, cognition, and values distinct from generations who came of age in a predigital era. Members of this cohort, born between the late 1970s and the early years of the millennium, function in ways that are more horizontal, interactive, participatory, open, collaborative, and mutually influential (Edmunds & Turner, 2005). Their tendency to be more collectivist oriented has led some to call them the "we" generation (Hewlett, 2009; Jenkins, 2008). Tapscott (2009) identifies eight features of the wired generation that relate directly to how its members experience digital communications: freedom, customization, scrutiny, integrity, collaboration, entertainment, speed, and innovation. A related characteristic stemming from this generation's media behavior is taking for granted the ability to practice what Shirky (2010) calls "symmetrical participation." These youth are not passive recipients of media and messages, as in the days when television and print media ruled, but they play an active role in the production, alteration, consumption, and dissemination of content; their relationship to the media is more interactive.

For all the seeming advantages and virtues of the wired generation, a parallel body of work points to its limitations and more degenerate sides. For example, consider the following titles of some well-known critiques of this cohort: *The dumbest generation: How the digital age stupefies young Americans and jeopardizes our future* (Bauerlein, 2009), *The narcissism epidemic: Living in the Age of Entitlement* (Twenge & Campbell, 2009), and *The shallows: What the internet is doing to our brains* (Carr, 2010). These cautionary works raise valid concerns about how members of this generation exhibit signs of having a short attention span, seeking instant gratification, being unable or unwilling to read and think deeply, and lacking the skills necessary for long-term vision and planning. This set of critical postulations does not cancel out the more positive qualities mentioned above but, rather, brings to the table a more multi-faceted picture of this cohort and the challenges it is likely to encounter over time. This combined literature touting virtues and vices leaves us wondering: As a whole, does the wired generation possess the skill sets, vision, resources, and organizational know-how necessary to build and sustain the type of democratic and just society it values? Before drawing on my own data to begin answering this question, I first turn to the sociology of generations and map out a conceptual framework.

Sociology of Generations

The enduring question posed by sociologists of generations is why, or under what conditions, does one generation become conscious of its common situation and rise to steer the reins of history while others follow the path paved by previous generations? Hungarian sociologist Karl Mannheim (1952) grappled with this question in Germany in the combustible period between the two world wars. Mannheim conceptualizes generations as a "social phenomenon" rather than a biological or life-course category, since generations consist of a cohort of people who share a "common location in the historical dimension of the social process" (p. 105; see also Pilcher, 1994). He asserts that members of a generation are not homogeneous, and differences among groups and individuals exist based on class, ideology, geography, and gender, to name a few axes of difference. According to Mannheim, members of a generation—like members of a social class—can achieve "actuality" when they develop a consciousness of their common interests and form group solidarity to harness their collective power: "It is a matter for historical and sociological research to discover at what stage in its development, and under what conditions [. . .] individual members of a generation become conscious of their common situation and make this consciousness the basis of their group solidarity" (p. 290).

He also notes that tectonic social shifts along generational lines usually occur as the result of a social trauma and/or acceleration in the "tempo of social change" (p. 309) through, for example, war, economic crisis (Wohl, 1979), or a social, political, and/or technological revolution (Klatch, 1999). During such times the young become less reliant on the "appropriated memories" of the older generations—those transmitted, for instance, through schools, mass media, and the family—and become more reliant on their own directly acquired experiences through a process of what Mannheim calls "fresh contact."[3] In these periods the young may cease to view the order of things as inevitable or desirable.

Mannheim treats generations as a cohort in a bounded nation state with distinctive national characteristics. But as youth around the globe develop common behaviors and attitudes stemming from their interaction with new media and communication tools, we can speak at some level of global youth culture (Castells, Fernandez-Ardevol, Qui, & Sey, 2007) and a global generation (Edmunds & Turner, 2005). Edmunds and Turner (2005) argue that global generations can rise and become active if they are able to access and exploit resources, innovate politically and culturally, and cultivate strategic leadership. They posit:

> Generations shift from being a passive cohort [. . .] into a politically active and self-conscious cohort [. . .] when they are able to exploit resources (political/educational/economic) to innovate in cultural, intellectual or political spheres [. . .] Resources, opportunity and strategic leadership combine to constitute active generations.
>
> (p. 562)

The wired members of this global generation have undoubtedly been able to innovate in cultural and intellectual spheres, as evidenced in the explosion of ideas and creative content online. This generational cohort has pioneered networked forms of online to offline organizing, whether for the sake of fun and irony, as with flash mobs (Wasik, 2006), or for more political purposes, as with smart mobs (Rheingold, 2003). Yet, even when a smart mob grows into a social movement—as happened with the Occupy Wall Street movement that started in New York City on the heels of the Egyptian revolution, Spain's Los Indignados movement, and the range of anti-austerity protests in Europe (Estes, 2011; Tharoor, 2011; Toussaint, 2012)—it remains to be seen if this online-to-offline crowdsourced organizing is itself proof that this generation is achieving what Mannheim calls "actuality."

To fully understand the rise of an active generation requires moving outside North America and Europe, where the bulk of research and theorizing about generations has occurred. A more inclusive global lens should reach to societies where high proportions of wired youth live under conditions of political repression and economic exclusion, where the stakes for change are at their most pressing. The Middle East and North Africa (MENA), characterized by authoritarian regimes, surging youth populations, and escalating rates of both youth connectivity and unemployment, provides an ideal vantage point to understand generations, justice, and power in the digital age.

The Case of Arab Youth Rising

The political and economic realities of growing up in the MENA region, where 65% of the population is under 30 years of age, distinguish youth there from their cohorts in North America and Europe in important ways. Youth in most of the Arab states, as in states in sub-Saharan Africa, live under authoritarian and militarized regimes ruled by oligarchies that seized power decades ago and continue to hold on to it well into their seventies and eighties. With the exception of the offspring of the political elite, younger citizens have, to a large degree, been locked out of the formal political establishment (Bayat & Herrera, 2010). Political exclusion of youth is made worse when it is met by economic marginalization (Dhillon & Yousef, 2009). The Arab states have among the highest youth unemployment rates in the world: roughly 25% in Egypt, 31% in Tunisia, and a staggering 77% in Syria (Chaaban, 2008). For those youth who find employment, the overwhelming majority labor in precarious circumstances with no fixed contract or benefits or in jobs incommensurate with their education and training (Silver, 2007).

Notably, Arab youth unemployment rates are highest among high-school and university graduates (Assaad & Roudi-Fahimi, 2007), a fact that bodes especially badly for the education system in this region. An underlying assumption guiding this research is that formal educational institutions have been losing their hold over the young and declining as sites of nation and citizenship building (Herrera, 2010). Neither schools nor universities seem capable of preparing Arab youth to deal effectively with the challenges the new age poses, whether with regard to securing livelihoods, confronting issues relating to economic insecurity and social injustice, or participating in the political system in meaningful ways. Yet, as this study shows, these youths have taken it on themselves to seek out such development through more informal, horizontal, and globally informed networks.

Young educated Arabs born in the 1980s and 1990s make up an exceedingly disaffected group. In interviews with 16- to 30-year-olds in 2006 (Herrera, 2006), a recurrent theme I found was their deep frustration with the corruption of the Mubarak regime and the lack of democracy and accountability at all layers of society, including schools and universities. A female university student in this study voiced a commonly expressed view when she said that

> the Egyptian political system [. . .] governs people with steel and fire (*hadid wa naar*) [. . .] Corruption spreads like fire on dry leaves. The government doesn't care about the demands of people or allow room for us to express our opinions or change the status quo. Security is the most important thing, but only wealthy people are protected by the police. The poor are always in state prisons.

Fatima, a 21-year-old student in the study, reinforced this view when she said with indignation, "We all know that we live in a dictatorial society far removed from the democracy that we all want, all of us."

Young people have been developing awareness of their common grievances—the consciousness to which Mannheim refers—and forming solidarities and strategies along generational lines with the aid of mobile and digital communication tools. Internet use in Egypt, the most populous Arab country with 82 million people, is spreading exponentially. In 2000 there were a mere 300,000 users, a number that increased to 6 million in 2006, 10.5 million in 2008, 17 million in 2010, and 21 million in March 2011.[4] People under 35 use the internet at far higher rates than other age cohorts. According to one study, 58% of Egyptians between the ages of 18 and 35 have access to computers, and among them 52% are internet literate. Thirty-six percent of youth have their own home computer, and the numbers are growing (Rakha, 2008). Digital inequality remains a reality, and large percentages of the population experience digital exclusion by virtue of their poverty, location, or other factors. But even in contexts where the young do not have access to the internet, the ones who do influence and drive generational changes with far-reaching civic, cultural, and political consequences (Bayat & Herrera, 2010).

Wired youth in Egypt have been in the global vanguard when it comes to using communication tools as a "weapon of opposition" (Eid, 2004), building coalitions, and engaging in civil disobedience. The first uses of the terms "Facebook Revolution" and "Twitter Revolution" in the Western media were in relation to Egypt in 2008 after two 20-something Egyptian college students used the social networking sites to coordinate a strike in solidarity with textile workers in Al-Mahalla al-Kubra, an industrial city in the Nile Delta region of Gharbia.[5] These social networking terms were later applied to Moldova, Iran, and Tunisia in 2009, 2010, and 2011, respectively. The term "Facebook Revolution" resurfaced after it became known that the call for the Egyptian revolution of January 25, 2011 originated from the Arabic Facebook page "We are all Khaled Said" (Kulina Khaled Said). Many have objected to the term since it ascribes agency to high-tech companies rather than to the people who use the technology (Aidi, 2011; Herrera, 2011a). But it remains valid to argue that the wave of prodemocracy movements in Tunisia, Egypt, Iran, and other countries of the region would probably not have been triggered at this historical moment in the ways they have been without social media and the availability of new connection tools and technologies.

The questions that beg to be asked at this juncture are: How have Egyptian youth been forming citizenship dispositions in the digital era? How has their use of communication tools evolved through different phases? And, a question of a more speculative nature, does this wired generation possess the tools and know-how necessary to play a meaningful role in long-term democracy building and economic reform?

Methodology

The sociology of generations and theories about global youth cultures emphasize the need for research that is attentive to two levels: the individual and the group. The concept of "fresh contact" that is so pivotal to Mannheim's (1952) generational theory plays out as "an event in one individual biography" and the experience of a cohort of people "who are in the literal sense beginning a 'new life'" (p. 293). It is therefore pertinent to come up with research strategies that allow for an understanding of autonomous individuals *and* age cohort collectivities. Biographical research offers such an approach.

Learning biographies are principally concerned with how, in a period of advanced globalization, individuals learn inside and outside of formal institutions, including during their leisure and consumer activities (Diepstraten, du Bois-Reymond, & Vinken, 2006). As Vinken (2005) has elucidated, "The domains of leisure and consumption might well be the playing fields where young people and their closest associates exercise their generational consciousness" (p. 153), where they "build a new community identity [. . .] as well as alternative routes to establish solidarity, community life and involvement in the common good" (p. 155).

The biographical interviews I conducted for this study are part of my ongoing research on youth, power, and educational and political change. The data come from narrative interviews that took place between 2006 and 2011. I designed the interviews to understand how, from childhood to the present time, Egyptians in the 16- to 30-year-old age group have been incorporating new media and communication tools into their everyday lives and how their internet use has been shaping their citizenship dispositions, or their awareness about society and their place within it. I adjusted interviews to keep in step with ever-changing communication tools and platforms. In 2006, for instance, my conversations revolved more around texting and email behavior, whereas by 2010 my interviews focused more on social networking activities.

The participants of this study, born between 1981 and 1993, are part of a generation insofar as they share a common historical location and have been coming of age in a similar political-economic context and communications environment. I chose them through a process of snowball sampling combined with selective sampling to ensure gender balance and the inclusion of individuals from diverse social, economic, and educational backgrounds. Participants heralded from the range of urban poor to affluent middle-class areas in Alexandria and Cairo, with a small sample from towns on the outskirts of the cities. I conducted a total of 28 in-depth interviews and two focus group meetings with university students in 2006, 2008, 2010, and 2011.[6] Due to the wealth of data and given space limitations, I use the biographical details of a small group of research participants— Mona, Fatin, Haisam, and Murad (pseudonyms)—to guide us through the findings. I chose their stories, though unique in some respects, because they complement one another and contain patterns common in the overall sample. The words of other youth are interspersed throughout the narrative to enrich the text and spotlight the multiplicity of voices informing this analysis. Unlike other kinds of research, biographical research by nature deals with a statistically small sample size and thus cannot claim representativeness or provide the basis for generalization. What this approach can offer is a means to arrive at a deeper understanding of "the 'personal' and its interlinking with the immediate and wider social context and political practices" (Roberts, 2002, p. 31).

Findings

Overall, this research shows that "ordinary" youth in Egypt and much of the region have been learning culture, forming a generational consciousness, and more actively engaging in politics away from schools and adult authority figures. In the process they have been gaining a greater awareness of their place in the world and experimenting with ways of challenging the status quo. According to this analysis, these changes have occurred in four phases that led to the revolution of January 25, 2011. A fifth, post-revolution phase, "Claiming the System," is ongoing.

Phase I: Opening Frontiers

For many young Egyptians with access to the internet in the early years of the twenty-first century, their cultural frontiers opened in unexpected ways as they took part in online gaming and chatting with strangers. Take the case of Mona, a 22-year-old agriculture student and amateur graphic artist from a semi-rural town in the north who comes from a conservative family associated with the Muslim Brotherhood. She recalls the excitement in 2006 when her parents bought a computer on installment for her and her siblings. She especially relished the time she spent in chat rooms, first ICQ and then Yahoo. Her English was limited, but that did not deter her. She was always curious about other cultures and dreamed about getting to know people from different parts of the world. Being from a religiously conservative family, she was not sure if she should chat with boys online. But when a guy from New Zealand was in a chat room asking questions about Islam, she began an online friendship "to talk more about Islam." Having broken that first taboo of chatting with boys, she later sought out "off-limits" groups. She chatted several times with Israelis because, as she explained, "we hear a lot about them in the news, and I wanted to know about them firsthand. It was normal. There was no big problem." She breached another national taboo in November 2009 during Egypt's "soccer war" with the rival Algerian team when she sought out Algerians online to hear their side of the story. For Mona, chat rooms provided an opportunity to talk about and spread Islam, to broaden her social circles, and to seek out contrary positions in order to form her own opinions about important issues of the day.

Murad, an architecture student at the University of Alexandria, was less inclined toward chat rooms and more drawn to massively multiplayer online role-playing games (MMORPGs). Murad grew up in Alexandria in the 1990s during the piety movement, when many of his classmates and peers were becoming more outwardly religious. He was ill at ease with the conservative youth culture, which he found to be hypocritical, and began feeling increasingly like an outcast. As he became more socially isolated, he slipped into depression. His lifeline at the time came from online gaming communities. At one point in high school he spent up to eight hours a day online, and his parents were concerned that he had an addiction. While that may have been true, what they did not understand was that these games provided him the interaction and social acceptance that was lacking in his actual physical environment. His preferred game was the World of Warcraft (11.5 million subscribers worldwide), which he played on a European server. Murad recounted how these games helped him not only to learn better English but also to "learn culture." For instance, during a game he taunted his opponent through the chat function with a homosexual slur. Other players immediately called him out for being homophobic. Their reactions took him by surprise and led to exchanges about discrimination and other related issues. The community of players formed and enforced its own codes of civility. Some of his online players became friends and even visited him in Egypt during their holidays.

Though Murad no longer has the time to play games, he is grateful for the many social, civil, and cognitive benefits they offered him at a crucial period in his life. His experiences echo studies of online gaming, which have found that these games can be much more than a way to pass time; they "epitomize the ways in which contemporary identities, expectations, and understandings about the world may be shaped and influenced" (Beavis, 2007, p. 52).

Phase II: Cultural Revolution

If early contact with the internet opened cultural frontiers, the second phase, which overlapped chronologically with the first one, heralded a cultural revolution. With the arrival of torrent peer-to-peer file sharing in the early 2000s, the world's cultural and scientific repertoires became accessible online. On recalling that time, when he had a gateway to art and music around the globe, 24-year-old

Haisam declared, "The computer changed my personality 180 degrees. It was the best thing that ever happened to me." Haisam, an Egyptian who spent his childhood in Saudi Arabia, returned to Egypt with his family when he was 13. He loved math and engineering but found that the Egyptian school system stifled rather than stimulated his avid mind. He searched outside of school for ways to feed his interests. Peer-to-peer file sharing supplied him with an endless and free, albeit illegal, supply of music, games, videos, films, and e-books. For Haisam, the computer became "like a gateway to heaven." For over a year he spent most of his waking hours downloading music and lyrics and meeting people with similar interests in online forums. He joined a group of Arabic music aficionados and worked on transferring 125 years of Arabic music recordings into digital format. If not for their labor, this music might have been lost.

Cinema was the next frontier, and Haisam discovered the world of foreign films. He recalls, "I was totally immersed in consuming the Internet. I wasn't working or reading, just consuming movies, songs, culture, and everything I didn't know before." Downloading a film was "painfully slow," but he had the tenacity to download the "100 Best Films of All Time" with Arabic subtitles. He took a liking to the Cohen brothers, Frances Ford Coppola, Woody Allen, Ingmar Bergman, Quentin Tarantino, and Danish Dogma cinema. After just two short years of using file-sharing programs, his cultural repertoire and English ability grew in ways that were unthinkable just a couple of years earlier. "Having this knowledge pumped into your head is like the Matrix," he observed. "Maybe someone who lived for seventy years wouldn't have the chance to know what we were able to learn in two years."

Haisam and scores of young people who grew up online when the internet was more or less unregulated and functioned as a global commons experienced a veritable cultural revolution. Their exposure to, and interaction with, ideas, people, images, virtual spaces, and cultural products outside their everyday environments led to a substantial change in their mentality and worldview.

In a society like Egypt's, where large segments of the population are culturally conservative and worried about negative exogenous influences, not everyone was as enthusiastic as Haisam about the cultural opening provided by the internet. In the interviews I conducted in 2006 and 2008, a number of respondents expressed concern that the internet could be a source of moral corruption. Dina, a student in a teacher's college, worried in 2006 that young people used the internet in "morally wrong ways." Her views were shared by 19-year-old Samer, who argued that unlike individualistic Western youth, Egyptians value marriage and family stability and are highly moralistic. He complained that the openness of the internet would tempt some users toward pornography or forming improper relationships. "We have our sexual mores from the prophetic traditions (*sunna nabawiyya*), the Holy Book, and not [atheist books] which may lead to illnesses like AIDS," he said. For him, it was important that Arab youth enjoy the knowledge benefits of the internet while understanding the limits dictated by religion and tradition.[7] In later years, however, respondents expressed less concern that the internet would be a source of temptation and corruption and more alarm that this s_ closed through regulation and censorship. Cognizant of the threat of a ıɔ. internet, Haisam has developed an interest in open-source operating systems and is working to keep the internet free and open.

Phase III: Citizen Media

By 2006–2008, scores of "ordinary" Egyptian youth were using mobile phones and computers for many familiar activities, such as chatting, exchanging photographs, playing games, passing on jokes, and flirting. But one activity that especially stood out was how they were using these tools to circumvent official media and construct an alternative news universe. High-school and university students had come to understand the power inherent in selecting, circulating, and commenting on a news story that contradicted the official version of an event or was absent altogether in mainstream news outlets. And research has shown that this generation has been thirsty for news. A 2008 survey on youth internet use in Egypt reported that 74% of respondents used the internet to stay current with the news, and 68% used it to download games, songs, movies, and programs (Rakha, 2008). With communication tools at their disposal, youth who may not have otherwise been especially political were acquiring political sensibilities. Shayma from the College of Arts said, "Many youths are trying to change things through the Internet. We are expressing our viewpoints through blogs and using the weapon of words to transform society."

Data on the Egyptian blogosphere are imprecise; size estimates range from 35,000 to 160,000 bloggers. A leading study presents a picture of bloggers as being predominantly in the 20- to 30-year-old age range and the majority males, but with adolescent girls and young women of 18 to 24 years a fast-growing force (Etling, Kelly, Faris, & Palfrey, 2009). There has been much speculation about the ideological character of the Arabic blogosphere—of whether it exhibits tendencies toward Islamism, democratic liberalism, secularism, or other affinities. The Arab blogosphere does not appear to be oriented toward a certain political ideology, though there is "very little support for terrorism or violent jihad in the Arabic blogosphere and quite a lot of criticism [of it]" (Etling et al., 2009, p. 10). It is more fitting to think of the new communication space as an expansion of the public sphere toward more participation (Lynch, 2007).

Fatin, a young woman from Cairo University, explained how it was a natural transition graduating from chat rooms to blogs. She began blogging with a group of friends, five boys and three girls, when she was 21. They blogged anonymously so that they could explore taboo subjects. Their blog dealt with Islamic feminism and delved into questions about whether pious and practicing Muslim women could be feminists; about gender and psychology; and about cinema, culture, and a range of other things. The act of writing to an unknown public gave Fatin great pleasure. She said, "I felt I wanted to open up, and I loved writing. Also, I wanted to see my words online. I don't know what's the difference [between seeing the words online versus in a notebook], but I just loved it."

Haisam also experimented with blogging in 2005. He became close virtual friends with a tight-knit group of six to seven male and female bloggers. They initially treated their blogs as private conversations with each other and a small circle of readers. But when a Syrian blogger from their group disappeared—just vanished from cyberspace with no word—they awoke to the risks of blogging in their respective police states.[8] For these pioneers, blogging did not start as a self-consciously political activity; rather, they were merely experimenting with a new kind of expressive art. Haisam used his blog to share anything that caught his attention, like music, films, current events, and rants about how much he hated school.

His blogging took a turn in 2005, however, during Egypt's parliamentary elections and first multi-candidate presidential elections. Then 19 years old, Haisam walked the early steps of citizen journalism.

> I was really interested in carrying out an experiment, of monitoring an election from inside a poll station. I went to a small village outside of Alexandria and started to observe what was happening. I saw how people would sell their votes and write "yes" for Mubarak just for money. I took pictures and posted them on my blog.

He wasn't working for a particular political party or candidate, just acting as an independent citizen with an online voice. Throughout Egypt, in Aswan, Mansoura, and Cairo, other bloggers, some as young as 15 and 16 years old, undertook similar experiments.

Among the pioneers of Egyptian youth citizen journalism was Wael Abbas.[9] He was one of the first bloggers to effectively connect his blog with the video-sharing website YouTube to agitate against police brutality and torture. In 2006 the Egyptian blogosphere was shaken after he posted a video clip of two police officers torturing and sodomizing a minibus driver, Emad al-Kabir. Not only did the horrifying and graphic video go viral, but al-Kabir came forward at the urging of human rights activists and pressed charges against the offenders, leading to the unprecedented conviction of each police officer to a three-year prison sentence.[10] This case emboldened many others to use their communications tools to "name and shame" perpetrators of crimes and corruption. Young citizen journalists anonymously founded anticorruption blogs and websites in different parts of the country, from the south to the north. It was also during this period that the US Department of State and international civil society groups working in human rights took an interest in Egypt's cyber citizens. They spearheaded training and networking initiatives with young activists, who came to be known as "cyberdissidents" (Herrera, forthcoming). It would not be off the mark to suggest that from this time the communication behavior of wired Egyptians was channeled toward political oppositional activities at least some of the time.

Phase IV: Becoming a Wired Generation

By 2007–2008 blogs were being surpassed by Facebook, the digital social media platform of choice for Egyptians. In March 2008 there were some 822,560 Facebook users in Egypt, and by February 2011 that number grew to more than 5.6 million (Burcher, 2010; Hui, 2011). During the early months of the Arab revolts alone (between January and April 2011), 2 million new Egyptian users joined Facebook. An overwhelming 75% of Egypt's Facebook users were now between the ages of 15 and 29, and 36% of those users were female (Mourtada & Salem, 2011). In 2007 Fatin, like many other bloggers, transitioned from blogging to Facebooking. She explained: "For a while I was putting my posts on my blog and on Facebook. Then I switched to Facebook only because you can filter the people you want to read your writings and tag people when you want to discuss an idea with them." A second reason for the shift had to do with security concerns. Fatin no longer felt comfortable transmitting her thoughts so openly in a blog to people she did not actually know. Facebook allowed her to tailor her audience and decide who could be in her networks, though she was under no illusion that Facebook was a secure or private space.

Murad also slowly phased out of blogging in favor of being the administrator (admin) of a Facebook group. By 2008 his group about tolerance and art gained a modest but loyal following of about 350 members of mainly Egyptians in their teens and early twenties. Many of them got to know each other offline, and some of them started their own Facebook pages devoted to such spinoff issues as religious freedom, the headscarf, graffiti, and cinema.

The organizing and movement building potentials of Facebook became more evident in 2008 after university student and part-time activist Israa Abdel Fatah received a text message from 28-year-old Ahmed Maher, an engineering student and fellow activist, suggesting they do something to support an April 6 strike planned by textile workers in the Nile Delta city of Al-Mahalla al-Kubra. Abdel Fatah set up a Facebook event for a general strike expecting to attract a small circle of activists. Unbeknownst to her, the event went viral, and the Facebook group, the April 6 Youth Movement (*Harakat Shabab 6 Abril*), was born (Shapiro, 2009). Yet for all the advantages and empowering features of Facebook organizing, it also carries heavy risks. The two creators of the April 6, 2008 event were arrested. In one confrontation, Maher was beaten for 12 hours by the state security police in order to get him to disclose his Facebook password. His friend Wael Abbas, in the spirit of the cyberdissidence, posted images of Maher's bruised and beaten body on his blog.

By this time Facebook had become such an integral part of Egyptian youth culture that it entered the local vernacular as "al-Face." This virtual space housed a cacophony of voices and innumerable groups ranging from biology study groups, fans of Arabic singers, car racing aficionados, and volunteer associations to hate pages against corrupt teachers, Quranic memorization clubs, fashion watchers, and everything in between.

In 2010 diverse individuals and groups from among Egypt's Facebook youth (*shabab al-Face*) came together around the cause of Mohamed ElBaradei, former diplomat, director general of the International Atomic Energy Agency (IAEA), 2005 Nobel Peace Prize recipient, and Egyptian presidential hopeful. ElBaradei founded the National Association for Change in Egypt to advocate for electoral reform and pave the way for representative democracy. Over a quarter of a million Egyptians from different religious, political, class, gender, and regional backgrounds joined the Mohamed ElBaradei Facebook page. As a critical mass of youth rallied behind ElBaradei, they came to realize that Mubarak and the system that kept the oligarchy in power were not inevitable. Using all the digital tools and online platforms at their disposal, members of this wired generation emboldened each other to challenge the status quo.

Mona, who by this time had joined a virtual community of female Arab graphic artists, made political cartoons that ridiculed President Mubarak. When asked if she was afraid of the possible consequences of her postings, she declared, "No! We're not afraid of them. What are they going to do, arrest millions of us? Because millions of us are doing this kind of thing." Fatin echoed this sentiment when she explained:

> There is something about being active on a social networking site that breaks all our concerns about anonymity. It's totally changing our attitude. No one can arrest thousands of people for what they're saying on Facebook, and they can't control the millions of conversations taking place there.

Two of the admins involved in running the ElBaradei Facebook page, 23-year-old Abdelrahman Mansour and 30-year-old Wael Ghonim, went on to create an even bigger online sensation, the anti-torture campaign "We are all Khaled Said," named after a victim of police brutality. The admins worked under the cover of anonymity partly for security reasons and partly to serve as the faceless, unifying voice of the youth. They spoke from behind the mask of the airbrushed "Every-youth" portrait of the martyr Khaled Said.

From its inception the page operated on a principle of online to offline street action. The page housed a unique cultural space that was youthful, Arab, Egyptian, Muslim oriented, educational, participatory, and subversive. Within hours of its launch, the admins called on members to get up from behind their computer screens and go out into the streets, initially to attend the public funeral of Khaled Said. The page continued to mobilize its members by organizing a series of anti-torture silent stands, or civil disobedience–styled flash mobs.

In the lead-up to the November 2010 presidential and parliamentary elections, the ElBaradei and "We are all Khaled Said" Facebook pages were blocked. The temporary loss of Facebook caused its young users great anxiety. Twenty-one-year-old Ahmed talked about how he was genuinely distressed that Facebook might be permanently "turned off." He said that depriving him of Facebook would be like "blocking the air to my lungs." The social networking site had become an extension of his social, political, psychological, and even spiritual life.

Ahmed explained how those on the "We are all Khaled Said" page abided by unwritten codes for participating in the community: members should not use the space to insult each other's religion, to make fun of each other, for pornography or sexual harassment, for advertising, for spreading false rumors, or for spying. When someone crossed these lines, others would intervene by way of posting a corrective comment, starting a conversation on the post in question, or by asking the admin to remove that person from the group. Members of the group expressed pride in knowing they had created a virtuous society that stood in contrast to the corrupt society outside (Herrera, 2011a).

When the Facebook pages came up again, following the direct intervention of a US-based human rights activist and high-level Facebook executive (Giglio, 2011), the "We are all Khaled Said" page surpassed even the ElBaradei page as Egypt's most active and consequential youth movement in over half a century. It had morphed into a unique community with its own identity, rebel culture, ethical codes, and politics. The true genius of the page was how it took the collective, generational "we" and branded it with a common identity, conviction, and purpose. Like the ElBaradei cause, the members of the "We are all Khaled Said" movement, though highly diverse, came to view themselves as a social collectivity with deepening ties of solidarity and overlapping sets of interests that converged on the need to claim and change the Egyptian system. The ElBaradei movement zeroed in on reform of the electoral process, whereas the "We are all Khaled Said" cause targeted the state's menacing security apparatus.

The "We are all Khaled Said" page issued a call for a march on January 25, 2011, the national holiday in honor of the police, to protest police corruption and torture. But on the heels of the Tunisian revolution and fleeing of its dictator, Zine El Abidine Ben Ali, on January 14, the protest became a call for a revolution against torture, corruption, poverty, and unemployment. This event became the trigger for the 18-day revolution that brought down the 30-year dictatorship of Hosni Mubarak. On the eve of the January 25 Revolution, the page had grown to 390,000 members and was receiving more than 9 million hits a day.

The page did not cause the revolution, and youth of the internet were not the only group active in the revolt, but it is hard to imagine the revolutionary movement unfolding in the way it did without the determination, tools, courage, training, networking, and changing political and cultural understandings of this wired generation. But, as it turned out, bringing down a dictator was the easy part; the hard work for deeper, structural, systemic change lay ahead.

Conclusions: Claiming the System?

Egypt's wired revolutionary generation that emerged on the world stage following the January 25 Revolution contributed in no small measure to the success of the first stage of the revolution, namely the toppling of President Hosni Mubarak. But like their generational counterparts engaged in various struggles throughout the Middle East and North Africa, Europe, sub-Saharan Africa, and the United States, young Egyptians grappled with questions about how to move forward. Even now, the hoped-for outcomes of the revolution—dignity, democracy, and equity—are far from inevitable.

The post-Mubarak period in Egypt has been fraught with uncertainty and conflict—and pregnant with risk. The country has had some success in the area of electoral democracy. It held its first ever multicandidate presidential election in June 2012. But the process favored two groups of entrenched power elites: the military and the 80-year-old opposition group—and ultimate victor—the Muslim Brotherhood. Both of these groups have had especially poor track records when it comes to democracy, transparency, and equity, as well as long proven records of cronyism, nepotism, and paternalism.

Egypt's young cyber citizens have been crowded out of the power game and are now struggling to find ways to more deeply dismantle and penetrate the old power structure. For all the dexterity and creativity they have shown in horizontal organizing, persistent civil disobedience, and networking and mobilizing across lines of difference—ideological, religious, class, gender, and otherwise—citizens of Egypt's wired generation have exhibited serious limitations when it comes to strategizing for the long term in ways that allow them to achieve their vision of a good society. This generation of young Egyptians faces debilitating obstacles resulting from the entrenchment of old power structures, the growing sophistication of surveillance systems, and the uncertainty that comes with long-term economic insecurity. Egypt's young aspire to live with dignity and freedom in accountable democratic systems with a standard of equity and justice. However, social media–based activism—whether the Khaled Said youth movement that sparked the 25 January uprising in Egypt or the Facebook activity around the Arabic exam—lends itself to short-term, single-issue campaigns. These campaigns can activate feelings of citizenship, start conversations, build coalitions, get people to the streets, and even trigger revolutions. But can they facilitate the sustained deliberation, organization, and leadership needed to imagine alternatives and rebuild structures of power?

The democratic movements of Egypt's wired generation have yet to develop an aptitude for planning over the long term; exploiting educational, economic, and political resources; and cultivating strategic leadership. At this critical juncture, it is important to consider how to best support citizens of Egypt's wired generation in their pursuit of deep democracy by developing educational systems—informally and formally—that provide the conceptual, methodological, and critical tools necessary to understand how power and counterpower operate. In the absence of critical and collaborative educational endeavors, the fear is that a dreaded counterrevolution, with its regressive and antidemocratic tendencies, may very well prevail.

Notes

1. This article was originally published by *Harvard Educational Review* Vol. 82 No. 3 Fall 2012. Many thanks go to the President and Fellows of Harvard College for permission to reprint the article for this volume.
2. Taken from the first-year Arabic exam administered in December 2011 at a high school for boys located in an educational district in the Governorate of Gharbia.
3. Mannheim (1952) posits that young people begin forming their own memories, distinct from the older generations', during late adolescence, at about age 17. In contemporary times, given the earlier onset of adolescence and the ubiquitous youth-oriented media and communications ecosystem, this is probably happening in the earlier teens.
4. For detailed country-specific and regional statistics on internet users worldwide, see internet World Stats at www.internetworldstats.com/stats1.htm.
5. Israa Abdel Fatah, who was dubbed the president of the "Facebook Republic," and Ahmed Maher used their Facebook networks to coordinate support for the striking workers. They were both arrested and detained as a result of their activism.
6. I am grateful for the invaluable help of two research assistants, Rawda Waguih and Hossam Basyoni, for the 2010 phase of research. The 2006 research was coordinated with Professor Kamal Naguib of Alexandria University. For an elaboration of those data in English and Arabic, see Herrera (2006) and Naguib (2008).
7. These attitudes were mirrored in a government survey on the internet use of 1,338 Egyptians between ages 18 and 35. It found that 72% of youth surveyed considered the internet "a bad influence on themselves"; 71% thought "the Internet is dangerous for children"; 43% believed "that the internet has negatively impacted family ties"; and 89% agreed to "having a law in place that monitors/censors internet content" (Rakha, 2008). Even accounting for biases of a governmental survey, it is highly plausible that in 2007–2008 young people were not entirely comfortable using a medium without adult supervision. But those attitudes appeared to have changed significantly in the succeeding years.
8. Howard's (2010) table "Blogger Arrests in the Muslim World, 2003–2010" is a very good source for understanding the risks of blogging in the region (pp. 113–116). See also Gasser, Maclay, and Palfrey (2010) on digital safety in developing countries.
9. Abbas's blog can be found at http://misrdigital.blogspirit.com/. See also a 2007 CNN story about how YouTube shut down and then restored Abbas's account and torture videos at www.cnn.com/2007/WORLD/meast/11/29/youtube.activist/.
10. The popular blog *The Arabist* played an important role in disseminating news about the case (see El-Amrani, 2007).

References

Aidi, H. (2011, Fall). Leveraging hip hop in US foreign policy. *Middle East Report, 260,* 25–39.

Assaad, R. & Roudi-Fahimi, F. (2007). *Youth in the Middle East and North Africa: Demographic opportunity or challenge?* Washington DC: Population Reference Bureau.

Bauerlein, M. (2009). *The dumbest generation: How the digital age stupefies young Americans and jeopardizes our future.* New York: Penguin.

Bayat, A. & Herrera, L. (2010). Being young and Muslim in neoliberal times. In L. Herrera & A. Bayat (Eds.), *Being young and Muslim: New cultural politics in the global south and north* (3–24). New York: Oxford University Press.

Beavis, C. (2007). New textual worlds: Young people and computer games. In N. Dolby & F. Rizvi (Eds.), *Youth moves: Identities and education in global perspective* (53–66). New York: Routledge.

Burcher, N. (2010, July 2). Facebook usage statistics by country—July 2010 compared to July 2009 and July 2008. Retrieved from www.nickburcher.com/2010/07/ facebook-usage-statistics-by-country.html

Carr, N. (2010). *The shallows: What the internet is doing to our brains.* New York: W. W. Norton.

Castells, M., Fernandez-Ardevol, M., Qui, J. & Sey, A. (2007). *Mobile communication and society: A global perspective.* Cambridge MA: Massachusetts Institute of Technology Press.

Chaaban, J. (2008, May). *The costs of youth exclusion in the Middle East* (Middle East Youth Initiative Working Paper No. 7). Retrieved from http://ssrn.com/abstract=1139172

Dhillon, N. & Yousef, T. (2009). *Generation in waiting: The unfulfilled promise of young people in the Middle East.* Washington, DC: Brookings Institution Press.

Diepstraten, I., du Bois-Reymond, M. & Vinken, H. (2006). Trendsetting learning biographies: Concepts of navigating through late-modern life and learning. *Journal of Youth Studies,* 9(2), 175–193.

Edmunds, J. & Turner, B. (2005). Global generations: Social change in the twentieth century. *British Journal of Sociology,* 56(4), 559–577.

Eid, G. (2004). The internet in the Arab world: A new space of repression? Retrieved from www.anhri.net/en/reports/net2004/all.shtml

El-Amrani, I. (2007). Three years in prison for Emad Al-Kabir torturers. *The Arabist.* Retrieved from www.arabist.net/blog/2007/11/5/three-years-in-prison-for-emad-al-kabir-torturers.html

Estes, A. C. (2011, November 1). The Arab Spring's advice for Occupy Wall Street. *Atlantic Wire.* Retrieved from www.theatlanticwire.com/global/2011/11/arab-springs-advice-occupy-wall-street/44419/

Etling, B., Kelly, J., Faris, R. & Palfrey, J. (2009). *Mapping the Arabic blogosphere: Politics, culture, and dissent* (Berkman Center Research Publication No. 2009–06). Cambridge, MA: Berkman Center for Internet and Society at Harvard University.

Gasser, U., Maclay, C. & Palfrey, J. (2010). *Working towards a deeper understanding of digital safety for children and young people in developing nations.* The Berkman Center for Internet and Society at Harvard University. Retrieved from http://cyber.law.harvard.edu/sites/cyber.law.harvard.edu/files/Gasser_Maclay_Palfrey_Digital_Safety_Developing_Nations_Jun2010.pdf

Giglio, M. (2011, February 24). Middle East uprising: Facebook's secret role in Egypt. *The Daily Beast.* Retrieved from www.thedailybeast.com/articles/2011/02/24/middle-east-uprising-facebooks-back-channel-diplomacy.html

Herrera, L. (2006). When does life begin? Youth perspectives from Egypt. *DevISSues,* 8(2), 7–9.

Herrera, L. (2010). Egyptian youths' quest for jobs and justice. In L. Herrera & A. Bayat (Eds.), *Being young and Muslim: New cultural politics in the global south and north* (127–143). New York: Oxford University Press.

Herrera, L. (2011a, February 12). Egypt's revolution 2.0: The Facebook factor. *Jadaliyya.* Retrieved from www.jadaliyya.com/pages/index/612/egypts-revolution-2.0_the-facebook-factor

Herrera, L. (2011b, October 14). Generation rev and the struggle for democracy: Interview with Aly El-Raggal. *Jadaliyya.* Retrieved from www.jadaliyya.com/pages/index/2869/generation-rev-and-the-struggle-for-democracy_inte

Herrera, L. (forthcoming). *Revolution in the age of social media: People vs. power in Egypt.* New York: Verso.

Hewlett, S. (2009, June 18). "Me" generation becomes the "we" generation. *Financial Times.* Retrieved from www.ft.com/cms/s/0/99e526a8–5c34–11de-aea3–00144feabdc0.html

Howard, P. N. (2010). *The digital origins of dictatorship and democracy: Information technology and political Islam.* New York: Oxford University Press.

Hui, L. Y. (2011, February 27). Which countries have over 1 million Facebook users? *GreyReview.* Retrieved from www.greyreview.com/2011/02/27/which-countries-have-over-1-million-facebook-users/

Jenkins, H. (2008, February 18). Obama and the "we" generation. *Aca-Fan.* Retrieved from www.henryjenkins.org/2008/02/obama_and_the_we_generation.html

Klatch, R. E. (1999). *A generation divided: The new left, the new right and the 1960s.* Berkeley: University of California Press.

Krause, K. (2007). Who is the e-generation and how are they faring in higher education? In J. Lockard & M. Pegrum (Eds.), *Brave new classrooms: Educational democracy and the internet* (125–140). New York: Peter Lang.

Lynch, M. (2007, Spring). Blogging the new Arab public. *Arab Media and Society*, 1. Retrieved from www.arabmediasociety.com/?article=10

Mannheim, K. (1952). The problem of generations. In P. Kecskemeti (Ed.), *Essays on the sociology of knowledge.* London: Routledge & Kegan Paul. (Originally published 1928.)

McDonald, D. (2010). The Twitter generation encounters the classroom. *SAIS 2010 Proceedings* (Paper 8). Retrieved from http://aisel.aisnet.org/sais2010/8

Mourtada, R. & Salem, F. (2011). Arab social media report: Civil movements: The impact of Facebook and Twitter. *Dubai School of Government*, 1(2). Retrieved from www.dsg.ae/en/publication/Description.aspx?PubID=236&PrimenuID=11&mnu=Pri

Naguib, K. (2008). *Thaqafat al-shabab al-Misri: Al-ihbatat wa'l-tattalu'at wa-ab'ad al-muqawama* (The children have grown up: The disappointments, ambitions, and scope of resistance in Egyptian youth culture). Cairo: Mahrousa Press.

Nielsen, L. & Webb, W. (2011). *Teaching generation text: Using cell phones to enhance learning.* San Francisco: Jossey-Bass.

Palfrey, J. & Gasser, U. (2008). *Born digital: Understanding the first generation of digital natives.* New York: Basic Books.

Pilcher, J. (1994). Mannheim's sociology of generations: An undervalued legacy. *British Journal of Sociology*, 45(30), 481–495.

Rafael, V. (2003). The cell phone and the crowd: Messianic politics in the contemporary Philippines. *Public Culture*, 15(3), 399–425.

Rakha, M. (2008, November 26). Egypt: 89% of youth support internet censorship law. *Global Voices Online.* Retrieved from http://globalvoicesonline.org/2008/11/26/89-of-egyptian-youth-are-pro-the-Internet-censorship-law/

Rheingold, H. (2003). *Smart mobs: The next social revolution.* Cambridge, MA: Basic Books.

Rideout, V., Foehr, U. & Roberts, D. (2010). *Generation M2: Media in the lives of 8-to-18 year olds* (A Kaiser Family Foundation Study). Menlo Park, CA: Henry J. Kaiser Family Foundation.

Rigby, B. (2008). *Mobilizing generation 2.0: A practical guide to using Web 2.0 technologies to recruit, organize, and engage youth.* San Francisco: Jossey-Bass.

Roberts, B. (2002). *Biographical research.* Glasgow: Open University Press.

Rosen, L. (2010). *Rewired: Understanding the iGeneration and the way they learn.* New York: Palgrave Macmillan.

Shapiro, S. M. (2009, January 22). Revolution, Facebook style. *New York Times.* Retrieved from www.nytimes.com/2009/01/25/magazine/25bloggers-t.html

Shirky, C. (2010). *Cognitive surplus: Creativity and generosity in a connected era*. New York: Penguin.

Silver, H. (2007). *Social exclusion: Comparative analysis of Europe and Middle East youth* (Middle East Youth Initiative Working Paper). Wolfensohn Center for Development and Dubai School of Government. Retrieved from www.shababinclusion.org/content/document/detail/558/

Tapscott, D. (1998). *Growing up digital: The rise of the net generation*. New York: McGraw-Hill.

Tapscott, D. (2009). *Grown up digital: How the net generation is changing your world*. New York: McGraw-Hill.

Tharoor, I. (2011, October 5). From Europe with love: US *"Indignados"* occupy Wall Street. *Globalspins Blogs*. Retrieved from http://globalspin.blogs.time.com/2011/10/05/from-europe-with-love-the-u-s-indignados-have-arrived/

Toussaint, E. (2012, January 10). The international context of global outrage, part 3: From the Arab Spring to the Indignados movement to Occupy Wall Street. *América Latina en Movimiento*. Retrieved from http://alainet.org/active/52025

Twenge, J. & Campbell, K. W. (2009). *The narcissism epidemic: Living in the Age of Entitlement*. New York: Free Press.

Vinken, H. (2005). Young people's civic engagement: The need for new perspectives. In H. Helve & G. Holm (Eds.), *Contemporary youth research: Local expressions and global connections* (147–158). Burlington, VT: Ashgate.

Wasik, B. (2006, March). My crowd: Or, Phase 5. *Harper's Magazine,* 312(1870), 56–66.

Wohl, R. (1979). *The generation of 1914*. Cambridge, MA: Harvard University Press.

3

MOROCCO ON-TRIAL

De-Colonial Logic and Transformative Practice in Cyberspace

Charis Boutieri

During a session of mathematics in a public high school in the coastal town of Kenitra in Morocco during the spring of 2008, Ibtissam, who was sitting at the desk next to me, listened covertly to music from her cell phone, having neatly tucked one earphone inside her hijab. Sensing the curious gaze of the anthropologist, she looked startled but swiftly regained her composure and winked at me: "I'm bored. What's the point of all this? I'm not gonna graduate, am I?" Responding to my ardent protestations, Ibtissam said in a resigned tone: "And even if I do graduate, all I will achieve is unemployment (*gilsa f-dar,* literally sitting at home)." Even though she was very disillusioned with public education, this was her third time repeating the senior year in pursuit of her Baccalaureate (high-school diploma). She went on: "Education here is bad (*khaib*), what more can we say? Teachers don't work, students don't study, we only come to spend time (*passer le temps*). Otherwise we would do chores at home." We continued our discussion during break until we were cut off by the bell. Rushing to her next class, Ibtissam asked for my *msn* address so that we could "chat some more." When I confessed I did not have one, she was stunned: "Really? I spend half, if not more, of my life online!" I asked, "Oh yeah? Doing what?" She replied:

> Everything! I learn about current affairs, talk to my friends, discuss issues such as racism, religion, culture, love, Morocco, and the world with random people . . . For me, this is another type of classroom, one where everyone gets to talk about any subject they want. It's great!

On a later occasion, Ibtissam and her best friend Houda elaborated on their lives online and talked about recent heated conversations between foreigners and Moroccans about life in Morocco, politics, and Islam. Ibtissam spent time almost every afternoon after school at her cousin's *cyber* (internet café), while Houda accessed the internet from home. Her family had recently purchased a second-hand desktop computer. The two giggled over the fact that they spent more time online than doing their homework: "The internet is a better school, I'm telling you!" insisted Ibtissam. Her cynicism towards formal schooling, in stark contrast with her enthusiasm towards virtual sociality and the learning practices it engenders, is very common among the Moroccan youth I have come to know through my fieldwork inside public high schools. Whereas their evaluation of the educational system has not changed since 2007, when I first entered a classroom, their online practices (surfing, social networking, and blogging) have flourished over the years. Not only do substantially more youth engage with cyberspace on a daily basis, but their online skills are developing at lightning speed.

This chapter draws on systematic research inside urban public high schools in Morocco and with Moroccan youth (students and graduates) in the period from 2005 to 2013. From 2007 to 2009 I made brief visits to 20 schools in the administrative districts of Rabat-Salé-Zemmour-Zaer and Gharb-Charda-Beni Hssen, and conducted in-depth ethnographic research in two high schools of a medium-sized town. I followed courses of the two main tracks, sciences and humanities, and spent time with junior- and senior-year students. This fieldwork brought me into close contact with a number of students who lacked enthusiasm about school but were very active online.[1] They turned to virtual spaces to creatively articulate ways to address the various hierarchies and discrepancies of their classroom experience.

I use the term "on-trial" as an allusion to "online" to capture ways that students use online spaces to indict their education system and the state structures that undergird it. They speak of schooling as an incomplete project of decolonization of knowledge following Morocco's independence from France in 1956. Decolonization in this context takes on the meaning of the possibility for indigenous creativity and innovation in the domain of learning. A feature of this struggle for emancipation is to allow equal place to all the languages of Morocco: *fusha* (Modern Standard Arabic), *darija* (Moroccan dialect), French, and Tamazight (a Berber language of the Imazighen). A decolonization of knowledge inside the school would translate into a vision for social justice and state commitment to diversity. As we will see, the performances in virtual spaces of class and gender significantly unsettle the image of a unified youth subjectivity struggling for equality and democratization.

The term "on-trial" also alludes to activism in the sense of contestation and indictment. Activism needs to be released from the binds of normative political behavior and expanded to encompass a plethora of endeavors to critique and request change. Students renegotiate the communicative repertoires as set out by formal education, and strive—though they do not always manage—to transform the socio-cultural frames that subjugate them. State-controlled formal schooling has foreclosed certain modes of learning and being that youth deem essential to their lives. The virtual sphere allows students to become a different public from the one envisaged by the state. The virtual public does not escape actual world coercion (physical or ideological) and hierarchy (material or gender), and it does not operate on an entirely different logic. Indeed, it often appropriates a number of dominant development paradigms regarding valuable knowledge and good learning. Even as it is fraught with tensions and paradoxes, virtual sociality designates a struggle for, and enactment of, change. This struggle speaks to changing enactments of citizenship that, to quote Ritty Lukose's observation in light of her research with Keralan youth, "mov[ed] beyond formal, legal, and constitutional definitions [. . .] [and] emphasized the everyday practices of belonging through which social membership is negotiated" (Lukose, 2009, p. 9).

My interrogation of the use of cyberspace among Moroccan high-school students builds on conversations about media and new media consumption in the region since the late 1990s (Eickelman & Anderson, 1999; Gonzalez-Quijano, 2010). Understanding the ways young people use and consume digital media can help to unsettle recent scholarship on the popular uprisings across the Arab world and challenge the idea that the spread of the internet is coterminous with a normative understanding of democratization and electoral politics (Etling, Kelly, Faris, & Palfrey, 2009). This teleology is problematic for three reasons: First, it risks attributing agency to the technology itself at the expense of a more thorough understanding of the publics that put this technology to work (a critique formulated by Escobar, 1994; Miller & Slater, 2000; Pfaffenberger, 1992). A second and related point is that when taken a priori, this equation invites what Carey (2005) calls "utopian or dystopian enthusiasms," whereas "the really interesting discoveries are to be made in locating the subtle social shifts taking place [. . .] as a consequence of technological change" (p. 443). Third, when this correlation between technology and democracy saturated analyses of the Middle East and North Africa during the Arab uprisings, it tended to obfuscate the ambiguous and somewhat neo-imperialist interventions of actors such as the US Department of State and certain international NGOs (Herrera, 2012; Kraidy & Khalil, 2008). Such actors have often played to their interests by directing cyber activism and moving it to the streets.[2] By asking *how* Moroccan high-school students situate the internet in their lives and *in what ways* "the tools of new media change the contexts and frames of communicative practices" (Wilson & Peterson, 2002, p. 459), I suggest that virtual sociality has certain "affordances" (Pfaffenberger, 1992, p. 503). By affordances I mean the potential for communicating a logic of decolonization not exclusively in the domain of electoral politics but also in relation to political economy. Such potential does not escape ambiguity or contradiction precisely because it is embedded in a specific socio-cultural and political context and undercut by gender, class, and locational differences. An ethnographic account of virtual activity is particularly apt at capturing and evaluating this specificity while acknowledging interconnections with larger frames of reference.

Conventional portrayals of the interface between online and offline activity have been inadequate and given rise to reductive interpretations of youth practices.

By taking a critical perspective, I show that Moroccan public education has been undergoing a crisis that is directly related to the rise of students' virtual sociality through a set of communicative and creative practices. As a concept, virtual sociality can complicate impoverished understandings of activism. Whereas activism is typically used to denote practice in the sphere of oppositional politics, I pay attention to the broader everyday reconfiguration of the actual social fabric in virtual environments. I argue that such an analytical angle is crucial for an appreciation of youth citizenship and can be more productive than the customary approach to virtual spheres that have recently captivated academic and public audiences alike. In sum, I seek to "reopen the problem of mediation" in culture and society (Mazzarella, 2004, p. 227).

In order to give visibility to such practices and highlight the critical shift I intend here, I use the terms "virtual" and "online" interchangeably to refer to social encounters in cyberspace. I juxtapose this engagement to "actual" and "offline" sociality, which I emphatically do not conflate with the notion of the "real." As advocated by Boellstorff (2011), "such an opposition wrongly encodes presumptions that the online is not real, and that the real is technology free" (p. 505). Therefore, I preserve a sense of the ontological gap between actual and virtual, which makes the virtual worthy of attention. I suggest that "ideas, metaphors, power relations, and even forms of materiality routinely move across this gap between the virtual and the actual" (Boellstorff, 2011, p. 513).[3] Students rehearse the future through virtual practices.

Moroccan Public Education and Cyberspace

When young people in Morocco, as in the rest of North Africa, the Middle East, and the Gulf, took to the streets during the Arab uprisings in 2011, they voiced their disapproval of current modes of governance and their profound frustration at structures of social (im)mobility. While not all unrest led to regime change, as it did in the Tunisian and Egyptian contexts, it was expressed in remarkably similar terms. In Morocco street protests erupted in about 50 urban settings, spearheaded by the activist movement *?Ashrine Febrair* (February 20). Unemployed graduates, who saw scarce prospects for anticipating what they called a "decent life," led the struggle by tirelessly voicing slogans on "work and dignity" (*shughl* and *karama*) that echoed in the Moroccan urban landscape and opened the curtains for highly symbolic acts of despair such as self-immolation across the kingdom.[4] One such act of self-immolation, which severely injured five young men and claimed the life of another, notably took place outside the occupied Ministry of Education in Rabat in January 2012.[5]

The location of these protests outside of the Ministry of Education is anything but random. The Moroccan public school, founded in the aftermath of independence from France, encapsulates the incomplete, contradictory, and frustrated anti-colonial nationalist vision. This vision hinged on a projection of mass public education as the panacea to socio-economic and cultural domination. Schools and universities were envisioned as the main mechanisms for scientific and technological development, both of which were necessary for remaking the nation. Today, schools are a painful reminder of how nationalist agendas recycle colonial relationships and dovetail with global neoliberal incentives. Hence, a mere 50 years after its founding, the Moroccan public school system is acknowledged—by multilateral agencies, the Moroccan government, and the general public—to be in a state of serious crisis (World Bank, 2008).

Moroccan public schools, similar to Egyptian schools (Herrera & Torres, 2006), face discrepancies that dominant development agencies like the World Bank classify as major structural hurdles: overcrowded classrooms, inadequate facilities, ineffective pedagogical methods, and differential access to education in relation to urban–rural and gender divides. Critics of such discourses point out that schools are further challenged by an explicit government endorsement of neoliberal policies of privatization and a turn towards a consumerist and entrepreneurial model of citizenship. However, taking these hurdles as universally meaningful is thorny for a comparative study of education. These critiques obscure the officially silenced linguistic and cultural tensions that undercut Moroccan student efforts at academic promotion. These tensions index the ambiguous relationship established between Morocco's post-Independence public school and the policy of educational Arabization (Boutieri, 2012).

The modern Moroccan school was founded upon the French protectorate model, which was highly elitist and linguistically and racially divisive. It was supposed to become the mechanism for consolidating national unity along Arabo-Muslim lines. This nationalist agenda was critically dependent on the expansive use of the Arabic language. Not only would Arabic replace academic subjects formerly taught in French, but it would also unite a population versed in varieties of *darija* and Tamazight.[6] Given political disagreement and the complexities of lived experience, the modern public school accommodated Arabization tenuously and unequally. Currently, education is ostensibly fully Arabized, but only until university level, at which point the most prestigious subjects are still taught in French. In addition, the current job market is inhospitable to exclusively Arabophone graduates. Many private schools (from pre-school to high school) promote a primarily francophone education (where Arabic and English feature as subjects), thus reifying colonial links between linguistic competence and social stratification.

Current and former students of the Arabized public school system are inadequately prepared in French (they receive three to four hours per week of foreign language instruction), and are unsure of the value of standard Arabic (*fusha*) in the job market, especially in light of the state's unequivocal turn towards market liberalization. At the same time, the school discourages the use of the languages of the everyday (*darija* and Tamazight) in relation to written speech. In my conversations with students, their impression of their linguistic predicament and, by extension, their social prospects appeared grim: "We don't have any language," said Mustafa, a student of a public high school in Temara. He added animatedly: "We are bilingual or trilingual illiterates!" Despite an official rhetoric about contemporary Morocco transcending its colonial past, such past is still strongly implicated in the mechanisms of social integration. Therefore, what we call the "post-colonial" or the "development" period in Morocco is in need of its own material and symbolic emancipation, a decolonization for which the battle is far from over. Cyberspace constitutes a central site where students raise the issue of the rudimentary nature of Moroccan decolonization in learning, and shape creative alternatives for moving forward.

On-Trial Part 1: The De-Colonial Logic of Memes

My student interlocutors were acutely aware of the overlap of colonial hierarchies with post-independence knowledge production and dissemination. As pointed out by anthropologists who work with youth in the region (Kastrinou-Theodoropoulou, 2012) and beyond (Masquelier, 2010), the ambivalence and contradictions that undercut youthful efforts to resist dominant structures are essential features of the fluidity of their, and all, self-fashioning projects. Even though my interlocutors deplored the entrenched prestige of the French language inside the theoretically Arabized school, they remained committed to certain liberal, modernist ideas around modes of pedagogy (dialogue, cultivation of critical spirit, and so on) that also partook in the French *mission civilisatrice* in Morocco and elsewhere. Such preference is not just the by-product of liberal democracy, but it is also instrumental to the reproduction of social stratification on both a local and global scale (Levinson, Foley, & Holland, 1996). Their critique neither escaped gender stereotypes nor evinced class elements. Nevertheless, cyberspace constituted one of the main arenas where they deliberated Morocco's educational system.[7] Some went online to enrich their schoolwork. Many students go to virtual space to access already prepared essays and quiz responses and these circulate for mass consumption. Teachers routinely discuss the online circulation of this material during their assemblies and exam board meetings. On at least one occasion, in 2006, the Ministry of Education had to officially cancel a module examination in June because the Baccalaureate exam topics were leaked the night before the exam (Benmahmoud, 2006). This is hardly unique to Morocco, but what is worth underscoring is the absence of guilt about using the internet to cheat at school. I maintain that such an attitude points to the internet as a medium of circumvention—through cheating—of what is perceived as an unjust and unproductive pedagogical space. Online, students outsmart school authorities, who are clearly losing control over the flow of information. What is more, the hierarchical classroom dynamics between teacher and student, the lecture format that dominates most modules, and general restrictions on political critique in public are being challenged. The internet serves as a more fertile terrain on which students venture to critique and reflect.

My inquiry into a widespread virtual conversation on education began when a student, Zakaria, emailed me in the summer of 2011 with a link to what appeared to be a well-known meme (an image propagated through the web) named Bouzebal. Bouzebal, which literally means "father of trash," comes from a disadvantaged social background and is evidently unemployed. He has an entourage of other memes, including a troll, an older male companion, and a female friend called Derpina. The link was accompanied by the comment: "This guy is trashing education online! He is terrific, you should have a look!" Bouzebal is the sketch of a young man who appears across a number of online spaces. He principally features on his own website (www.bouzebal.com), but his stories and opinions circulate widely on Facebook and YouTube. The figure of the distinctly Moroccan Bouzebal materializes out of a template employed by various online users outside Morocco. He also appears on Lebanese and Egyptian sites under different names.[8] The students I worked with neither knew nor cared to find out where the meme originated, nor were they especially curious about who created it. In 2013 there were at least four different Moroccan Bouzebal pages on Facebook featuring, among others, *Bouzebal in High School* (http://on.fb.me/YCQIpQ), and *Bouzebal Oujda* (town in northeast Morocco) (http://on.fb.me/YCQLSB). In this sense, the meme has a rhizomatic quality. It spreads horizontally and its origins are not known.[9] Bouzebal and his critique of the system are interactive, informal, and horizontal. They contrast to modes of knowledge production and transmission within pedagogical institutions.

Bouzebal was not explicitly made into a symbol of the uprisings in Morocco, but the critique he embodies around structural inequality and hypocrisy was paramount to the mass demonstrations that took place during 2011–2012 and beyond. Bouzebal appears in a variety of comic strips (sketched out, collaged, and sometimes animated) that address the disconcerting aspects of Moroccan society. Education features prominently on this list. In one of these comic strips, Bouzebal aspires to win over a foreign girl through the use of French (see Figure 3.1).

As in other former settings, speaking French fluently in Morocco is an indication of holding a good educational level and respectable social standing. Bouzebal decides to learn French by buying and memorizing a novel, memorization being a dominant pedagogical feature of the public school. When he eventually meets up with this girl, this is how their dialogue unfolds:

FOREIGN GIRL: *Cheri, je t'aime* (Darling, I love you.)
BOUZEBAL: *Moi aussi, murmura-t-il* (Me too, he whispered.)

In his various appearances, where he usually speaks in Latinized and computerized *darija,* Bouzebal appears to be acutely aware of the lingering social role of French in Moroccan society. Through the exposure of these educational, and consequently social and linguistic incongruities, Bouzebal and his entourage shed light on the predicament of the current generation of lower-class public school graduates. One such sketch focuses on Derpina, Bouzebal's female friend, and

FIGURE 3.1 Bouzebal meets a foreign girl.
Source: www.bouzebal.com, November 28, 2012.

her difficulties in succeeding in the Baccalaureate (see Figure 3.2). Unsure of her future prospects and without recourse to the appropriate channels, Derpina resorts to the traditional character of the *chwwafa* (fortune teller):

FRAME 1: *Derpina 3nd chwwafa* (Derpina goes to the fortune teller.)

FRAME 2: Chwwafa: *Ach bghiti t3rfi a bnti?* (What do you want to know, my girl?)
Derpina: *3afak choufili wach ghadi ndi lbac* (Please, see whether I'll get the Bac.)

FRAME 3: Chwwafa: *Iyyah, hiya luwla a bnti* (Yes, definitely, my girl.)

FRAME 4: Chwwafa: *Ghadi tddih o twldi m3ah jouj drari!* (You'll get him and have two children with him!)

In the last frame, Derpina finds out that she will most likely marry someone called Bac (short for Baccalaureate) and have two children with him. The strip plays on the multiple meanings of the verb *dar*: "to do, make" and, here, as "to have children."

Opinions online were often conflicted over the degree of vulgarity and sexism of Bouzebal sketches. The meme obviously privileges a masculine experience of disenfranchisement that, while critical towards state mechanisms, replicates challenging aspects of offline gender relations such as the over-sexualization of

FIGURE 3.2 Derpina visits a fortune teller.
Source: www.bouzebal.com, n.d.

women. However, female commentators were quick to put Bouzebal in his place by posting remarks to counter his machismo.

Students followed the meme across its online appearances as they also adopted his jokes and mannerisms offline. For instance, one of Bouzebal's famous catchphrases is "Bouzebal Plzzzzz!," an indication that he is either being too funny or too offensive. This catchphrase became very popular among youth offline. Indicatively, the troublemaker of a senior-year class, Mehdi, was nicknamed "Bouzebal," which he readily embraced. Aicha, a student of the same class, justified the attribution of the nickname in this manner: "Maybe he adopted stuff from the online Bouzebal, maybe the online Bouzebal is inspired by him! Who knows . . ." The identification of this youth with the Bouzebal meme in linguistic, educational, and material terms suggests that it functioned as a collective virtual incarnation (an avatar if you wish). The avatar does not stand for the Moroccan public school student but for a more general student critique against the school. If Bouzebal embodies—even if tenuously—a collective "we" by virtue of his rhizomatic production and the anti-school messages he communicates, what are the features of this collectivity? Herrera's research on digital media in Egypt (2012, p. 335) suggests that the communicative behavior of youth online reveals their "cognitive makeup, which changes their relationship to political and social systems and their notion of themselves as citizens." In a similar vein, I propose that the avatar points to a youth disposition towards engaged citizenship that is imaginative and invested in dialogue. This disposition is avowedly, yet not uncritically, modernist and is also undercut by gender stereotypes evident in the over-sexualization of female memes such as Derpina.

Similar to Bouzebal, Le Prasson is an actual-person-turned-meme, who exemplifies similar aspects of the public educational system. The meme originates in a home video uploaded on YouTube (Commir, 2012). The video features two street urchins of a popular neighborhood of Casablanca on their way to class who are asked on camera why they like school and whether they are learning useful things. During the interview, it becomes apparent to the interviewer that one of the boys, who is wearing a T-shirt featuring French-Algerian football idol Zinedine Zidane, cannot actually read the name Zidane. Instead, the boy vocalizes the written name as "le Prasson," a nonsensical French-sounding word that causes both interviewer and cameraman to laugh hysterically. The interviewer, whose social background is more privileged and who is evidently more fluent in French, is blatantly mocking these kids. In his laughter and his probing, he demonstrates how class plays out in these online cultural productions even at moments of critique. Despite this performance of class disparity, the purpose of the video was to underline the highly problematic educational experience of public school students. Such a critique must have resonated with many internet users as the video went viral. Migrating to Facebook, the image of this nicknamed Le Prasson began featuring in caricature sequences that contrasted the vulnerable state of Moroccan education with that of other countries.

One of these sequences features the Turkish prime minister, Recep Tayyip Erdoğan, and the Moroccan prime minister, Abdelillah Benkirane, who are both the leaders of the moderate Islamic parties of their countries. The sequence (originally posted in Latinized *darija*) is based on the rumor that Erdoğan considered investing in iPad tablets, which he would distribute to 15 million students and 1 million teachers instead of textbooks (Obama Pacman, 2011). The dialogue reads as follows:

ERDOĞAN:	I am Recep Erdoğan. I distributed iPad tablets to students so that they could study well.
TURKISH STUDENT:	Thank you, Uncle Erdoğan.
LE PRASSON:	And how about us, Uncle Benkirane?
CAPTION 4:	Benkirane—The Prasson wants an iPad! Hhhhh.
BENKIRANE:	Fuck off! Slate and chalk please.
LE PRASSON:	Education in Morocco . . .
ERDOĞAN:	Hm . . . [just] a rumor!

The criticism of the new Moroccan government headed by the Islamist Justice and Development Party (PJD) is candid and the online endorsement of such criticism against the state's educational prerogatives is evident. Since early 2012, three

Le Prasson pages on Facebook have been inundated by fans who enthusiastically show their support towards the figure of the poorly educated street urchin.[10]

Bouzebal and Le Prasson appear together on www.bouzebal.com as the subject matter of a mock Baccalaureate exam paper (www.bouzebal.com, May 20, 2012). Imitating the format and tone of an actual exam paper, this satirical version asks students to demonstrate their familiarity with the memes of Bouzebal, his entourage, and Le Prasson. At the top of the page, the exam advises students that: "The use of Facebook is permitted but re-posting is forbidden." The questions are farcical: "In four lines, write everything you know about the figure of Bouzebal," "What does Le Prasson want to become when he grows up?" "Which one of the following is part of Bouzebal's crowd?" and so on. At first sight, such questions enact the absurdity and perceived worthlessness of the examination and the modules studied at school. Yet this type of reference is also suggestive of the general familiarity of internet users with online activity (notice the reference to re-posting). The mock Bac constitutes an invitation to elaborate on shared knowledge. The mock Bac circulated widely across Moroccan cyberspace during the exam period in 2012. Teasing her poorly performing classmate, Soufia re-posted the mock Bac to his Facebook wall saying: "At last, an exam you can get 100% in! lol" (personal communication, June 12, 2012).

Artifacts such as memes, dynamically appropriated by students to deplore and debate their education, appear next to postings of photos of run-down schools and commentaries on inappropriate teaching methods. Similarly to Bouzebal, such postings, distributed on Facebook by groups such as *Al Maghreb Zwin* (Morocco is Beautiful), or *Maroc Follie* (Morocco Madness), that were active during 2011–2012 are not exclusively created by and for a Moroccan public. Originating anywhere in the world, these postings find fertile ground among students and graduates who have endured the inconsistencies of public school pedagogy. One of these postings is a three-part sequence of a class scene written in English that exposes the rupture between the content of school messages and the reality of teaching and learning in class (see Figure 3.3).

> TEACHER: Dear kids today we are going to talk about democracy.
> STUDENT: Why?
> TEACHER: Because I said it [= so].

Many Moroccan commentators on this posting related similar incidents and reminisced about the lack of opportunity to express themselves and disagree with their teacher for fear of verbal rebuke or physical punishment. Taking his cue from the latest sketch, one of the students I knew well from my fieldwork, Simo, joked that the first verb he ever learned at school was *skout!* (shut up!).

While neither conventionally political (they do not target a change of regime), nor conventionally economic (they do not transform structures of social mobility), such cultural products are actively implicated in both domains by anticipating a

FIGURE 3.3 A lesson in democracy.

Source: www.bouzebal.com, 2012.

different social experience. Some might argue that Bouzebal and Le Prasson are not pre-figurative of emerging forms of citizenship but rather, a form of venting and a divergence from activism. I find this viewpoint unsatisfactory. So long as we can accept that the radical separateness between virtual and actual is not the result of technology but of motivation, we should remain open to the possibility that reworking socio-cultural and political subjectivities, inherent in reconfigurations of citizenship, may be *actually* happening in the *virtual* sphere.

My interpretation of the symbiotic and locally specific relationship between virtual and actual is underscored by a number of postulations about the role of digital practices as both "cultural products and social processes as well as extremely potent arenas of political struggle" (Spitulnik, 1993, p. 303). This earlier elaboration of mass media by Spitulnik serves as a reminder that the internet is neither entirely novel nor a fully separate domain of engagement but, rather, the most recent instantiation of the relationship between technology and socio-cultural arrangements (Abu-Lughod, 1989; Armbrust, 1998; Kraidy, 2009). Surely, the internet offers certain possibilities of engagement and interactivity that are qualitatively different from pre-digital media: self-generated content, speed of communication, and the existence of a space that can accommodate huge numbers of users at a time. Yet it is at the intersection of such qualities and located practices of consumption that we can gain insight into the actual role of digital media in people's lives. For instance, when Armbrust (1989) traces habits of spectatorship in commercial cinemas in downtown Cairo, he explicitly seeks the link between leisure and social transformation. Interesting, he takes his cue not from the context of the film itself, but from the in-hall practices of cinema-goers. Armbrust shows that downtown commercial cinemas provide enough anonymity for a degree of political transgression—such as mocking President Mubarak at a time when such behavior was not accepted in normal public spaces—during the newsreels that precede film screenings. Drawing on his insight, we can argue that the internet, through anonymity or usage of pseudonyms, has not invented, but it has breathed new life into, this type of public participation.

Insofar as mainstream media in Morocco and other parts of the region has been controlled by the state, new media has enabled alternative ways of relating (Eickelman & Anderson, 1999).[11] Looking at digital media as imbued with what Buckingham (2008, p. 12) calls "potentialities," a certain leveling out of expertise in knowledge production and dissemination, scholars have investigated online struggles over moral authority. These struggles took their cue from the technical features of digital media but gained momentum with the loosening grip of the state over this domain of sociality and the expansion of mass literacy (Hirschkind, 2012).[12] Researchers of Morocco will readily admit that a precondition for considering virtual practices emancipatory is our familiarity with a regime that restricts political dissent and censors political expression. It is known that some opinions that cannot circulate among an offline public or in print may find their way into cyberspace, which engenders a quasi-unique relationship between private and public. Such is the dynamic that saturates the dissemination of student critiques of the Moroccan educational system.

It is important, however, not to overstate this point. The internet is closely monitored in Morocco, as it is in Tunisia and Egypt (Aouragh & Alexander, 2011; Ben Mhenni, 2009), as evidenced by the number and speed of arrests of bloggers and other users who broach taboo topics such as the King of Morocco. In 2008, university student Fouad Mourtada was arrested and imprisoned for having created a fake portrait of Mohammed VI's younger brother, Moulay Rachid (Ben Gharbia, 2008). In 2012, 19-year-old Walid Bahomane was arrested for posting caricatures of the King on Facebook (Errazouki, 2012). Clearly, it would be misleading to treat the internet as autonomous and even more so to assume that it is location-less and immaterial.[13] Probing the interface between virtual and actual experience without predetermining it helps us remember that, as Lila Abu-Lughod writes, some people can be "caught between several worlds whose borders the new media technologies can cross but most individual lives cannot" (1989, p. 47). Notwithstanding such awareness, I argue that online sociality in Morocco contests the existing educational order and, in so doing, envisages and demands socio-economic and political change. To confer such power to virtual practice requires us to see that a conventional understanding of political activism may well be part of this anticipation, yet it is not its indexical example.[14]

On-Trial Part 2: Registers of a Transformed Public

The student critiques above address the pedagogical messages of public education and the vulnerable social status of public school graduates. There is more to this activity: the semiotic space carved out by Moroccan high-school students unsettles official linguistic categories and conventional rules of linguistic competence. Bidding us all goodnight, Fati, a university student, wrote on her Facebook page: "*Mohim, ana daba nmchi n3ss. Il fait dega tart et demain je me reveille tot. Peace out*" ("Alright, I'm going to bed. It is getting late and tomorrow I'm getting up early. Peace Out") (personal communication, July 10, 2013). This goodnight note is remarkable in that it is written in computerized *darija*, idiosyncratically spelled French, and English that recalls American urban culture. The quote omits Arabic *fusha*, the formal language of the state and modern school. In both its inclusiveness and its omission, the quote demarcates the domain of virtual youth sociality—inescapably reliant on language—at the same time as it redefines the Ministry of Education's definition of "correct" Arabic, French, and English. Therefore the decolonial quality of student virtual activity takes on a different appearance: it becomes the reconfiguration of their offline socio-cultural communicative repertoires. Language remains a central consideration and becomes a key instrument to this reconfiguration. By remaining close to the dynamics of ambivalence and contradiction, students seek to reverse certain aspects of colonial hierarchy and its recycling into contemporary experience. They remain complicit in some rules of interaction such as the preservation of French fluency as a class feature.

I managed to understand the virtual linguistic code used by youth and their online productions (among which are Bouzebal and Le Prasson sketches) rather quickly for reasons that demonstrate the transformative nature of this practice. First, since this code made ample use of French words (more so than face-to-face interactions), I, a foreigner, felt free to mix my *darija* with French whenever I reached the limits of my vocabulary. Second, the rules of transcription of both Arabic and French are loose enough so that I did not feel self-conscious about correct spelling. I realized that similar concerns made students more comfortable about using their linguistic skills online. There is no space here for a detailed morphological presentation of this language, which I call *virtual darija,* but it is important to mention that the code is an evolution of cell phone *darija* used for sending text messages and therefore emerges out of users' own communicative and creative needs. Interestingly, virtual *darija* uses a few basic principles for consonant transcription that point to a francisized version of Latinization. For example, the letter *shin* is transcribed as ch. As for vocalization, it is more of an individual choice. For instance, the word for country can be: *blad, bled or bld*.[15] Generally, the malleability of virtual *darija* at the hands of each writer distinguishes it from the French that is required by school and the job market. Even though some degree of standardization is beginning to emerge, students engage in an ongoing rewriting of this code. When asked about how virtual *darija* works, or how they learned how to write it, the students were unable to explain. They answered, "If you use the internet, you know how to do it."

Online use of *darija* legitimizes *darija* as a written register. On another level, it empowers youth to innovate linguistically rather than submit to the recommendations of their government. Hence I suggest that virtual *darija* emerges as a new skill, more horizontally cultivated and less formally sanctioned, which is implicated in subjective and collective operations. From this angle, literacy gained at school (no matter how insufficient for the current job market), and the sociality encouraged through schooling, become platforms for a whole range of other activities.

Juxtaposed to the exclusion experienced through the hierarchical multilingualism of formal education, it would seem that online chatting entirely circumvents issues of social positioning through an incessant mixture of linguistic codes. Nonetheless, for the initiated, virtual *darija* does not entirely escape social labeling. Usually, students of a certain background made use of their French fluency on *msn* or Facebook by employing more sophisticated terms or the latest French argot. Other students, who did not have this linguistic ability, strove to incorporate as much French as possible in order to impress their interlocutors. This was confirmed by a close friend who was a university student and fluent in French. He explained that he used sophisticated French in order to screen interlocutors on *msn.* Virtual *darija* cannot take credit for the disappearance of social distinctions, yet the social *passing* that virtual *darija* permits is considerably easier than face-to-face communication, where issues of accent and appearance come into play. I consider this passing significant, not just as another indication that students are acute commentators of social stratification, but equally as evidence of what Tsing calls, "the necessity and power of the guise" (1993, p. 253), reminiscent of Armbrust's claims about cinema-goers. By using French online, students deploy a language that had shaped Moroccan socio-cultural hierarchy for 100 years in order to "forge creative self-positionings" (Tsing, 1993, p. 253). To what end this register serves the politics of this transformed citizenry that I am tracing here is too early to tell, yet I contend that virtual *darija*'s effectiveness should not be limited to a parody of hegemonic language ideologies. I view this activity as being at the intersection of rehearsing and remaking culture. It is for this reason that it constitutes a *techne*, that is, an art or craft for staging sociality otherwise (Boellstorff, 2008, p. 25). In fact, these novel writing techniques have long begun to filter into offline written communication as more Moroccans use them to produce poetry, theater, and songs (for a comparative perspective, see Cook, 2004, p. 104).

Consequently, it is fair to say that the register in question partakes in virtual sociality as a cultural product and a social process and that it is worthy of our attention because it expands—as do the memes—conventional definitions of the political. Were this not the case, Moroccan state mechanisms would not be threatened by the artistic enunciations of the arrested rapper al-Haqid (the Enraged) (Schemm, 2012), and the Facebook pranks of the prosecuted Mourtada and Bahomane. If we see the constitutive gap between virtual and actual as porous but fundamental, we will better appreciate the expectation and transformation embodied in the memes as well as the linguistic ingenuity among students.

Mediated Worlds

Moving away from romanticizing virtual sociality, this chapter has interrogated memes and linguistic registers that evince the emergence of a new public among Moroccan students. These students hold their educational system, and by extension their state, "on-trial" for not having assisted them in emancipating from older and recycled socio-cultural hierarchies and their economic implications. They also "try out" alternative ways of producing and disseminating knowledge foreclosed to them by official state mechanisms. Insisting that the impression of apartness between virtual and actual risks classifying certain emancipatory and transformative practices as "less real," I expanded the notions of activism, citizenship, and politics to encompass these student practices. It is possible to think of instances where people construct "a world apart" (Miller & Slater, 2000, p. 5) from their actual lives, but this distance is an outcome of their motives and not a feature of virtuality. More gravely, when apartness becomes tautological to freedom—of expression, of movement, of identity—it reiterates a normative postmodern notion of the self as unbound and fluid.[16] Mapping virtual sociality onto the broader domain of media,

I normalized the interrogation of online practices by framing them as "cultural products that exist in the social and political worlds within which they were developed, and they are not exempt from the rules and norms of these worlds" (Wilson & Peterson, 2002, p. 462). That the online sociality explored in this chapter should be seen for its decolonial features and transformative potential is undeniable. Simultaneously, this sociality is anchored in modernist understandings of pedagogy that should not necessarily be taken at face value and is constrained both by high politics through censorship and lingering gender and social stratifications. Inconclusive as this assessment of the nature of digital mediation may be, it reflects more accurately the inchoate nature of citizenship than a pre-formulated template about technology and human agency that conflates prescription with analysis.

Notes

1. In 2006 Moroccan education witnessed dropout rates of about 370,000 students a year, a number that has been steadily rising. Especially noticeable in the primary school level, dropout rates are quite significant in middle-school and high-school levels as well (Mdidech, 2007).
2. Scholarship suggests that online activity of all types by far preceded the Egyptian 25 January Revolution of 2011 (Otterman, 2007; Weyman, 2007), marking a dynamic field of negotiation of privacy, intimacy, identity, and authority. Radsch (2008) has gone as far as to claim that the symbiotic relationship between offline activism in Egypt (the *Kifaya* movement) and the development of an activist blogosphere has been a specific convergence and is rather unusual for the region. She has equally highlighted the fact that American media actively shaped a discourse around "citizen journalism" and sanctioned from early on what she calls an "organizational identity" for bloggers (p. 5).
3. Boellstorff (2011) looks at virtuality, originally understood as life in the mind, as intrinsic to all lived experience and therefore suggests that it would be a mistake to exaggerate its separation from physical reality, or, adversely, prophesize about the eventual convergence of the two. Whereas Boellstorff argues that social networking sites do not constitute virtual worlds, I claim that there is considerable overlap in the way they engage with subjectivity and creativity. Interestingly, in a parallel move, the anthropology of politics has also disengaged from positivism with regards to the nature of reality as "what is solid, tangible, constant, and visible" (Yael Navaro-Yashin, 2007, p. 6).
4. For over 20 years, Moroccan urban life has been saturated with discontent. Large numbers of unemployed graduates spend their days in front of trade unions and demonstrate outside government buildings (Cohen, 2004). The concept of a "decent life" invites a thorough empirical exploration that lies beyond the scope of this chapter. In my experience with Moroccan youth, the concept alludes to financial independence, social validation (including the fulfillment of culturally sanctioned gender roles), inclusion in political decision-making, and encouragement of individual and collective creativity. As is obvious from the above, the criteria for the accomplishment of such goals are by no means unique to Morocco.
5. In reality, demonstrators belonged to different age groups, yet they appeared to collectively identify with the term *al-shabab* (youth), which alludes both to their dynamism and to their perceived liminality within existing socio-cultural and economic frames. Throughout this chapter, I use the term "youth" not as a universal category of

experience (as commonly understood by a developmental psychology framework), but as a term of individual and collective identification put forward by my interlocutors.

6. I need to clarify that the labels of "French," "Arabic," and "Tamazight" are deployed to speedily introduce a cultural landscape but in essence constitute artificial and hegemonic categories of linguistic usage as bound and homogeneous (see Blommaert, 2005).

7. Despite its pronounced intention to engage students with IT since the early 2000s, the Moroccan Ministry of Education has not yet materialized such goals. The Emergency Plan, announced in 2009 by the High Commission on Education, aspired to install eight to twelve PCs, a video-projector, and a laptop in every public school and strongly encouraged the use of multi-media by teachers (Program Nafida@) and students. This ambitious agenda clashes with the material circumstances of many public schools that lack working restrooms, heating installation, and windows. As a result, students familiarize themselves with ICT as an extracurricular activity.

8. Insofar as he embodies a youth perspective (privileging its male components), Bouzebal's appearances concur with the views of organized activist groups in Morocco, both online and offline, though an instrumental link between the two does not seem to exist.

9. The concept of the "rhizome" as social formation was famously developed by Deleuze and Guattari (1987), but it also emerged in discussions of actual and virtual activism during the Egyptian 25 January Revolution in 2011 (Herrera, 2011).

10. According to his website (www.bouzebal.com), Bouzebal has 491,435 followers on Facebook and 1,977 on Twitter. One of the three official profile pages of Le Prasson has 57,455 "likes" and another has 14,254 "likes." Indicatively, the profile of Benkirane has 13,417 "likes" and the unofficial profile of the current king, Mohammed VI, has 27,209 "likes."

11. The discipline of anthropology has judiciously explored religious education and new media in an effort to undo what had theoretically been posited as a contradiction between religion and modernity. It has demonstrated how cognitive and affective states of moral cultivation not only adapt but also creatively put to work new technologies of communication.

12. These struggles reveal what may be at stake when debating Moroccan education online, which, even though it does not exactly fall under the rubric of either morality or cultural production, is occasionally interlaced with both. For example, students who engage in novel learning and teaching practices online are also intensely interested in religious pedagogy outside the domain of the state and are equally enthusiastic about cultural production (art, poetry, photography, film, and music).

13. As Aouragh (2012) and Bernal (2005) have persuasively argued in the case of Palestinian and the Eritrean diaspora online practices respectively, neither nationhood nor the nation state—as aspirations, emotional attachments, or frames of activity—truly collapses online. Arguing against the immateriality and non-locational aspects of the internet, Fish reminds us that "censorship and deregulation are explicit messages of how place-based national laws impact the way people engage with the internet" (2011, p. 17).

14. Ulrich (2009) likened Arab blogs to earlier print media and coffeehouses that disseminated alternative types of information and contested (subtly or not) existing forms of authority. While he views blogs as democratizing vehicles, Ulrich does not attribute democratization to the medium but, rather, to the historically persistent motivation of actors to seek dialogue and pluralism.

15. More pronounced differences in alphabet are compensated by the use of numbers that are readily available on the computer keyboard and the cell phone: the letter ḥa becomes 7, ʿayn becomes 3, and qaf becomes 9. The correspondence between number and letter, standardized in many Arabophone contexts, does not have a phonetic connection but a visual one: in short, there is a presumed visual resemblance between the consonant ʿayn and the number 3. To put all these principles in an expression: the online version of the sentence "kanḥamaq lih" (I'm crazy about him) is "kan7ma9 3lih."

16. Even though some of our interlocutors may empirically associate with this type of personhood, this is definitely not the case for all of them (Reed, 2006) and neither is their encounter with the internet an equalizing experience (Facer & Furlong, 2010). These concerns are pertinent to another set of arguments about the gradual redefinition of education online, often assumed to be horizontal, democratic, critical, and communicative. Such views disregard inequalities of access or the real limitations in legitimizing web-acquired knowledge and skills in actual society (Buckingham, 2008; Drotner, 2008).

References

Abu-Lughod, L. (1989). Bedouins, cassettes and technologies of public culture. *Middle East Report*, 159, 7–11.

Aouragh, M. (2012). *Palestine online*. London: I. B. Tauris.

Aouragh, M. & Alexander, A. (2011). The Egyptian experience: Sense and nonsense of the internet revolution. *International Journal of Communication*, 5, 1344–1358.

Armbrust, W. (1998). When the lights go down in Cairo: Cinema as secular ritual. *Visual Anthropology*, 10, 413–442.

Ben Gharbia, S. (2008, February 19). Morocco: Facebook's fake prince could face five years in prison. *Global Voices*. Retrieved from http://advocacy.globalvoicesonline.org/2008/02/19/morocco-facebooks-fake-prince-could-face-five-years-in-prison/

Benmahmoud, S. (2006, June 12). Fuite des épreuves du baccalauréat à Meknes. *L'Opinion*. Retrieved from http://lejournaldumaroc.canalblog.com/archives/2006/06/12/2076831.html

Ben Mhenni, L. (2009, May 15). Tunisia: Ammar 404 is back and censoring blogs again. *Global Voices*. Retrieved from http://globalvoicesonline.org/2009/05/15/tunisia-ammar-404-is-back-and-censoring-blogs-again/

Bernal, V. (2005). Eritrea on-line: Diaspora, cyberspace, and the public sphere. *American Ethnologist*, 32(4), 660–675.

Blommaert, J. (2005). Situating language rights: English and Swahili in Tanzania revisited. *Journal of Sociolinguistics*, 9(3), 390–417.

Boellstorff, T. (2008). *Coming of age in second life*. Princeton: Princeton University Press.

Boellstorff, T. (2011). Virtuality, placing the virtual body: Avatar, chora, cypherg. In F. E. Mascia-Lees (Ed.), *A companion to the anthropology of the body and embodiment* (504–520). Malden, MA: Wiley Blackwell.

Boutieri, C. (2012). A deux vitesses (in two speeds): Linguistic pluralism and educational anxiety in the Moroccan state school. *International Journal of Middle East Studies*, 44(3), 445–456.

Buckingham, D. (Ed.). (2008). *Youth, identity and digital media*. Cambridge, MA: Massachusetts Institute of Technology Press.

Carey, J. W. (2005). Historical pragmatism and the internet. *New Media & Society*, 7(4), 443–455.

Cohen, S. (2004). *Searching for a different future: The rise of global middle class in Morocco*. Durham: Duke University Press.

Commir, H. (2012, February 29). *Messi et Le Prasson* (video file). Retrieved from www.youtube.com/watch?v=Etk5vaejqRQ

Cook, S. (2004). New technologies and language change: Toward an anthropology of linguistic frontiers. *Annual Review of Anthropology*, 33, 103–115.

Deleuze, G. & Guattari, F. (1987). *A thousand plateaus*. Minneapolis: University of Minnesota Press.

Drotner, K. (2008). Leisure is hard work: Digital practices and future competencies. In D. Buckingham (Ed.), *Youth, identity and digital media* (167–184). Cambridge, MA: Massachusetts Institute of Technology Press.

Eickelman, D. F. & Anderson, J. (Eds.). (1999). *New media in the Muslim world: The emerging public sphere*. Bloomington: Indiana University Press.

Errazouki, S. (2012, February 17). "Violating sacred values" in Morocco: Free speech with an exception. *Jadaliyya*. Retrieved from www.jadaliyya.com/pages/index/4418/violating-sacred-values-in-morocco_free-speech-wit

Escobar, A. (1994). Welcome to cyberia: Notes on the anthropology of cyberculture. *Current Anthropology*, 35(3), 211–231.

Etling, B., Kelly, J., Faris, R. & Palfrey, J. (2009). *Mapping the Arabic blogosphere: Politics, culture, and dissent*. Harvard, MA: Berkman Center Research Publications.

Facer, K. & Furlong, R. (2010). Beyond the myth of the "cyberkid": Young people at the margins of the information revolution. *Journal of Youth Studies*, 4(4), 451–469.

Fish, A. (2011). The place of the internet in anthropology. *Anthropology News*, 52(3), 17.

Gonzalez-Quijano, Y. (2010). La fabrique sociale de l'internet Arabe: Une démocratisation du ou part le numérique? *Afkar/Idées*, 27. Retrieved from www.afkar-ideas.com/fr/article/?id=4451

Herrera, L. (2011, October 14). Generation rev and the struggle for democracy: Interview with Aly El-Raggal. *Jadaliyya*. Retrieved from www.jadaliyya.com/pages/index/2869/generation-rev-and-the-struggle-for-democracy_inte

Herrera, L. (2012). Youth and citizenship in the digital age: A view from Egypt. *Harvard Educational Review*, 82(3), 333–352.

Herrera, L. & Torres, C.A. (Eds.). (2006). *Cultures of Arab schooling: Critical ethnographies from Egypt*. Albany: State University of New York Press.

Hirschkind, C. (2012). Experiments in devotion online: The youtube khutba. *International Journal of Middle East Studies*, 44(1), 5–21.

Jacobson, D. (1999). Doing research in cyberspace. *Field Methods*, 11, 127–145.

Kastrinou-Theodoropoulou, M. (2012). A different struggle for Syria: Becoming young in the Middle East. *Mediterranean Politics*, 17(1), 59–76.

Kraidy, M. (2009). Reality television, gender and authenticity in Saudi Arabia. *Journal of Communication*, 53, 345–366.

Kraidy, M. M. & Khalil, J. F. (2008). Youth, media and culture in the Arab world. In S. Livingstone and K. Drotner (Eds.), *The international handbook of children, media and culture* (337–350). London & Thousand Oaks, CA: Sage Publications Ltd.

Levinson, B. A., Foley, D. E. & Holland, D.C. (Eds.). (1996). *The cultural production of the educated person: Critical ethnographies of schooling and local practice*. Albany: State University of New York.

Lukose, R. (2009). *Liberalization's children: Gender, youth, and consumer citizenship in globalizing India*. Durham: Duke University Press.

Masquelier, A. (2010). Securing futures: Youth, generation, and Muslim identities in Niger. In L. Herrera and A. Bayat (Eds.), *Being young and Muslim: New cultural politics in the global south and north* (225–239). Oxford: Oxford University Press.

Mazzarella, W. (2004). Culture, globalization, mediation. *Annual Review of Anthropology*, 33, 345–367.

Mdidech, J. (2007, April 17). Maroc: 370.000 élèves ont abandonné l'école en 2006. *Bladi. Net*. Retrieved from www.bladi.net/maroc-education.html

Miller, D. & Slater, D. (2000). *The internet: An ethnographic approach*. London: Berg Publishers.

Navaro-Yashin, Y. (2007). Introduction: Fantasy and the real in the work of Begona Aretxaga. *Anthropological Theory*, 7(1), 1–7.

Obama Pacman (2011). *Prime minister of Turkey uses iPad*. Retrieved from http://obamapacman.com/2011/12/prime-minister-erdogan-of-turkey-ipad-user/

Otterman, S. (2007, Spring). Publicizing the private: Egyptian women bloggers speak out. *Arabic Media and Society*, 1. Retrieved from http://arabmediasociety.sqgd.co.uk/?article=13

Pfaffenberger, B. (1992). Social anthropology of technology. *Annual Review of Anthropology*, 21, 491–516.

Radsch, C. (2008, Fall). Core to commonplace: The evolution of Egypt's blogosphere. *Arab Media and Society*, 6. Retrieved from http://arabmediasociety.sqgd.co.uk/?article=692

Reed, A. (2006). "My Blog is Me": Texts and Persons in UK online journal culture (and anthropology). *Ethnos: Journal of Anthropology*, 70(2), 220–242.

Schemm, P. (2012, April 4). Moroccan rapper "Al-Haqid" charged for anti-police song. *The Associated Press*. Retrieved from http://readingmorocco.blogspot.co.uk/2012/04/moroccan-rapper-al-haqid-charged-for.html

Spitulnik, D. (1993). Anthropology and mass media. *Annual Review of Anthropology*, 22, 293–315.

Tsing, A. (1993). *In the realm of the diamond queen: Marginality in an out-of-the-way place*. Princeton: Princeton University Press.

Ulrich, B. (2009, Spring). Historicizing Arab blogs: Reflections on the transmission of ideas and information in Middle Eastern history. *Arab Media and Society*, 8. Retrieved from www.arabmediasociety.com/?article=711

Weyman, G. (2007, October). Personal blogging in Egypt: Pushing social boundaries or reinforcing them? *Arab Media and Society*. Retrieved from www.arabmediasociety.com/?article=425

Wilson S. M. & Peterson, L. C. (2002). The anthropology of online communities. *Annual Review of Anthropology*, 31, 449–467.

World Bank. (2008). *The road not traveled: Education reform in the Middle East and North Africa*. Washington DC: Author. Retrieved from http://econpapers.repec.org/bookchap/wbkwbpubs/6303.htm

4

CHILDREN'S CITIZENSHIP

Revolution and the Seeds of an Alternative Future in Egypt

Chiara Diana

> Children must be seen as actively involved in the construction of their own social lives, the lives of those around them and of the societies in which they live. They can no longer be regarded as simply the passive subjects of structural determinations.
>
> (James & Prout, 1990, p. 4)

Introduction

Suleiman is an Egyptian child aged 6, and he is one of the child protagonists of a report dealing with feelings and experiences of children during Egypt's political uprising. Suleiman describes how he came to know about the revolutionary mobilizations from home, and his strong concerns when his family members took part in street protests. Like Suleiman, Aya, aged 14, also inquired about the street protests from her home and was explicitly prevented by her family from taking part in demonstrations. Despite her family's refusal to let her go to the streets, she was determined to find a way to support mobilization movements, so she turned to the internet. She created a Facebook group called *Thawra ma'hash bitaqa* (Revolution has no identity card) to disseminate information, and opinions, and to enter into dialogue with other online groups. Children like Suleiman, who have been emotionally affected by the uprisings, and others, like Aya, who have been politically involved, are becoming commonplace in Egyptian society.

The political involvement of children in the events leading up to and following Egypt's January 25 Revolution of 2011 has gone almost unnoticed. A handful of journalists and international organizations have written about the presence of children in public squares during the uprising. Yet, no valuable analysis has been made about how experiencing the uprising could have an ongoing impact on the personality and political preferences of these children as they enter different life stages. This chapter seeks to give voice and visibility (Brighenti, 2007) to a social group whose opinions are not usually taken into account and whose initiatives do not always reach the headlines. It explores the role of children in recent political changes and how they inspired a novel political and civic consciousness in public, private, institutional, and digital spaces. The uprising has stimulated children's imaginations, creativity, and sense of initiative, and expanded their awareness about issues such as political corruption, social justice, human rights, educational equity, and inequality. It has also strengthened children's sense of their own Egyptian citizenship and sense of community.

This chapter begins with the social, economic, and political reasons that sparked off revolutionary events in Egypt. Then, using the theoretical framework of the new social studies of childhood (NSSC), I highlight children's status, their attitudes to citizenship, and political practices. Egyptian children experienced the revolution in different settings, both virtual and physical, at school, in social media spaces, in the streets, and at home. Did any of their political attitudes and action derive from the formal teachings they were exposed to in school about citizenship education and "education for democracy"? How did revolutionary events affect their daily lives? Did they bring children into the world of politics and lead to a new citizenship consciousness?

Egyptian Children: New Social Actors in Revolutionary Times

In Egypt the image of children was traditionally used by the state to serve political ends and to show how their lives were integral to the process of nation building and national development (Karimi & Gruber, 2012). In the years leading up to the revolution, another experience of children, outside this normative development model, has been emerging. Children of Egypt today have not directly witnessed war or anti-colonial struggles, but they have grown up under the dictatorship of the Mubarak regime and experienced the ravages of the neo-liberal economic and political reforms. These reforms, which dismantled the social welfare state and exacerbated inequality, have been applied through Structural Adjustment Programs (SAPs) imposed by global financial institutions, among other means. Children, especially from the lower and middle classes, bear witness to their families' everyday life troubles and the deprivations of their basic rights. They are affected by economic reforms that result in the reduction and privatization of government services like education and health. Indeed, the economic reforms aimed at developing economic liberalization and promoting political liberalization in the Arab states since the middle of 1980s have led rather to a political stagnation, a so-called "political deliberalization" (Kienle, 2001).

At the same time, these policies have Janus-faced results. Simultaneous with the deterioration of basic civil rights and pauperization of the lower social classes, school enrolments in pre-school, primary, preparatory, secondary as well as higher education have risen throughout the Arab world in the last decades (Assaad &

Roudi-Fahimi, 2007; Filiu, 2011). In Egypt, it is worthwhile highlighting the significant progress in enrolling pre-school children into kindergarten education between 2001/2002 (13.69%) and 2008/2009 (25.12%) (Ministry of Education, 2010, p. 67). What bearing do all these economic, social, and educational indicators have on the lives and socialization of children? Such a question is difficult to answer with any authority since the topic of childhood and children's citizenship has been neglected in research and in the social history of the Middle East.[1] This chapter seeks to highlight these still unexplored issues by situating Egyptian children in the theoretical framework of the new social studies of childhood (NSSC) to help to clarify concepts about children, citizenship, and political participation.

The NSSC theories developed in the last decades of the twentieth century as an interdisciplinary approach to studying childhood. During the 1970s and 1980s concerns had been developing about the way in which the social sciences had traditionally conceptualized children and childhood. Those concerns resulted in the emergence of a new paradigm for the study of childhood (James & Prout, 1990).[2] It tried to give a voice to children who, for a long time, had been considered as "muted groups" (Hardman, 1973, p. 85), "passive receptors of adult culture," or 'in progress' of becoming full, rational adults" (Caputo, 1995, pp. 22–24). The latter was strongly determined by the theories of development of Piaget (1964) and Piaget & Inhelder (1966).

The new paradigm attempted to analyze childhood in relation to socio-political contexts; it tried to study them as a social category rather than a group. Some of the main features of the paradigm are: understanding childhood as a social construction and as a variable of social analysis that can never be separated from other variables; considering children's social relationships and cultures worthy of study in their own right and independent of the perspective of adults; seeing children as active in the construction of their own social lives and not just passive subjects. This theory encouraged scholars to look at the multiple meanings of childhood across cultures and societies, time and space.

Variables such as gender, religion, responsibilities, class, race, and ethnicity play important roles in defining how individual children experience their childhood. Moreover, these variables also affect the transition out of childhood and into the next life phase. The transitions between childhood and youth, and youth and adulthood, are not the same everywhere; they vary across and within societies and cultures over time (Honwana & De Boeck, 2005). Therefore, in some social and cultural settings, the age of children and its *temporal* dimension can even lose their importance as factors such as the time that adult people give them responsibilities, work, and even military tasks become more significant.

The sociological concept of socialization, based upon adult concern for the reproduction of social order and social transformation from child to adult, deliberately erased children's present tense because of its orientation analysis towards the past or the future. According to Caputo (1995), children are not passive recipients of social structures and processes, but they actively construct the world. Children must be seen as agents involved in social interactions, citizen cultures, and political actions.

Assuming that children's cultural development takes place on the social and individual levels (Vygotsky, 1978), then social interactions play a fundamental role in the formation of a child's cognitive development, the time when children acquire basic cultural ideas and formulate their own views. Children's everyday social interactions with adults and peers can provide a key to knowing about their citizenship values and even political attitudes. Children are social and political actors very early in life and not only after they learn about government, adult political roles, and major political events (Maynard, 1985).

In light of these approaches and theories about child's development and participation in their social and cultural contexts, I will go on to analyze children's attitudes to citizenship and political practices during current revolutionary times in Egypt in different spaces: in public (in the street); in private (in the family); in institutions (at school); as well as in digital society (on the internet).

Street Mobilization

During the initial and central period of the 25 January Revolution schools in Cairo were closed for half-term. Freed from school tasks and activities, children had the time to follow revolutionary events from home through television, radio, and adult conversations. They even attended protests, alone or together with their families. It was also common in the street mobilizations to find Cairo's homeless children wandering and sometimes taking part in demonstrations and clashes between pro-Mubarak and anti-Mubarak protesters (Fisk, 2011).[3]

Despite the scant attention paid to the role of children—whether school pupils or street children—in the revolution, a good number of them participated in events in Tahrir Square, the center of revolutionary events. The presence of children has been documented largely on amateur videos and mobile phones (Preston & Stelter, 2011), then uploaded on YouTube, Citizentube, or on the more militant Bambuser (O'Neill, 2011: Messieh, 2011).[4] The most common images in these homemade videos are of children carried by adults amidst the protesters, shouting out slogans against the (old) system (*nizam*) in order to demand Mubarak's resignation. Sometimes a child leads the protest from the shoulders of an adult, chanting slogans from a piece of paper, or improvising them on the spot.

The revolution was not the first time in recent history that children had been involved in street protests. In 2005, encouraged by a flurry of anti-Mubarak initiatives led by the *Kefaya* (Enough) movement, public demonstrations by the group "Children for Change" took place in Cairo. This group of children, aged between 5 and 16, was led by 13-year-old Mohamed El-Kazzaz following his father's arrest during a *Kefaya* demonstration (Howeidy, 2005).

Children from politicized family backgrounds, like young members of "Children for Change," show themselves to be more politically active than the average child (Dupoirier & Percheron, 1975). However, we see that young people from a more depoliticized milieu can acquire a "political socialization." Indeed, for them, political circumstances can prompt them to be involved in public protests, either alone or with their families. Street children, in particular, spent time in Tahrir Square hoping that the uprising would change their everyday street reality and terrifying conditions. Alone on the streets they face the horrors of rape, abuse, and arrest, and are sometimes forced to pose as drug dealers or prostitutes by the police themselves (Ali, 2013; Itameri, 2011).

Hosni Mubarak stepped down as president on February 11, 2011 and in July, 2011 the second phase of the revolution began. In Tahrir Square the community set up a tent city that included a library, a school that took on the name "Tahrir School," and a playground for children (Doss, 2011). Tahrir School was an initiative of the protesters to allow children to keep learning and expressing themselves through games and drawings. A video posted on YouTube shows children enthusiastically taking part in the school's activities, particularly children who had never before attended an actual school (*Daily News Egypt*, 2011).

In another video, a school science teacher by the name of Rabah talks about her initiative for the children of Tahrir Square. She created a public tent-space where children could express their feelings about the revolution and the current political situation through drawings. The children, aged between 8 and 11, explain their drawings. Nine-year old Fatma talks about how she supports the revolution since it forced corrupt leaders to leave the government. According to Islam, an 11-year-old boy, although many things have already changed thanks to the revolution, he advocates continuing the protests because the corrupt people are still in power.[5] In yet other videos, children as young as 7 talk with clarity about Mubarak's incarceration, the complicity of his wife Suzanne Mubarak, and the need for justice and respecting the civil rights of poor people. They are also up to date on the young martyrs whose lives had been taken during violent clashes between the protesters and the police (Raheb, 2011b). These children come across as well informed about current events and they have strong opinions about political change, which they are keen to express.

Outside of Tahrir Square other initiatives took shape. *Al Fan Midan* (Art is a Square) was launched two months after the fall of Mubarak by the Independent Artists Coalition and it was supported by civil society volunteers. *Al Fan Midan* holds monthly workshops in cities all over Egypt. Thanks to this initiative, Abdeen Square in Cairo, the site where it was born, has become the public place of street art, cultural events, and exhibitions for artists, musicians, performers, including children (Habib, 2011; Montasser, 2012). Through these cultural and public experiences, organizers and volunteers explore ways of expressing democracy and citizenship through art.

Student Initiatives

Soaked in revolutionary principles like justice and democracy, Egyptian school children organized their own revolution in schools, launching initiatives and calling meetings with other students and school staff in order to discuss and improve school conditions (BBC News, 2011). Some of them created the movement *Harakat tullab madaris masr li taghyyr* (Egypt's School Students for Change Movement) with various sections in different Egyptian cities founded by primary, secondary, and college students. The movement, in coordination with other student associations and organizations, called for a general strike on February 11, 2012, the date that marked a year since President Hosni Mubarak had been ousted (Laila, 2011).

Students for Change represents another student initiative launched on September 5, 2011 by four high-school students aged between 16 and 17 from different schools. They united around a common enthusiasm to find viable solutions to educational issues, especially disparities between private and public schools. Their model is to work through a type of school parliament that includes students and teachers, to hold stimulating workshops for students, organize scientific debates, sports competitions, and collaborative activities with student groups from foreign countries.

Online Action

Some children had the opportunity to experience the uprisings first hand in the streets and public squares, but many were confined to the home because of the risks of what was taking place in the streets. From their domestic and protected space, children experienced feelings of fear and danger towards their family and friends who were protesting in the street. They also felt feelings of happiness and enthusiasm for the successful moments of the revolution. Many children turned to the internet to participate in the revolution and they created groups and pages on social networks sites, Facebook and Twitter.

Fourteen-year-old Aya was forbidden by her parents to go down to the street, so she decided to support the revolution in her own way. She started by posting comments on the Facebook page of the Military Council (incidentally, her father is in the military). She then became more involved in revolutionary and political issues through her Twitter account, although she was technically too young to hold such an account. In collaboration with other children, she launched the Facebook page *Thawra ma'hash bitaqa* (Revolution has no identity card),[6] which is for Egyptian children and young people under 18 who wanted to contribute to the Egyptian revolution. Five boys and three girls served as the page administrators (admins). Even though they did not know each other, they worked together in order to plan activities and upload news and information onto the page. They also drafted a declaration in which they explained the reasons for creating the page. Some of these reasons were to use their creative capacities for the development of Egypt and to disseminate their messages, opinions, and remarks. Their only condition was that views expressed on the page did not "clash with religious values."[7] On February 15, 2011 the group was interviewed on *Akher Kalam*, one of Egypt's most popular talk shows, hosted by Yousri Fouda. They explained that one of the admins was a young Salafist, who had suggested they include the last sentence about religious values (ONtveg, 2012).

Aya's experience shows how the boundaries between "childhood" and "adulthood" are becoming increasingly blurred. I dare add that in changing and unstable political contexts like the Egyptian revolutionary period, it is more difficult to distinguish boundary lines which are separating children's action and spaces from adult ones. The revolutionary context, combined with technological social media, has given children the opportunity to explore "adult" aspects of life such as politics, and instill some concepts and ideas necessary to build a political consciousness, and citizenship values.

Raising Political Socialization and Citizen Consciousness

The results of the opinion poll "How to make a better Egypt," undertaken by Edrak for Edutainment Project Development[8] in the months following the 25 January Revolution, measured political concerns and commitments of the young generation during those crucial moments of Egyptian history. The poll, which contained 20 questions, targeted children between 6 and 15 years old. Those aged 6 represented the smallest portion of respondents (10), the 13–15 range the highest (312), followed by children aged 10 (188). The respondents were from public, national, and international schools in Cairo (85%) and in Alexandria (15%).

The poll revealed that children were highly affected by the revolutionary events. To the question, "What do you know about the revolution?" 52% answered that the population was protesting because people were angry, and 42% thought it was a Facebook revolution, because Facebook was the protesters' communication tool. Twenty-seven percent of the respondents had been present in Tahrir Square with their family or friends during the 18-day revolution, and 20% had been to Tahrir afterwards. Seventy-nine percent of the children answered that they would have taken an active part in the revolution had they been older. Sixty-five percent helped to clean the streets after the revolution, and 38% of them declared that dirt was one of the negative aspects of Egypt. One question asked about role models and many respondents pointed to the "youth of the revolution" (*shabab al-thawra*), while some others expressed their admiration for some important Egyptian bloggers. Since Mubarak's resignation, Egyptian children wondered about the personality of their next president. The majority (61%) asserted that the new president should help people solve their problems giving priority to the eradication of poverty (50%), to education issues (35%), and Egyptian foreign policy (14%). The question of national unity and nationhood were the major concern for the children, as was shown by the drawings with the symbols of the two main religions (Islam and Christianity) and expressive images of love for the country and its people. In the end, the most relevant point resulting from the opinion poll was that the revolution had instilled a strong sense of belonging and a political conscience in children (Helmy, 2011).

To put it in Durkheimian terms (1966), Egyptian children who experienced revolutionary moments have acquired a "collective conscience" that arises from the sharing of a "community of ideas and feelings" and an "ideological proximity" that is indispensable to political socialization.[9] The development of this kind of consciousness endowed Egyptian children with strong partisan and political preferences that could last until adulthood (Hyman, 1959). As Cullingford argues, "children develop 'political' concepts at a very early stage, through their everyday experiences of institutions such as the school and the family: notions of authority, fairness and justice, rules and laws, power and control, are all formed long before they are required to express their views in the form of voting" (quoted in Buckingham, 2000, p. 177). The results of the opinion poll proved that Egyptian children possessed a well-developed conceptual understanding of current political issues, even if they lacked information on specific topics, or parents and other adults had influenced their views. Their political consciousness is not independent of the family and social milieu in which they are living and growing up. Moreover, as Aya's experience demonstrates, the new technologies and social media also contribute to the development of children's political personality and expression of their citizenship values.

Citizenship Values in Egyptian Education?

According to the American philospher and educational reformer John Dewey, the school is a small community where an embryonic society is formed (1916). Democracy can be achieved through the education system, if the political system establishes an educational system that incorporates norms and democratic values, one in which students are educated to participate actively in society. The acquisition of direct political knowledge represents an important step in the political socialization process (Campbell, 2008). The term "citizenship education" refers to institutionalized forms of political knowledge, values, and attitudes that take place within formal and informal educational frameworks. The content of citizenship education is complex and multidimensional in nature, time, and space.

Foucault takes an entirely different view of educational institutions. He views them as a "block of capacity-communication-power" in which relations of power and knowledge are legitimized and exercised. In this logic, teaching and learning are developed through "regulated communications" and "power processes," which adjust abilities and inculcate behavior producing effects of power (Dreyfus & Rabinow, 1983, pp. 217–218). In light of these perspectives, it is worthwhile to explore citizenship values and practices transmitted and experienced by children in Egyptian school contexts and evaluate how they differ from those experienced in other contexts, like the public sphere and digital spaces.

In Egypt a juridical framework mandates an important relationship between education and citizenship. The Education Law 139 of 1981 states, "the purpose of basic education is to develop the students' abilities and readiness [. . .] to prepare the individual to be a productive citizen in their environment and community." During the 1990s, the Ministry of Education introduced important innovations in the curricula of primary schooling, with particular attention to democratic education. Governmental education policies have been founded on the slogan: "From democratic education to education for democracy" in order to encourage educating students to acquire democracy and citizenship values in the school, the family, and society (Mourad, 2010, pp. 48–49). There are nevertheless no programs with specific goals for teaching citizenship in public schools. They are still traditional institutions based on traditional curricula that do not prepare citizens for social participation.

Social sciences curricula, for instance, rather than encouraging freedom of thought and critical thinking instill obedience and submission to the regime in order to produce dependent and submissive students. The teachers, curricula, activities, and administration in public schools have failed to promote or support democratic values and practices. Basic concepts in citizenship education are rarely mentioned. The term "authority" prevails in the social studies textbooks over the term "citizen" (Baraka, 2007; Qasim, 2006, quoted in Faour & Muasher, 2011, p. 11). Discipline, obedience, oppression, and commitment are the principal aspects of the educational system, which begins with the decision makers at the top level and extends to pupils in the classrooms. As a consequence, the concept of citizenship education disappears from the Egyptian education system (Moughith, 2002, quoted in El-Nagar & Krugly-Smolka, 2009, pp. 48–49).

In Egypt educational institutions represent a hideout of power and authoritarianism on behalf of obedience (to the regime) and discipline, imposed by the highest actors to the lowest actors. Although young generations do not acquire democratic and citizenship attitudes in the school institutions, that does not mean they do not have democratic or citizenship attitudes and leanings. The young generations' active engagement in public life as citizens rises from different learning *venues* (family, extra-school activities, and associations) and through platforms like social media. The media, and social media in particular, are strongly implicated in changing the nature of the younger generation today. In the digital era, children are increasingly spurred to develop imagination, creativity, and awareness by electronic and technological means.

By using the new communication and information tools, children shift from being passive recipients to active producers of knowledge, and become themselves messengers of information (Herrera, 2012). Indeed, the flourishing of educational, cultural, and informative content on the internet is a visible demonstration of the new media's capacity to play a significant role in helping children become informed and engaged citizens for the future. In some cases, they can also fill the gap left by the school institutions concerning civic and democratic education, and be able to build new forms of knowledge and learning, which is an expression of informal education.

Conclusion: Being the Seeds of an Alternative Future

The events leading up to and following Egypt's January 25 Revolution in 2011 permanently changed the political path of the Egyptian society as a whole, including the everyday life of its youngest citizens. Like adults, children from 6 to 17 have been emotionally and politically involved in Egypt's revolutionary movement.

They have experienced and participated in it in different settings, both virtual and physical. Since 2005 when children were actively involved in the *Kefaya* movement and anti-Mubarak initiatives, they have been familiarizing themselves with issues commonly considered to be adult domains, such as corruption, cronyism, social justice, human rights, and inequality.

New initiatives launched by Egyptians under 18 in various settings, public, private, institutional or virtual, reveal children's capacities for the development of the country. The *Harakat tullab madaris masr li taghyyr* (Egypt's School Students for Change Movement), organized in the post-revolution period, called for a general school strike on the first anniversary of Mubarak being ousted. Moreover, children's participation in protests in Tahrir Square demonstrates how revolutionary experiences can concretely mold the youngest generation's political socialization—understood as the process by which citizens acquire their attitudes and beliefs about the political system in which they live and their roles within that system (Rimmerman, 2011, p. 19). They have also been articulating their visions for the future.

Digital social media have also contributed to the development of children's political personality. The new media allow children to develop imagination and awareness and make the shift away from being passive recipients to active producers of knowledge and messengers of information. New technological and digital tools have also filled the gap left by the school institution regarding citizenship and democratic education. Schools continue to work to instill in children dispositions of discipline and obedience to authority, rather than freedom of thought and participation in decision making.

Supported by new forms of informal education and thanks to such an early political and citizenship consciousness, children could well be the vectors of change and the bearers of an alternative future for Egyptian society, as well as for educational institutions. The latter could become the place where all newborn aspirations and experiences find an immediate application. Such a case has already occurred in a school where a group of children brought their experiences from Tahrir Square into their school. They presented the authorities with a list of demands to improve the structure and the management of their school (BBC News, 2011). Following the spirit of the revolution, the teachers are bound to change their vision about students, who until now have been considered as second-class citizens without rights to express their opinions, and to give them a whole new place in their schools as well as in their society. The school can become a laboratory for developing long-lasting democratic skills and values such as freedom, equality, social justice, and respect for basic human rights, which are the main demands of the Arab uprisings.

Notes

1. A reference book about contemporary children's experiences and childhood in Middle East still remains the book edited by Elizabeth Warnock Fernea (1995). Avner Giladi's

(1999) work has also contributed to the development of childhood studies in Islamic contexts. Recently, the latest edited volume entitled "Images of the child and childhood in modern Muslim contexts" (2012) of the journal *Comparative Studies of South Asia, Africa and Middle East* seems to bring new scientific interest to the issue, as will Heidi Morrison's monograph (currently under peer review).

2. Recently some researchers have raised the question of whether a "new paradigm" or an "epistemological break," as some leaders of the NSSC have usually called it, has really occurred in the study of childhood (Ryan, 2008). Nevertheless, this chapter does not intend to come down in favor of one school of thought over another, or engage deeply in this kind of debate because it is not its main focus.

3. According to a report on the situation of street children in Cairo and Alexandria (WFP, UNICEF & UNODCCP, 2001), the general profile of street children in Cairo is the following: children less than 18 years old, males or females, who spend all or most of their time on the street, with minimal or no contact with their families, who lack supervision, protection, or guidance, are vulnerable to a wide range of health and psychological hazards. At governmental level, street children in Egypt have historically been labeled as "delinquents," and "juvenile delinquents," until recently when they were recognized as "children exposed to delinquency," according to the Child Law 12/1996, in order to change the negative attitude of society towards street children and consider them as victims and at risk rather than as criminals.

4. Interviewed in Cairo during the revolutionary protests, the founders of Bambuser described their platform as a tool used by citizen journalists, friends and family not only to disseminate information, but also to act as a vanguard of justice. When Egyptian activists like Ramy Roof started to use the service to live-stream the protests, the Bambuser staff contacted Egyptian users in order to better understand what they could do to improve the service for them on the ground. Moreover, Bambuser was also used to monitor the Egyptian parliamentary elections and over 10,000 broadcasts from the one-day election were disseminated by its platform (Messieh, 2011).

5. The *Children of Tahrir Square* video was uploaded on December 22, 2011 but it was shot before the military's recent attacks on protesters and the dismantling of the tent city in Tahrir Square (*The Real News*, 2011).

6. From when it was started in 2011 to April 2013 the Facebook page *Thawra ma'hash bitaqa* of the group of young people under 18 (www.facebook.com/Thawra.ma3hash.beta2a) was followed by more than 52,300 people.

7. During an interview in the TV program *Akher Kalam* (The Last Word), one of Egypt's most popular talk shows, hosted by the presenter Yousri Fouda on February 15, 2011, members of the group explained that a Salafist young member had suggested the last sentence (ONtveg, 2012).

8. The Edrak for Edutainment Project Development Company is an Egyptian shareholding company established in Cairo in 2010. It manages three international brands: KidZania, a real city for playing for kids from 4 to 14 years old; The Little Gym, a space where children between 4 months and 12 years old can develop motor skills in a fun and supportive environment; and Jazzercise, a workout program that fuses jazz dance, resistance training, pilates, yoga, and kickboxing movements for women of all ages. According to the managing director, Tarek Zidan, the ambition of the company is "to reach out to the community in order to create positive change through innovative and life changing development projects" as the three innovative brands described above. For more information, see the Edrak website www.edrak.com.eg/web/edrak. This kind of company is an example of trans-nationalization and globalization of education

concepts such as "edutainment" (a combination of "education" and "entertainment"): "this concept gives children aged 4–14 role-play opportunities and exposure to real world professions." It has branches in different countries of the world: the United Arab Emirates, Mexico, Japan, Indonesia, Portugal, India, and so on (AME info, 2010).

9. According to Annick Percheron, "ideological proximity" is actually the only explanatory concept of "political socialization" (Reginensi, 2005).

References

Ali, N. (2013, February 2). Mob sex attacks and the everyday reality of street. *Egypt Independent*. Retrieved from www.egyptindependent.com/opinion/mob-sex-attacks-and-everyday-reality-street-children

AME Info. (2010). Edrak for Edutainment Projects Development launches new investments in Egypt. Retrieved May 12, 2013 from www.ameinfo.com/247203.html

Assaad, R. & Roudi-Fahimi, F. (2007). Youth in the Middle East and North Africa: Demographic opportunity or challenge? *Population Reference Bureau*. Retrieved May 12, 2013 from www.prb.org/pdf07/youthinMENA.pdf

Baraka, P. (2007, Spring). Citizenship education in Egyptian public schools: What values to teach and in which administrative and political contexts. *Journal of Education for International Development*, 3(3). Retrieved May 12, 2013 from www.equip123.net/jeid/articles/7/Baraka-CitizenshipEducation.pdf

Barthe, B. (2011, January 19). Al-Jazira à la pointe de la couverture de la révolution tunisienne. *Le Monde*. Retrieved from www.lemonde.fr/proche-orient/article/2011/01/19/al-jazeera-a-la-pointe-de-la-couverture-de-la-revolution-tunisienne_1467521_3218.html

BBC News (2011, May 9). Egyptian children tell revolution tales. Retrieved from www.bbc.co.uk/news/education-13312429

Berlin, I. (1969). Two concepts of liberty. In I. Berlin (Ed.), *Four essays on liberty* (118–172). Oxford: Oxford University Press.

Blitzer, W., Cooper, A., Gorani, H. et al. (2011). *Egypt uprising: Hosni Mubarak steps down. Interview with Wael Ghonim: The Egyptian people are the leaders and heroes of this revolution*. Retrieved February 11, 2011 from http://transcripts.cnn.com/TRANSCRIPTS/1102/11/bn.02.html

Bourdieu, P. (1977). Questions de politique. *Actes de la recherche en sciences sociales*, 16, 55–89.

Brighenti, A. (2007). Visibility. A category for the social sciences. *Current Sociology*, 55(3), 323–342.

Buckingham, D. (2000). *After the death of childhood: Growing up in the age of electronic media*. Cambridge: Polity Press.

Campbell, D. (2008). Voice in the classroom: How an open classroom climate fosters political engagement among adolescents. *Political Behavior*, 30(4), 437–454.

Caputo, V. (1995). Anthropology's silent "others." A consideration of some conceptual and methodological issues for the study of youth and children's cultures. In V. Amit-Talai & H. Wulff (Eds.), *Youth cultures. A cross-cultural perspective* (19–42). London, New York: Routledge.

Central Agency for Public Mobilization and Statistics (CAPMAS). (2006). *Population and housing census 2006*. Retrieved from www.msrintranet.capmas.gov.eg/pls/indcs/cens_typ?lang=0&lname=

Colla, E. (2012, Summer). The People want. *Middle East Report*, 263(42). Retrieved from www.merip.org/mer/mer263/people-want

Cullingford, C. (1992). *Children and society: Children's attitudes to politics and power*. London: Cassell.

Daily News Egypt. (2011, July 20). *Tahrir School* (video file). Retrieved from www.youtube. com/watch?v=KZwouv_-ynE

Danziger, K. (Ed.). (1970). *Readings in child socialization*. London: Pergamon Press Ltd.

Dewey, J. (1916). *Democracy and education*. Illinois: Southern Illinois University Press.

Doss, L. (2011, July 20). Nearing 2-week mark, Tahrir sit-in becomes Tahrir city. *Egypt Independent*. Retrieved from www.egyptindependent.com/node/478914

Dreyfus, H. L. & Rabinow, P. (1983). *Michel Foucault: Beyond structuralism and hermeneutics*. Chicago: University of Chicago Press.

Dupoirier, E. & Percheron, A. (1975). Choix idéologique, attitudes politiques des préado-lescents et contexte politique. *Revue Française de Science Politique*, 25(5), 870–900.

Durkheim, É. (1966). *Education et sociologie*. Paris: Puf.

Egyptian Gazette. (2012, February 27). Egypt's street children in need of help. Retrieved from http://213.158.162.45/~egyptian/index.php?action=news&id=23332&title= Egypt%27s+street+children+in+need+of+help

El-Nagar, A. H. M. & Krugly-Smolka, E. (2009). Citizenship education and liberal democratic change: The Egyptian case. *Canadian and International Education/Education canadienne et internationale*, 38(2), 36–54. Retrieved from http://ir.lib.uwo.ca/cgi/ viewcontent.cgi?article=1012&context=cie-eci

Faour, M. & Muasher, M. (2011). *Education and citizenship in the Arab World*. Washington: Carnegie Middle East Center.

Filiu, J.-P. (2011). *La révolution arabe. Dix leçons sur le soulèvement démocratique*. Paris: Fayard.

Fisk, R. (2011, February 13). Cairo's 50,000 street children were abused by this regime. *The Independent*. Retrieved from www.independent.co.uk/voices/commentators/ fisk/robert-fisk-cairos-50000-street-children-were-abused-by-this-regime-2213295. html

Giddens, A. (1986). *The constitution of society: Outline of the theory of structuration*. Berkeley: University of California Press.

Giladi, A. (1999). *Infant, parents and wet nurses: Medieval Islamic views on breastfeeding and their social implications*. Leiden: Brill.

Government of Egypt (GOE) & United Nations Development Programme (UNDP). (2006). *Empowering and connecting the community through ICT: Egypt—Emergence of the regional digital hub. Plan of action (2007–2012)*. UNDP/MCIT Project Egypt.

Guaaybess, T. (2005). *Télévisions Arabes sur orbite. Un système médiatique en mutation (1960–2004)*. Paris: CNRS Editions.

Habermas, J. (1974). The public sphere: An encyclopaedia article (1964). *New German Critique*, 3, 49–55.

Habib, H. (2011, May 8). Al fan midan again takes culture to the streets. *Ahram online*. Retrieved from http://english.ahram.org.eg/News/11664.aspx

Hardman, C. (1973). Can there be an anthropology of children? *Journal of the Anthropological Society of Oxford*, 4(2), 85–99.

Helmy, H. (2011, May 21). Poll indicates high political consciousness among Egyptian children. *Al Masry al Youm*. Retrieved from www.egyptindependent.com/node/446252

Herrera, L. (2012). Youth and citizenship in the digital age: A view from Egypt. *Harvard Educational Review*, 82(3), 333–353.

Honwana, A. (2005). The pain of agency: The agency of pain. In A. Honwana & F. De Boeck (Eds.), *Makers and breakers: Children and youth in postcolonial Africa* (31–51). Oxford: James Currey Ltd.

Honwana, A. & De Boeck, F. (Eds.). (2005). *Makers and breakers. Children and youth in postcolonial Africa.* Oxford: James Currey Ltd.

Howeidy, A. (2005, September 8–14). Enough is still enough. *Al-Ahram Weekly.* Retrieved from http://weekly.ahram.org.eg/2005/759/eg8.htm

Hyman, H. (1959). *Political socialisation. A study of the psychology of political behavior.* Glencoe: The Free Press.

Institute of National Planning (INP) & United Nations Development Programme (UNDP). (2000). *Egypt human development report 1998/99.* Cairo: Author.

Internet World Stats (2012). *Internet usage in the Middle East.* Retrieved May 12, 2013 from www.internetworldstats.com/stats5.htm

Itameri, K. (2011, July 25). Street children among those who stand to gain from revolution. *Egypt Independent.* Retrieved from www.egyptindependent.com/news/street-children-among-those-who-stand-gain-revolution

James, A. & Prout, A. (Eds.). (1990). *Constructing and reconstructing childhood: Contemporary issues in the sociological study of childhood.* London, New York, Philadelphia: The Falmer Press.

Karam, I. N. K. (2010). Arab youth, education and satellite broadcasting. In A. E. Mazawi & R. G. Sultana (Eds.), *Education and the Arab world: Political projects, struggles, and geometries of power* (300–316). World Yearbook of Education. New York, London: Routledge.

Karimi, P. & Gruber, C. (2012). Introduction: The politics and poetics of the child image in Muslim contexts. *Comparative Studies of South Asia, Africa and the Middle East,* 32(2), 273–293.

Kienle, E. (2001). *A grand delusion: Democracy and economic reform in Egypt.* London: I. B. Tauris.

Kienle, E. (2008). Libéralisation économique et déliberalisation politique: Le nouveau visage de l'autoritarisme? In O. Dabène, V. Geisser, & G. Massardier (Eds.), *Autoritarismes démocratiques et démocraties autoritaires au XXI siècle. Convergences Nord-Sud* (251–265). Paris: La Découverte.

Laila, R. (2011, February 16–22). Students in action. *Al-Ahram Weekly Online.* Retrieved from http://weekly.ahram.org.eg/2012/1085/eg6.htm

Lipman, P. (2005). Educational ethnography and the politics of globalization, war and resistance. *Anthropology and Education Quarterly,* 36(4), 315–328.

Marshall, T. H. (1977). *Class, citizenship and social development: Essays.* Chicago: University of Chicago Press.

Maynard, D. W. (1985). On the functions of social conflict among children. *American Sociological Review,* 50(2), 207–223.

Mazawi, A. E. & Sultana, R. G. (Eds.). (2010). *Education and the Arab world: Political projects, struggles, and geometries of power.* World Yearbook of Education. New York, London: Routledge.

Messieh, N. (2011, November 29). Live-streaming service Bambuser goes for Egypt's revolution to its elections. *The Next Web.* Retrieved from http://thenextweb.com/me/2011/11/29/live-streaming-service-bambuser-goes-from-egypts-revolution-to-its-elections/

Ministry of Education (MOE). (2010). *Condition of education in Egypt 2010. Report on the national education indicators.* Cairo: Ministry of Education.

Montasser, F. (2012, April 10). A year of Al-fan midan in Egypt. *Ahram online.* Retrieved from http://english.ahram.org.eg/News/38785.aspx

Morrison, H. (under peer review). *State of children: Egyptian childhoods in an age of modernity, nationalism and emotion.* Syracuse, NY: Syracuse University Press.

Moughith, K. (2002). Civic education in Egypt. In K. Mougheeth & M. Darwish (Eds.), *Civic education in Arab world* (104–112). Amman: Arab Civic Education Network.

Mourad, S. N. (2010). *Educational reform in Egyptian primary schools in the 1990s. A study of the political values and behaviour of sixth grade students.* Lewiston: The Edwin Mellen Press.

National Centre for Education Resource Development (NCERD). (2001). *Education development. National report of Arab republic of Egypt (1990–2000).* Cairo: NCERD.

Neveu, C. (2004). Les enjeux d'une approche anthropologique de la citoyenneté. *Revue européenne des migrations internationales,* 20(3), 89–101. Retrieved from http://remi. revues.org/2024

O'Neill, M. (2011, February 1). Egyptian protests erupting on YouTube, not just in the streets of Egypt. *Social Times.* Retrieved from http://socialtimes.com/egyptian-protests-youtube_b36797

Ontveg. (2012, February 15). *Akher Kalam* (video file). Retrieved May 12, 2013 from www. youtube.com/watch?v=lP-213N7oAU

Pagès-El Karoui, D. & Vignal, L. (2011). Les racines de la révolution du 25 janvier en Egypte: Une réflexion géographique. *EchoGéo. Sur le vif.*

Parolin, G. P. (2009). *Citizenship in the Arab world: Kin, religion and nation-state.* Amsterdam: Amsterdam University Press.

Piaget, J. (1964). *Six études de psychologie.* Paris: Denoël.

Piaget, J. & Inhelder, B. (1966). *La psychologie de l'enfant.* Paris: Puf.

Preston, J. & Stelter, B. (2011, February 18). Cellophones become the world's eyes and ears on protests. *The New York Times.* Retrieved from www.nytimes.com/2011/02/19/world/middleeast/19video.html?_r=3

Qasim, M. (2006). *Education and citizenship.* Cairo: Cairo Institute for Human Rights.

Raheb, E. (2011a, May 20). *Suleiman Abdel Hakam (Egypt)* (television broadcast). Issy-les-Moulineaux, Baden: Itar Productions, les Films Sauvage, ARTE, ZDF/ARTE. Retrieved from www.arte.tv/fr/Generation-Revolution/3922644.html

Raheb, E. (2011b, June 7). *Suleiman Abdel Hakam (Egypt)* (television broadcast). Issy-les-Moulineaux, Baden: Itar Productions, les Films Sauvage, ARTE, ZDF/ARTE. Retrieved from www.arte.tv/fr/Generation-Revolution/3955420.html

Reginensi, L. (2005). Annick Percheron et l'univers politique des enfants. *Revue d'histoire des sciences humaines,* 1(12), 173–192.

Rimmerman, G. A. (2011). *The new citizenship. Unconventional politics, activism and service.* Boulder: Westview Press.

Ryan, P. J. (2008). How new is the "new" social study of childhood? The myth of a paradigm shift. *Journal of Interdisciplinary History,* 38(4), 553–576.

Sabae, A. (2011a, September 5). *Students for change Nadwa 1* (video file). Retrieved from www.youtube.com/watch?v=1dZZj4U3HFs&feature=player_embedded

Sabae, A. (2011b, September 5). *Students for change Nadwa 2* (video file). Retrieved from www.youtube.com/watch?v=4NOkudmaEAU&feature=share

Sayed, N. (2011, May 26). These are their words. *Al-Ahram weekly online.* Retrieved from http://weekly.ahram.org.eg/2011/1049/li1.htm

The Real News. (2011, December 22). *Children of Tahrir Square* (video file). Retrieved from www.youtube.com/watch?v=oDB0XJ2hfH4

The Telegraph. (2011, February 1). Egypt's march of a million people. Retrieved from www. telegraph.co.uk/news/worldnews/africaandindianocean/egypt/8296026/Egypts-march-of-a-million-people.html

United Nations Development Programme (UNDP). (2009). *Arab human development report 2009. Challenges to human security in the Arab countries.* Retrieved from www.arab-hdr. org/contents/index.aspx?rid=5

United Nations Development Programme (UNDP). (2010). *Egypt human development report 2010. Youth in Egypt: Building our future.* Retrieved from www.undp.org.eg/Portals/0/NHDR%202010%20english.pdf

Viney, S. (2012, May 11). Profile: Junior Malek brings street politics to high school. *Egypt Independent.* Retrieved from www.egyptindependent.com/news/profile-junior-malek-brings-street-politics-high-school

Vygotsky, L. S. (1978). *Mind in society.* Cambridge, MA: Massachusetts Institute of Technology Press.

Warnock Fernea, E. (Ed.). (1995). *Children in the Muslim Middle East.* Cairo: The American University in Cairo Press.

World Food Programme (WFP), United Nations Children's Emergency Fund (UNICEF), & United Nations Office for Drug Control and Crime Prevention (UNODCCP). (2001). *Rapid situation assessment report on the situation of street children in Cairo and Alexandria, including the children's drug abuse and health/nutritional status.* Cairo: WFP, UNICEF, UNODCCP. Retrieved from www.unicef.org/evaldatabase/index_14268.html

5

CYBERSPACE IN TURKEY

A "Youthful" Space for Expressing Powerful Discontent and Suffering

Demet Lüküslü

Introduction

The dominant literature on young people's political participation either views the contemporary young generation as disengaged and apolitical (particularly dominant in the Turkish case), or as engaged and political, but using nontraditional forms of engagement like volunteerism. This chapter aims to pursue Ulrich Beck's alternative way of analyzing young people's participation and political attitudes by transcending this engaged/disengaged or political/apolitical dichotomy (see Farthing, 2010).

In the decades following the 1980s, young people appeared to be largely absent from the political scene. Recent developments such as the Arab uprisings, the anti-austerity movements in the southern Mediterranean countries, the student protests in Great Britain, as well as various youth protests in Turkey, bring young people back to the "stage" as key actors. This sudden change from young people being "inactive" and "apolitical" to becoming "actors" may have come as a surprise to those who defined the young generation as silent and obedient. However, for researchers who track traces of "discontent" and "resistance" in acts of silence and obedience, this situation has been no mystery. Drawing on empirical evidence from Turkey, this chapter underlines the importance of offering an alternative analytical framework that transcends the engaged/disengaged or political/apolitical dichotomy in young people's relationship to politics. The internet has become an important tool in the everyday life of urban youth in Turkey. Cyberspace in Turkey has served as an active and "youthful," to use Asef Bayat's terminology (2010), reference source for expressing powerful discontent and suffering that cannot always be expressed through either conventional politics or open resistance.

Youth and Politics in Turkey

Turkey's population of 15- to 29-year-olds is the third largest in Europe and eighteenth largest worldwide. The cohort of 15–29s, a total of 18.8 million people, makes up 25.2% of Turkey's overall population. The state is proud of its young population, which it views as an asset. The history of modern Turkey, from the nineteenth century to the 1980s, is in large measure a history about how youth movements played a central role in Turkish political life (Georgeon, 2007; Lüküslü. 2009). After the military coup of 1980 and the subsequent implementation of neoliberal economic policies by Prime Minister Turgut Özal's government, youth movements were no longer at the forefront of Turkish political life. The young people of the post-1980 generation have been labeled the "children of the military coup," the "neoliberals," and members of a globalized, consumer society. All these terms imply that this generation is characterized by being individualistic, apathetic, and self-centered, and is incapable of forming youth movements like previous generations have.

Given these historical contrasts, a brief history of youth in Turkey is warranted for better comprehension of the contemporary generation. If youth, as a social category, is indeed a construct of industrialization, urbanization, and modernity, then the emergence of youth as a social category in the history of modern Turkey dates from the nineteenth-century modernization movements of the Ottoman Empire. That era witnessed the emergence of "modern" Western-style schools where the generation underwent a "modern" form of socialization. Interestingly, this modernization process constructed youth as a political category whose ultimate objective was to save the Ottoman Empire from collapse and to restore its glory. I argue that youth has been a key component of Turkish political culture since the nineteenth century and I refer to this definition of youth as a political category as the "myth of youth" (Lüküslü, 2009).

Although the empire's young generation accepted its political mission, it also believed that the way to save the empire was to rebel against the Sultan and his oppressive regime. Hence, the Young Turk movement and the revolution of 1908 were in fact products of the modernization process. Likewise, those who founded the Republic of Turkey in 1923 were all members of the last generation of the empire who had inherited this "myth of youth," which became the symbol of the young republic. Only a small proportion of the Republic's first generation (1923–1950) received a formal education. This group, schooled according to the Kemalist ideology, was seen as the "vanguard" of the Republic (Neyzi, 2001). The second generation, the so-called 60s and 70s generations, were equally active as actors on the political scene. Whether they adhered to leftist or rightist movements, their ideologies centered on the state, and even when in conflict, each was loyal to the myth of youth and claimed to be the state's real vanguard.

The third generation of the Republic, the so-called post-1980 generation, was born after the 1980 military coup "defeated" political movements in the period between 1980 and 1983 when the military regime was depoliticizing Turkish society. The influence of this military regime remained even after the 1983 transition to democracy and implementation by the ruling Motherland Party (*Anavatan Partisi*–ANAP) of neoliberal economic policies that soon changed the economic structure of Turkish society. Under these neoliberal economic policies, the Turkish market opened to international markets and Turkish society consequently became a consumer society. As a result, youth who came of age in the post-1980 period are seen as the generation of the military coup, neoliberalism, and the consumer society. This image, when added to inactivity on the political scene in comparison to previous generations, has further deepened the criticism of this younger generation.

Even though over 30 years have passed since the military coup of 1980 and three different age cohorts from the 1980s, 1990s, and 2000s have emerged, I argue that due to their common characteristics, all these belong to the same generation. As Xavier Gaullier notes, generations are larger than age cohorts and generations continue their existence until a new deal between generations is needed (1998, p. 6). The post-1980 generation symbolizes the end of the "myth of youth," in which young people are actively involved in the political space, a notion that has existed in Turkish political culture since the late nineteenth century.

The UNDP *Human development report* 2008 *Youth in Turkey* (p. 9) further confirms the notion that young people harbor widespread mistrust of politics and urges a change of attitude and activity: "While the youth's distrust towards politics seems to be rather widespread, civil society can offer some adequate participation tools for the youth. Youth's perception of politics too needs to change. Political participation is one of the most important means for youth to become responsible citizens." In fact, surveys on youth in Turkey published from 1999 to the present indicate that young people feel a certain apathy towards the political sphere and their participation in political parties, political organizations, and NGOs is low. Only 3% claim to be a member of any political party, social group, or association, and only 10% state that they talk about politics among friends (Lüküslü, 2013).

I have been involved in three qualitative research studies in the 10-year period between 2000 and 2010 that assessed the political attitudes and social experiences of young people in Turkey. My doctoral research at the École des Hautes Études en Sciences Sociales (EHESS) from 2000 to 2004 comprised 80 intensive hour-long interviews with 18- to 25-year-old Istanbul residents from different socio-economic groups who were not actively engaged in political movements or civil society. The second study, conducted in 2008 by a six-member research team at TÜSES (the Social, Economic and Political Studies Foundation of Turkey), consisted of 26 focus group sessions with three different types of 18- to 25-year-olds active in civil society: those active in the youth branches of political parties; those active in different NGOs, initiatives, and platforms; and those in the too often neglected category of disadvantaged youth. The third study, carried out between 2009 and 2010 under the auspices of the İstanbul Bilgi University Youth Studies

Unit, aimed to better understand the success indicators for youth policy in Turkey. It comprised a total of 20 focus group sessions conducted in seven different cities (İstanbul, Ankara, İzmir, Adana, Samsun, Diyarbakır, and Van) with 135 socially active young people aged between 16 and 26. Based on the findings of these research studies, I object to the dominant view defining the young generation in Turkey as disengaged and apolitical. In fact, the young people I interviewed, rather than seeming ignorant about the problems of society or the world, exhibited awareness of such problems and expressed unhappiness about living in a problem-ridden society. They were also highly critical of the political space, which they viewed as far removed from their desires and needs. Thus, in their minds, the political space appeared as a devalued one, a corrupted and clientelistic space that was extremely rigid and untransformable, with all political organizations being "authoritarian" entities; individuals could choose either to join a group or become a militant, but they had little chance to express their individuality outside these two options. They expressed a clear lack of trust in political institutions and political organizations. Since they believed that the system was so rigid and irreversible, they expressed little hope for change, which explains their failure to react and protest that the situation be improved. Their lack of reaction does not mean that they are not paying attention to what is happening. Rather, I could observe how their dissatisfaction reflected a latent desire to change things. The current situation requires new research lenses and terminology about youth and citizenship that transcend simple binaries of apathetic or political, loyal or disloyal.

I have argued that the general characteristic of the young in Turkey is the "necessary conformism" that they adopt as a tactic, as "an art" of living (Lüküslü, 2009, 2010, 2013). Michel de Certeau (1988) distinguishes between "tactic" and "strategy." He defines tactic as the "art of the weak," whereas "strategy" is the "art of the powerful." The young generation in Turkey seemingly chooses to act in conformity with society's rules without really believing in them by inventing "tactics" rather than directly rebelling. It is, however, important to note that "necessary conformism" is not synonymous with apathy, but rather hides a real and strong discontent and can mask a profound agony. According to the logic of necessary conformism, young people are only conformist when they believe it to be necessary, but they try to escape being so whenever possible.

Necessary conformism turns institutions into entities that are both dead and alive or, as Beck explains it, the young generation in individualized societies is an "actively unpolitical younger generation which has taken the life out of the political institutions and is turning them into zombie categories" (Beck, 2008, pp. 202–213). In fact, this so-called unpolitical younger generation strategically employs the tactic of necessary conformism to turn institutions—whether family, educational, or political—into zombie categories. In the presence of many "zombie categories," cyberspace, in which the young generation is especially active, offers a very "alive" and, using Asef Bayat's terminology, "youthful," space characterized by "a particular habitus, behavioral and cognitive dispositions that are associated with the fact of being 'young'—that is, a distinct social location between child-hood and adulthood, where the youngster experiences 'relative autonomy' and is neither totally dependent (on adults) nor independent, and is free from responsi-bility for other dependents" (Bayat, 2010, p. 28).

Cyberspace: A Source for Expressing Powerful Discontent and Suffering?

Recent protest movements in the Arab world, southern Mediterranean countries, and European societies not only brought young people to the "stage" as key actors, but also underlined the role of the new information technologies in these events. Linda Herrera and Asef Bayat in their edited book, *Being young and Mus-lim*, published just before the revolts in the Arab world, had already underlined the impact of new information technologies on the lives of the young generation:

> Muslim youth, like their global counterparts, have come of age during a technological and communications revolution. New information commu-nication technologies (ICT), from the mobile phone to the Internet, have changed the landscape of youth learning, culture, sociability, and political engagement. [. . .] On a massive and growing scale, youth use the new media as a tool for peer interaction, leisure, [. . .] consuming information, and an array of direct and indirect political action-uses that are not mutu-ally exclusive.

> (2010, p. 10)

Despite stating that new information technologies had been a part of everyday life of the young generation, it is important to keep in mind what Charles Tilly reminds us about technological determinism and information technologies exclud-ing much more strongly those who do not have access to these technologies (2004, p. 98). The high-tech moment gives rise to a new type of inequality, what Pippa Norris calls the "digital divide" (2001). This new stratification in society creates divides within the same generation (differences of position, ideology, and practice). Notwithstanding inequalities arising from the digital divide, the younger genera-tion has an advantageous position over the older generation in the current com-munications environment (Anduiza, Cantijoch, & Gallego, 2009, p. 871). There is also research that shows how youth are expressing political participation in new ways with new information technologies (Della Porta and Mosca, 2005; DiMaggio, Hargittai, Neuman, & Robinson, 2001; Norris, 2002). In this chapter, I will be under-lining the role of the internet and new information technologies in the everyday life of urban middle and upper-middle class youth in Turkey and arguing that cyberspace can be an active and youthful reference source for youth researchers.

Internet use in Turkey became popular first in the mid-1990s with the intro-duction of home dial-up connection services. In 2003 the government launched

the E-Transformation Turkey Project for facilitating the transition to an information society and since 2006 the number of ADSL broadband users has increased
significantly.[1] According to the Turkish Statistical Institute (TurkStat), in 2012,
47.2% of households had access to the Internet, up from 42.9% in April 2011.
The highest internet and computer usage is among the 16–24 age group. Popular
social networks such as Facebook, Twitter, and MySpace, as well as applications like
Skype, can be used in Turkish.

The Turkish government initially had a hands-off approach to the internet,
but over time it has exercised more censorship in the virtual sphere. Freedom
House's "Turkey" report of *Freedom on the Net 2011* argues that since 2001 the
Turkish government has "taken considerable legal steps to limit access to certain
information, including some political content. According to various estimates,
there were over 5,000 blocked websites as of July 2010, and this blocking spurred
street demonstrations against internet censorship" (Freedom House, 2011, p. 329).

The video-sharing website YouTube was first blocked in Turkey on March 2007
and "access was blocked roughly 20 times between March 2007 and November
2010" by court order (Freedom House, 2011, p. 330). Users evaded this block,
however, by inventing "tactics" that take advantage of the cracks in the system.
For instance, they accessed the website by modifying the connection parameters
to use alternative DNS (domain name system) servers. In fact, according to the
web information company Alexa, YouTube was still the eighth most accessed site
in Turkey during the two-and-a-half-year block (Freedom House, 2011, p. 333).

Turkish Youth in Cyberspace

Cyberspace offers a large platform for studying young people. I analyze three
different websites that have gained popularity in Turkey and serve as important
examples of how the young generation uses new information technologies as a
creative tool for making a youthful space. These three websites, which are very
different, share three features: a rejection of traditional politics; preoccupation with
the present life and with drawing substance from everyday life; and the usage of
humor, in particular black humor.

The first of the websites, EkşiSözlük, or "Sourtimes" (www.sozluk.sourtimes.
org), was created by a young computer engineer named Sedat Kapanoğlu on February 14, 1999. This website was built up by user contribution, similar to Wikipedia, and very quickly became popular (Turgut, 2006). According to the website's
analytics from January 2013, there are a total of 17,313,397 entries, 2,765,051
titles, 39,308 writers, and 280,945 users. The site requires that users go through a
rigorous process to become a writer. Before gaining "writer" status, a user must
begin as an elementary writer and then wait to be recognized as a full writer.
Elementary writers are evaluated by writers, who have the right to vote on the
basis of the quality of their entries and how many times their entries and titles
were read by visitors. Even though becoming a writer is a demanding process,

anyone who wants to read EkşiSözlük can access the website and view the entries. To submit an entry, one must be a subscribed user. The site is managed by a team of volunteers called, ironically, *gammaz* (informers) and they inform the moderators about entries that are incompatible with the principles of EkşiSözlük; these entries are then erased by the moderators.

Through a process of crowdsourcing, young people assemble their generation's "dictionary" or "reference book," which is of course very different from "traditional" dictionaries or reference books. As Telli Aydemir notes, EkşiSözlük serves as an "interactive platform and database and functions as an alternative dictionary that criticizes standard paradigms of what is true" (2007, p. 89). On the main page of the website it is stated that: "This site is not a forum, nor a chat platform. It is a source of sacred information." In other words, the slogan, "A source of sacred information," is a way of mocking the Enlightenment, which took its own ideas and knowledge to be "sacred." A number of copycat websites, humorously referred to as "clones" of EkşiSözlük emerged, attesting to the site's popularity. Additionally, it would be a mistake to consider the site to be a virtual space only, since face-to-face summits are organized regularly in various cities.

The second website is by the movement, GençSiviller (Young Civilians) (www.gencsiviller.net). The movement arose following the 1999 earthquake in the Marmara region of Turkey, which marked a turning point for Turkey's civil society. Apart from being active on the internet and transmitting its messages through an e-group, the movement also tries to be active offline and organizes different meetings, events, and protests. One of the student clubs of the Middle Eastern Technical University in Ankara organized a day of assembly in Van on May 19, 2000 in commemoration of the start of the Turkish Independence War and the Youth and Sports Day. Various groups of young people from different Turkish universities took part in this gathering. The main idea was to develop an alternative way of celebrating the Youth and Sports Day, rather than celebrating it in the stadiums with gymnastics ceremonies. On May 19, 2003 at a gathering that they had organized in the parliament, the movement released a manifesto entitled, "Let's Save the 19th of May from Stadiums." In this manifesto, as displayed in the English version of the website, the group declared, "these stadium ceremonies existed only in totalitarian countries and they are an old-fashioned way of ceremony." The manifesto garnered a good deal of critical attention, as reported on the website: "Our manifest[o] was in the headlines of many newspapers the next day. We were subjected to scathing criticism for two weeks." The *Cumhuriyet* newspaper, which claims to uphold the principles of the Republic and Kemalism, ran the headline "Young army officers are worried." These officers could not begin to fathom why a debate about the Youth and Sports Day ceremonies should take place. The slogan of the Young Civilians, "Young civilians are worried," is an explicit reference to that headline. However, the usage of the name "Young Civilians" began only after a manifesto was published on May 19, 2006, demanding a peaceful solution to the Kurdish issue in Turkey. The group's symbol was a pair of sneakers in the style of

Converse. When asked what kind of Turkey they dream of, the movement, via its English website, gives the following answer:

> Actually, we don't have big assertions. When we are asked, we only answer ironically by "we are coming to the power." We are doing some things by running away from big ideologies. We think that not power-focused but civil society-based politics is significant. We get up to following our consciences. We are engaged in conscientious politics. It is a quite hard job itself. It is not like saying "the end of ideologies." However, the problems in Turkey are so destructive. One does not need to be a liberal, socialist or Islamist to demand Hrant Dink's [the Armenian journalist assassinated in Istanbul on January 19, 2007] murderers being detected, to call for being removed the unjust treatment against Kurds, or to rise against treating women wearing head scar[ves] as blacks [*sic*].

The Young Civilian movement is influenced by a wide range of different intellectuals from inside and outside Turkey. They make references to writers from Hannah Arendt to Gramsci, Foucault and de Certeau, to Turkish poets like Namık Kemal. They also draw on figures from Turkish popular culture such as Sezen Aksu and Orhan Gencebay. For example, in the first manifesto on the Kurdish issue, one of their slogans was: "If Kurds and Turks cannot live together in this world, then, go down with the world!" This slogan makes an explicit reference to Orhan Gencebay's classic Arabesque song, "Batsın Bu Dünya!" (Let the World Sink!). The movement draws a good deal on popular culture and humor. The website makes explicit reference to ways in which humor plays an important role in communicating ideas to people. It underlines the importance of changing the "classic" language of politics and developing "a new, original and creative language."[2] In 2007 it also published a book concerning the history and the declarations of the movement entitled, *İçerde Eylem Var! Genç Siviller* (Action Inside! Young Civilians). The movement has recently been criticized for its close links to the ruling Justice and Development party and has therefore been losing its oppositional characteristic (Tuna, 2011).

The third website, which is currently not online, is called "52 Percent" (www. yuzde52.org) because 52% of the population in Turkey is under the age of 26. This youth movement, which used the slogan "Imaginative power in action against tyrants' power!" was an activist site and used to announce demonstrations, raids, and other related events that could only be found on their website. The movement and website gained popularity after it organized a raid at Boğaziçi University in Istanbul on March 29, 2007 during the Career Days. 52 Percent called this event "slave bazaars." The protesters wore Guy Fawke's masks from *V for Vendetta*, threw eggs at the representative of the Koç Group, one of the oldest and largest industrial groups in Turkey in terms of revenue, and protested the fusion of the university with the business world and its large holdings in the Istanbul Stock Exchange.

52 Percent organized another demonstration in Beyazıt Square in front of Istanbul University on June 15, 2007, just two days before the university entrance exams. They planned to carry a coffin, symbolizing the death of 12 young people who had been driven to suicide because of the pressure of the university entrance exam. The police confiscated the coffin, but the protesters still marched from Beyazıt mosque to the gate of the university to symbolically bury these 12 young people. Instead of crying and ululating, they shouted: "In spite of the university entrance exam, long live life!" A racehorse was also brought to Beyazıt Square to make the point that young students are seen as "racehorses" who compete in the university entrance exams. A banner placed on the horse read, "We won't become racehorses!"

Another demonstration was organized at Istanbul University, Faculty of Literature, on May 23, 2007 in protest against the campus security's attack on a woman who was trying to enter the university grounds while wearing a headscarf. Young men and women protesters wore headscarves and shouted, "Zulme İnat, Hepimiz Baş Örtülüyüz!" (In spite of oppression all of us are with headscarves). This was simultaneously a protest against the rector and the entire administrative body, which 52 Percent called *cüppeli generaller* (generals with academic gowns). On May 18–19, 2007, members of 52 Percent handed out manifestos against ceremonies in the stadiums on Youth and Sports Day, calling on people to "run away" from these ceremonies. Other protests organized by the movement used similar tactics for dramatic effect. As it is noted by Aslı Telli Aydemir (2007, p. 97), "[T]he visuals of their demonstrations are always demonstrated on the website [during the events the group members capture the action from several angles with their handy-cams and run away] and the format is generally medium-quality video. [. . .] They have their own style of civic participation remaining under cover as group, but the events they organise are often unusual and effective."

The movement published a book of their collected manifestos, which shows its anarchist tendencies and reasons for rejecting politics in the formal sense. In the second article of 52 Percent's "Manifesto of Rage," it states:

> We are here! The God of politics, we are here! You are political and we are not! We will not be your tools for your dreams for power. Because we are rejecting all sorts of power and power relationships. [. . .] We will not lose time with your sweet lies. And we exclaim with all of our rage: "We are here! We will respond to every attack on life. We will not get lost in the dark corridors of politics, full of labyrinths. We will exist with our imaginative power against the power of the tyrants. We are not a part of the world of lies of politics.

These three websites, very different in nature, speak to some common features of this generation of young Turks of the digital age. First of all, none of these websites claim to contain political content in the traditional sense of politics. In fact, each movement devalues or rejects traditional political organizations and ideologies because of the understanding that politics is corrupt, unable to bring about real transformative change, and cultivates "militants" as opposed to free individuals. For these reasons, many young people "choose" to stay outside of formal politics. In fact many youth groups criticize the Young Civilians for not putting enough distance between themselves and the ruling Justice and Development party. In response the Young Civilians, even as they position themselves beside the ruling party, claim in their manifestos that they wish to remain outside of traditional politics and ideologies: "We are doing some things by running away from big ideologies. We think that not power-focused but civil society-based politics is significant." When they talk about running away from "big ideologies" they do not mean this is a time of "the end of ideologies," but rather that it is a time for coalition building across ideological differences. They stress that people who belong to different ideologies can unite under some fundamental democratic basics.

A second common characteristic of these websites is a preoccupation with the present (not the past or future, which is the preoccupation of ideologies and political movements), a concern with life over death, and an effort to protect private spaces (as opposed to public space). In fact, each one of these three groups criticizes the restrictions felt in the private spaces of their present everyday life, especially restrictions on personal liberties. This is a characteristic that unites these three youth movements and separates them from traditional political movements. This characteristic also marks the end of what I call the "myth of youth." Since these movements reject involvement in political life and choose to be involved in private space rather than public or political space, they also reject the definition of youth as a political category destined to save or advance the state. With the post-1980 generation, movements that focused on the individual and personal liberties emerged. Since these new youth movements are not state-centered, it seems that they are usually neglected and named as "apolitical" or "depoliticized" movements.

Third, the content of these websites draws substance from everyday life and also from popular culture. They incorporate a language from everyday life rooted in humor, especially black humor. Many of the entries and titles in EkşiSözlük originate from the everyday life experiences of young people or from popular culture. In a similar manner, the Young Civilians make references to stand-up comedians and other figures and products of popular culture. 52 Percent focuses on everyday life experiences of young people such as the trauma of university entrance exams. The anger they stage in their protests comes from anger they experience because of neoliberalism, repressive policies of the military coup regime, gerontocratic politicians, and the oppressive policies of the education system.

Despite all that had been happening among youth groups in cyberspace, the dominant view of the young generation as passive and apathetic remained the same, until recently. The emerging younger cohort of high-school students has been entering the public sphere, galvanized around issues of internet censorship. After the government instituted a filtering block, young people followed their online dissent with offline protests, which led to the mass media rethinking the image of the "silent" youth in Turkey. In July 2010 there was a major protest gathering approximately 2,000 people in Istanbul demanding the abolishment of the "Internet Law" No. 5651 of Turkey, "which has served since 2007 as the basis of a mass blocking of websites in Turkey" (Akdeniz, 2010, p. 2). Similarly, on May 15, 2011 a march was organized in 36 cities in Turkey. In Taksim, Istanbul, thousands of protesters took part.

Around the same time high-school students from different parts of Turkey took to the streets to protest an educational issue. Scores of high-school students skipped classes and organized various events and marches to protest a cheating scandal affecting that year's university entrance exam. In fact, even before the rise of these protests, it was possible to observe the discontent of the high-school students with the education system and the university entrance exam. High-school students preparing for the university entrance exam cannot escape the education system. Even though they believe that an exam cannot be the only indicator of their success, and despite the suffering and injustice they endure because of the exam, they feel obliged to conform to the system and take it. A documentary, *Three Hours*, produced by Serdar Değirmencioğlu and Can Candan (2008) demonstrates the mix of fear, hope, and agony experienced by high-school students preparing for the "three hour" university entrance exam. Even after the exam, it is uncertain whether students will be allowed to choose their course of study because of restrictions based on scores or family dictates. That is why it was no surprise to see the rise of a protest movement from high-school students since, even before the scandal, they had wanted a way to express their anger and discontent with the educational system. In that sense, what Asef Bayat argued for the Arab street in 2003, long before the Arab uprisings, is also true for the "cyberspace" created by young people in Turkey:

> The Arab street is neither "irrational" nor "dead," but is undergoing a major transformation caused both by old constraints and new opportunities brought about by global restructuring. As a means and mode of expression, the Arab street may be shifting, but the collective grievance that it conveys remains. To ignore it is to do injustice to both moral sensibility and rational conduct of politics.
>
> (Bayat, 2003)

Conclusion

It is important to note that there are common characteristics between the websites created and followed by young people and the protests in which young people appeared as actors such as the protests against internet censorship and high-school students' protests. Just like the websites, these movements, rather than directly targeting the decisions or acts of the government, aim to separate themselves from politics and ideologies; they have a preoccupation with the present and private space, drawing substance from everyday life and popular culture, and they all use humor actively. It seems that offline and online activities of the young generation have common characteristics even though online activities most of the time remain "invisible." The online world needs to be more visible, it is very important that youth research focuses more on the study of the internet and social media since they offer a "youthful" space where the young generation expresses itself. Urban youth in Turkey incorporate online activities as part of their everyday lives, and cyberspace serves as a source for them to express powerful discontent and suffering that is not always expressed through either conventional politics or open resistance.

Notes

1. According to Annick Percheron, "ideological proximity" is actually the only explanatory concept of "political socialization" (Reginensi, 2005).
2. The website makes specific reference to figures and productions from real popular arts. For instance, it cites stand-up comedian Cem Yılmaz, and a film directed by Çağan Irmak, *Babam ve Oğlum* (My father and my son).

References

Akdeniz, Y. (2010). *Report of the OSCE representative on freedom of the media on Turkey and internet censorship.* Vienna: OSCE. Retrieved May 4, 2013 from www.osce.org/fom/41091

Anduiza, E., Cantijoch, M. & Gallego, A. (2009). Political participation and the internet. *Information, Communication & Society,* 12(6), 860–878.

Bayat, A. (2003, Spring). "The Street" and the politics of dissent in the Arab world. *Middle East Report,* 226 (33). Retrieved from www.merip.org/mer/mer226/street-politics-dissent-arab-world

Bayat, A. (2010). Muslim youth and the claim of youthfulness. In L. Herrera & A. Bayat (Eds.), *Being young and Muslim: New cultural politics in the global south and north.* Oxford and New York: Oxford University Press.

Beck, U. (1992). *Risk society: Towards a new modernity.* Mark Ritter (Trans.). London: Sage Publications.

Beck, U. (1997). *The reinvention of politics: Rethinking modernity in the global social order.* Cambridge: Polity Press.

Beck, U. (2008). Zombie categories: Interview with Ulrich Beck. In U. Beck & E. Beck-Gernsheim, *Individualization* (202–213). London: Sage Publications.

Beck, U. & Beck-Gernsheim, E. (2008). *Individualization.* London: Sage Publications.

Can, C. & Serdar, D. (2008). *3 Saat* (movie). Istanbul.

De Certeau, M. (1988). *The practice of everyday life.* Steven Rendall (Trans.). Berkeley, CA, London: University of California Press.

Della Porta, D. & Mosca, L. (2005). Global-net for global movements? A network of networks for a movement of movements. *Journal of Public Policy,* 25(1), 165–190.

Della Porta, D. & Mosca, L. (2009). Searching the net. *Information, Communication & Society,* 12(6), 771–792.

DiMaggio, P., Hargittai, E., Neuman, R. & Robinson, J. (2001). Social implications of the internet. *Annual Review of Sociology,* 27, 307–336.

DiMaggio, P., Hargittai, E., Neuman, R. & Robinson, J. (2002). *Le déclin de l'institution.* Paris: Seuil.

Dubet, F. (1987). *La galère: Jeunes en survie.* Paris: Fayard.

European Commission White Paper (2002). *A new impetus for European youth.* Luxembourg: European Commission.

Farthing, R. (2010). The politics of youthful antipolitics: Representing the "issue" of youth participation in politics. *Journal of Youth Studies,* 13(2), 181–195.

Freedom House (2011). *Freedom on the net 2011. A global assessment of internet and digital Media.* Retrieved May 9, 2013 from www.freedomhouse.org/report/freedom-net/freedom-net-2011

Gaullier, X. (1998). Ages mobiles et générations incertaines, *Esprit,* 246, 5–44.

Georgeon, F. (2007). Les Jeunes Turcs étaient-ils jeunes? Sur le phénomène des générations de l'Empire ottoman à la République turque. In F. Georgeon and K. Kreiser (Eds.), *Childhood and Youth in the Muslim World* (146–173). Paris: Maisonneuve & Larose.

Herrera, L. & Bayat, A. (2010). Introduction: Being young and Muslim in neoliberal times. In L. Herrera & A. Bayat (Eds.), *Being young and Muslim: New cultural politics in the global south and north* (3–17). Oxford and New York: Oxford University Press.

Hirschman, A. O. (1970). *Exit, voice, loyalty: Responses to decline in firms, organizations, and states.* Cambridge, MA, London: Harvard University Press.

Lüküslü, D. (2009). *Türkiye'de "gençlikMiti." 1980 sonrası Türkiye gençliği.* Istanbul: Iletisim Yayinlari.

Lüküslü, D. (2010). *Gençlik örgütlenmelerindeki gençlerin sorunları, ihtiyaçları, istekleri ve önerileri Temelinde Türkiye' de Gençlik Politikaları Göstergelerinin Oluşturulması Araştırma Projesi Raporu.* Istanbul: Istanbul Bilgi Üniversitesi Gençlik Çalışmaları Birimi.

Lüküslü, D. (2011). Bilişim teknolojileriyle örgütlenen gençlik hareketleri ve yeni bir siyaset arayışı. In A. Telli Aydemir (Ed.), *Katılımın "e-hali".gençlerin sanal alemi* (48–67). Istanbul: Alternatif Bilişim Derneği.

Lüküslü, D. (forthcoming). Necessary conformism: An art of living for the young people in Turkey. *New Perspectives on Turkey.*

Mannheim, K. (1952). The problem of generations. In P. Kecskemeti (Ed.), *Essays on the Sociology of Knowledge* (276–320). New York: Oxford University Press.

Neyzi, L. (2001). Object or subject? The paradox of "youth" in Turkey. *International Journal of Middle East Studies,* 33, 411–432.

Norris, P. (2001). *Digital divide? Civic engagement, information poverty and the internet worldwide.* Cambridge & New York: Cambridge University Press.

Norris, P. (2002). *Democratic phoenix: Reinventing political activism.* Cambridge: Cambridge University Press.

Telli Aydemir, A. (2007). *Report on Turkey, websites and civic participation: A European overview.* Retrieved May 12, 2013 from www.civicweb.edu

Tilly, C. (2004). Social movements enter the twenty-first century. Paper presented to the Conference on Contentious Politics and the Economic Opportunity Structure: Mediterranean perspectives. Boulder, CO: Paradigm Publishers.

Tuna, Y. B. (2011). Internet et militantism ni utopie ni dystopie: Usage de nouvelles technologies d'une association contestataire en Turquie. MA thesis. Paris: Université de Paris I–Panthéon Sorbonne.

Turgut, A. (August, 14, 2006). EkşiSözlük: A Turkish internet phenomenon. *Turkish Daily News.*

United Nations Development Programme. (2008). *Human development report Turkey 2008: Youth in Turkey.* Ankara: UNDP.

6

DISTORTING DIGITAL CITIZENSHIP

Khaled Said, Facebook, and Egypt's Streets

Amro Ali and Dina El-Sharnouby

Introduction: Citizenship and the Youth Bulge in the Republic of Egypt

The concept of citizenship in relation to youth was hollowed out under the former Egyptian president Hosni Mubarak's authoritarian state, and further gutted by a dysfunctional education system and the *wasta* (connections) plague. The swindled young generation grew up in despair; they were not able to find work, marriage, or a voice. As the numbers of youth increased exponentially, so too did their frantic attempts to address their disorientation in a patronizing state that viewed them as a burden, even if the formal rhetoric referred to youth as "the future" and the "hope of the nation."

The focus on youth within the last few decades has increased tremendously on a global scale, and more so in the Arab world due to the region's significant youth bulge. In Egypt, the most populated Arab country, a full 62% of the population is under the age of 29 (Barsoum, 2010, p. 2). Despite making up the majority of the population, youth have consistently been absent from the formal political sphere. During the era of Hosni Mubarak (1981–2011), under 30s were totally marginalized by the ruling National Democratic Party (NDP). When neoliberal economic policies, such as the Structural Adjustment Programs (SAPs), were introduced into Egypt in 1992 (Atia, 2008), the NDP relegated youth to objects of economic advancement rather than being agents of socio-political change (Herrera, 2009; Jeffrey & Mc Dowell, 2004).

The discourse on youth since Egypt's independence from colonial rule has situated youth as pillars of the nation. They were essential to the project of rebuilding Egypt and forging a path of Arab unity, as articulated by Gamal Abdel Nasser (1954–1970). Under the *Infitah* (open-door) policies of President Anwar

Sadat (1970–1981), the youth were the keys to Egypt's economic advancement (El-Sharnouby, 2011; Ibrahim, 2008). With the start of the Mubarak era in 1981, youth continued to be viewed as important productive forces. However, the ruling NDP did not manage to put policies into place that would absorb the high numbers of young people into the labor force. Without access to steady employment and income, large numbers of youth could not make the transition to adulthood, form families, and live independently of their parents.

Starting from the 1990s, generations have been coming of age politically and economically marginalized; they stopped being integral to the project of nation building and started to become "a problem." The voices representing power from inside and outside the nation worried that youth were susceptible to becoming religiously radicalized, Westernized, and morally lax (Assaad & Barsoum, 2007; Handoussa, 2010; Ibrahim & Wassef, 2000; Sobhy, 2009). It does not come as a surprise, then, that young people were the main drivers of the 25 January Revolution in Egypt.

Tackling "the youth question" is proving far more challenging than toppling Mubarak. While young people succeeded in mobilizing the Egyptian population during and after the 18-day uprising that led to the fall of Mubarak, they have not been as effective in finding some kind of solution or impasse out of the youth quagmire. There have been no real attempts on the part of youth activists and revolutionaries to deal with the problems and realities of being young, to search for new meanings, approaches, and prospects. Young activists are still falling into the trap of idealizing young Egyptians through heroic stories of martyrdom and sacrifice, rather than addressing the social, economic, and political-cultural dimensions of youth in a more realistic and holistic way. In other words, they are not dealing with the tough conditions of being young in Egypt, or the uncomfortable realities of drug abuse, religious extremism, poor-quality education, unemployment, sexual frustration, late marriage, and the other big issues that make being young in Egypt such a struggle (Herrera, 2010).

This chapter aims to analyze one of the most important youth movements in Egypt in decades, the "We are all Khaled Said" (WAAKS) Facebook page. The page was named after 28-year-old Alexandrian Khaled Said, who suffered a brutal death on June 6, 2010 at the hands of two police officers. The incident sparked national outrage, helping to make WAAKS a driving force for the 25 January Revolution. It will be argued that the WAAKS youth movement was an opportunity for the youth to mobilize on many different fronts, not just on anti-torture and security ones. Looking back, it seems that the page avoided dealing with the range of socio-economic and political-cultural problems that youth face in Egypt. The page even alienated youth from their own day-to-day experiences of unemployment, poor-quality education, sexual harassment, marriage, and political exclusion. The page was able to galvanize large swaths of young people around issues of police abuse and torture. Khaled Said, the martyr of police torture, was elevated to the role of an archetypical young Egyptian from the lower middle class who was the victim of torture. While WAAKS appropriated the final 20 minutes of Said's life and culled all the troubling aspects of the martyr's life away, it did illustrate that social media could enable young people to find new opportunities to explore their citizenship, identity, and share their problems. The three-dimensional life of the troubled youth Khaled Said differed considerably from the two-dimensional martyr who has been reconstructed by the WAAKS Facebook page. While the two-dimensional construct of Said served the purpose of gathering support for the 25 January Revolution, it has been found wanting during the transition period and the subsequent rise of the Muslim Brotherhood, their fall and rise of the Egyptian military. Consequently, there is the implicit feeling that the Said poster child is becoming difficult to relate to beyond a security dimension.

The "We are all Khaled Said" Social Movement

To better understand youth collective action through the WAAKS page, we turn to social movement theory. Social movements can generally be defined as a collective or joint action with change-oriented goals that require some degree of organization and carry some degree of temporal continuity (Snow, Soule, & Kriesi, 2004, p. 6). The Political Process Approach (PPA) claims "that activists do not choose goals, strategies, and tactics in a vacuum" but, rather, within a larger political context (Meyer, 2004, p. 127). Hence, according to certain historical moments and events, activists claim certain demands, ways of mobilization, and develop strategies over others creating a dialectic relation between activists' mobilization and the external environment (Meyer, 2004). PPA is strongly based on a structural understanding of the political sphere which helps in comprehending political opportunities and threats for activists through their mobilization structures, cultural framings, and political opportunity structures (POS).

From the 1990s, with the dismantling of the rentier state system, the Egyptian state lost its grip over its citizens and citizenship education. At the same time, digital technologies were spreading rapidly and were developing into a new mobilization structure. Doug McAdam has theorized these new tools as, "those collective vehicles, informal as well as formal through which people mobilize and engage in collective action" (McAdam, 2004, p. 204). Communication spaces became an alternative space, a virtual public sphere where many disenchanted youth developed their own methods for learning citizenship and acting politically (Herrera, 2010, p. 128).

Using social media tools like Facebook, Twitter, and blogs, youth were finding new means of mobilization (Aitamurto & Sistek, 2011). As Marc Lynch notes, "Activist youth proved creative, determined, and able to stay a step ahead of the authorities through new uses of social media and protest techniques. The deteriorating economic conditions and closing political space kept grievances high and rising, with new protestors entering the fray" (Lynch, 2012, pp. 66–67). Such protests and popular mobilizations were not unprecedented, but, as Lynch notes, they were "the first to take place within the intensely unified political space shaped by new media technologies [. . .] [and] the new social media profoundly shaped the character and orientation of these protest movements' avant garde" (Lynch, 2012, p. 65). Social media–driven movements, despite their perceived horizontal organization, crowd-sourced features, and space for democratic deliberation, can also over-simplify the digitally engaged segments of the society. These movements have a tendency to co-opt their followers into towing a particular narrative that can alienate some citizens more than create consensus among them through their usage of slogans, incidents, and cultural symbolism in their mobilization strategies. The case that most vividly illustrates the digital co-option is the WAAKS Facebook page. WAAKS saw in Said's death a political opportunity to focus national attention on the victims of the Emergency Law. Under this law, which has been in place for most of the time since 1967, police powers were expanded to the extent that the police did not require arrest warrants and their powers basically went unchecked, constitutional rights were suspended, street demonstrations banned, and censorship enforced. Thousands of political prisoners were victims of the Emergency Law. The Khaled Said page and youth movement expedited the rapid countdown to the 25 January Revolution.

A Digital Movement that Sought out a Martyr

For many years, Egypt's digital activism was without a unifying figure or martyr. Activists needed to find a cause that would unite members of this struggling generation. Activists and human rights workers were trying in particular to galvanize people around the issues of torture and human rights abuses committed by the police state. A turning point came in 2006 when a young bus driver by the name of Emad al-Kabir was filmed being tortured and sodomized with a rod by officers in a police station. The officers filmed al-Kabir's torture at the Bulaq police station to humiliate him. They sent the video to other minibus drivers' cell phones as a warning that the same could happen to them if they refused to cooperate with security officials (Radwan, 2007). The film ended up in the hands of an activist who posted it on YouTube. The bloggers drew attention to it and the video went viral in Egypt. This incident became well known and it caused a public outcry that ended with the police officers being given prison terms. But, as Ashraf Khalil has noted, "Nobody formed a 'We are all Emad al-Kabir' website because they simply didn't feel that kind of instant kinship and sympathy" (Khalil, 2012, p. 77). The kinship would be formed four years later with Khaled Said, who became the human face and lynchpin to unite and spearhead disparate youth movements.

Not just any Egyptian victim was good enough to be a unifying figure; a symbol for the youth needed to be of a certain type, to die in a certain way, at a certain place, and in a certain context. One factor that aided Khaled Said's ascendency to the pinnacle of celebrity martyrdom was that he was a young Egyptian man who came from a middle-class background. This class dimension was critical since Egypt's online society is often more sympathetic to individuals of the middle class than those from lower socio-economic or impoverished backgrounds. Another factor is that Said had no known connection to religious or political movements. The absence of any obvious ideological bent in his background enabled many to claim ownership of Said as "their" everyday Egyptian. The social media savvy generation could also identify with Said. He was martyred at an internet café where he was allegedly about to upload a video to YouTube of crooked cops sharing the spoils of drug money. Yet the biggest push to make Khaled Said the youth martyr was the horrific image of Said's mangled face. The infamous photograph of a disfigured Said ensured that the youths' emotions would run high. The Facebook page, "We are all Khaled Said," created by 23-year-old cyberactivist Abdelrahman Mansour, and 30-year-old Google executive, Wael Ghonim, channeled those emotions. That image, which was taken by his relative at the morgue the night of Said's death and sent to an activist blogger who put it into circulation, transformed Said into a focal point for the nation; inspired by him, citizens rallied together against the hated Emergency Law, which essentially robbed citizens of due process and their rights for the sake of "national security." Said became the human face of Egypt's tragedy, but also the galvanizer of its digital youth.

The page underwent a series of intentional and unintentional rewritings to sanitize Said and elevate him to a saint. The page used an airbrushed passport photo of Said as its profile picture and this photo became the eternal engraved image. Said was given an activist profile makeover to turn him into a hero of citizen journalism. In reality, he was a young man who was known locally for his drug abuse, and the question of whether he was ever in possession of an anti-police video remains open. These "redeeming" features all served to propel Said to the status of chief martyr. This was problematic. It is not that WAAKS wanted to intentionally distort Said, but they thought they had little choice if they wanted to channel their grievances and activism into one dead man. They allowed the figure of Khaled Said to posthumously personalize and humanize complex issues. All the complexities and inner contradictions of Said were stripped away as he was repackaged for the consumption of Egyptians. There was one problem with this appropriation: it did not do justice to the real day-to-day problems faced by youth, and ended up censoring the questions of what pushes many of them to drugs, depression, sexism, sectarianism, and religious extremism, to name but a few youth issues. In other words, the range of problems that brought Said to his fateful day that have to do with the dynamics of drug abuse, unemployment, and conscription were made redundant by the youth movement that took his name. The Khaled Said movement became synonymous with anti-torture and the Emergency Law, nothing more, nothing less. In this manner, WAAKS created a one-dimensional Khaled Said to represent middle-class urban youth, neglecting the countless Khaled Saids with social problems so intense that police abuse is the least of their worries.

Even if Khaled Said does not represent the problems of all Egyptians, that is not to say that they do not identify with him. Said has become integral to national identity in the post-revolutionary period. The Egyptian media circuit, nationalist commentators, activists, and the public discourse in general became involved, inflating the importance of Said to distinguish him from, and maybe even eclipse, Mohamed Bouazizi, the Tunisian fruit seller whose desperate act of self-immolation to protest his indignity and the injustice in society sparked off the Arab uprisings.

Dismantling Khaled Said's World

Khaled Said means "eternally happy" in Arabic, but his story is anything but that. The actual life of Khaled Said was "ordinary," often troubled, and not especially heroic. When he was serving his mandatory military service, the harshness of the conscript's life made him go AWOL. He served only a light military prison sentence of 10 months between 2006 and 2007 because of some family connections and a voluntary return to the army. Said was known in the military jail as someone who amused the other inmates with his witty antics. Some of those he made friends with there would later visit him after their release (Ali, 2012).

In his years at school people rarely knew him by his full name. He was called "Khaled Tayara" (Khaled Kite) for attaching razor blades to his kite to threaten kite rivals, causing all kite-flying enthusiasts to flee the scene upon sighting the winged predator over Alexandria's beaches (Mohamed W., personal communication, April 29, 2011). Inspired by his revered older brother, Ahmed Wave, who lived in the US during large parts of Said's life, Said took on the nickname "Kaled Wave," which he used until his death. This name was also a nod to his love for rap music and DJ-ing. Said's neighbors knew he was home if his music system was blasting out of his second-floor apartment. Being resourceful, he would power up his stereo on the beach from streetlight wires. Finally, he had the less than flattering nickname of "Abu Sena" in reference to a crooked tooth (Ali, 2012b).

His mother was often in Cairo, where her daughter Zahra lived with her children, leaving Said alone in the apartment. It is rare in this neighborhood to find a young man living alone. Most unmarried youth live with their families. The judgmental mindset of society assumes that the worst is taking place in the home of a single man (that is, women are being brought home). Said had a strong compassionate side; when he was running out of money he would sometimes forgo meals just to feed his 12 cats (Ali, 2012). Said's hospitality, politeness, helpfulness, and youthfulness left him susceptible to all sorts of social parasites and opportunists. His new set of "friends" exploited the privacy of his home for substance abuse, which was made easier by his autophobic nature. The impressionable Said soon succumbed to variations of cannabis. His need to "fit in" could at times reach abnormal lengths; in one instance, a friend dared him to drink the contents of a medicine bottle from the bathroom cabinet and he complied (Ali, 2012b).

In the final months of the Mubarak regime, the authorities attempted to justify Said's death by insensitively painting Said's suburb, Cleopatra Hamamat, as a den of drug dealers and substance abuse, though without the statistics to back up the claim. Still, the neighborhood does reflect the decline in the situation of Egypt's youth, which had been taking place between 1999 and 2009. Over this decade the quality of life in the supposedly middle-class suburbs deteriorated as the result of rising unemployment, delayed marriages, and the rapid rise of apartment complexes that placed extra pressure on the district's utilities and traffic. A predatory culture of self-interest arose in some sections where neighbors were less inclined to look after each other's welfare and friendships were commonly formed based on economic interests. Tensions were on the rise between Muslims and Christians. Through the difficulties, the effects of hashish were visible on young faces throughout the streets.

While the authoritarian order had entered its fifth decade, the rise of the digital world reshaped the rules of engagement across Egypt. Tourism was no longer the sole bastion of cross-cultural interaction as the internet became a formidable force in opening the way to forming new relations (Ali, 2011). This was also Said's world. Said spent much of his time on the internet as a form of escapism, and it was here that he developed relationships with foreign girls abroad. There was nothing unusual about Said that would have made anyone give him a second look. He was hardly the idealized cyberactivist that others subsequently made him out to be. His internet use was mainly limited to downloading the latest movies and songs to distribute to his friends on the street, as well as conducting the romantic relationships he had with two girls living abroad.

Khaled Said lived in a youth cultural world where he was influenced by the strong overtones of black American subculture. Aspects of its language, clothing style, mannerisms, and even anti-police views weaved their way into his thinking, but it stopped at that; he never translated it into any form of activism (Ali, 2012b). Said developed a disdain for Arabic music. Like so many young people, he harbored aspirations of being famous and imagined rap music would be his ticket to fame and the good life. Little did he know that a posthumous fame was awaiting him. Said exhibited a strong desire to find true love. As he once said to a friend in a moment of despair: "I just wish to love and be loved by somebody" (Ali, 2012c). He became the object of love and affection of an entire nation. Khaled Said's story was one of mental dispossession in his own land, where the pillars of identity, belonging, and citizenship collapsed one after the other like the dangerously built apartment complexes that often cave in throughout the coastal city.

In the social media world of Facebook, there are at least two contrasting Khaled Saids. There was the WAAKS page that started off with the famous passport photo of an Alexandrian youth with slick, gelled back hair. There was another and more authentic Khaled Said tucked deep away in the catacombs of social media, where a Facebook corpse rests, and this was Kaled Wave (Said's alias). The latter profile speaks volumes about the real Said, the one who was robbed of hope and a future. The Alexandria he depicts for his virtual life is not the once-thriving cosmopolitan city of Egypt 60 years ago, but the Alexandria Bay in New York ("Kaled Wave," Facebook, 2012). It was his obsession to immigrate, particularly to the US, after having lived in Pennsylvania for a short period of time (Wesam, personal communication,

April 29, 2011). The Khaled Said of WAAKS represents the inclusive youth of the Egyptian revolution, while the other Khaled Said represents the exiled Egyptian.

Khaled Said fits perfectly well into the deteriorating social tapestry of an Egypt where emigration attempts, drug abuse, street mistrust, and questionable friendships characterize the life of a young Egyptian. This is not to mention the extreme example of his "friend," "Mohamed Hashish," who sold him out to the police, a betrayal that ultimately resulted in Khaled Said's death and altered Egyptian history. On that fateful humid summer Sunday night, Hashish, long suspected by the street of being an informant for the police, contacted Said and informed him that a drug dealer would meet them on the corner of their street facing the coast. After the sun had set over the Mediterranean just after 7 p.m., Said walked with Hashish and bought his "bango" (cannabis). Later on, according to second-hand testimony, Said suggested that they both go to his place. Hashish replied, "Just come with me to the *cyber* [Spacenet Café] as I have to see something." They continued walking towards the Spacenet Café. As Hashish was speaking on his mobile through an earpiece, he was sighted doing a hand wave and slowly walked away from Said, although remaining close enough to maintain a conversation. At that point two police officers followed Said into the internet café and Hashish parted. An anonymous source recounted that Hashish ran towards the Sidi Gaber police station and returned to the scene of the crime in a police van. This claim transforms Hashish from being a snitch to a barefaced accomplice. It would be incredulous if it were not for sightings of Mohamed Hashish with two *mokhbereen* (informers) for his protection in the period following Khaled Said's death.

We are not all Khaled Said: Limits and Backlash

For all the noble causes of cyber campaigns, the energies put into digital citizenship can skew or mask Egypt's dysfunctional social system. Once the revolution passed its zenith, it was not surprising that the limits of WAAKS would surface. After all, it was set up to attack the Emergency Law, with which the Mubarak regime had been closely associated during his 30-year rule. Mubarak arguably abused the law more than his predecessors. Bringing down Mubarak was seen to give justice to Said's death and to the society at large. With time, the page became less confrontational and backed away from the mobilization efforts that had characterized its purpose in the past; it went from "catalyst of the revolution to becoming the memory of the revolution" (Khamis & Vaughn, 2011, p. 155). While WAAKS had played a pivotal role in the lead-up to the 25 January Revolution, it was not able to continue as a youth movement after the revolution. This failure derived in part from the fact that the page had always fixated on the dramatic ending of Khaled Said's life, while eschewing the everyday socio-economic problems that had driven Said to that fateful day.

The events on June 6, 2012, the second anniversary of Khaled Said's death, went a long way to revealing the extent to which he had been turned into a political prop. Hamdeen Sabahi, the presidential candidate who came so close to being in the run-offs, visited the cemetery with Said's family, and Al Jazeera and other media outlets traipsed behind them. By 5 p.m. the scene was spectacular in the Cleopatra Hamamat district. There were thousands of marchers, many from Cairo, steadfastly approaching the area with a sea of black, red, and white Egyptian flags, with old nationalist songs by Om Kalthum and other Egyptian singers blaring out. Members of the April 6 Youth Movement (*Harakat Shabab 6 Abril*) were spray-painting Khaled Said's face on every available space on walls. The sight was hypnotic. The day before activists had blogged and tweeted instructions on how to get to the area. Thousands converged on the streets of the neighborhood of Cleopatra Hamamat, including the who's who of the revolutionary movement. In addition to Hamdeen Sabahi, there were other presidential hopefuls and leaders, such as Abul Fotouh, Ahmed Harara, Khaled Youssef, and others.

There was a conspicuous absence of local residents in the lively crowds. To be sure, some were able to use their balconies as they were more convenient, but not all. It was almost as if residents were unaware of the magnitude of Khaled Said as a history changing figure. One shop owner stated bluntly to one of the authors of this article (Ali): "No one from this neighborhood has ever come out for Khaled Said since he died." Had Said's transformation by WAAKS alienated the people in his own neighborhood? It is quite possible that this is the case.

In the months following the revolution, standing on my balcony overlooking the bustling Cleopatra Square, Said's friend, Wesam, made an unexpected comment to me (Ali): "Once Khaled said something so bizarre, he asked me 'Have you thought of going to the US? I can help you get there through Nigeria as I have contacts there" (Wesam Mohamed, personal communication, April 29, 2011). After we had both had a chuckle at the suggestion, my smile quickly turned to a frown as I remembered the three generous Egyptians I had bumped into in northern Paris in 2009 who had illegally entered France and were therefore forced to work in the country's shadow economy with all the difficulties it entails. At the heart of the young Egyptian psyche was escape. It only reaffirmed the obvious, that Said was not a saint or from another planet, but he was the product of Egypt's contemporary society and a member of the troubled youth generation.

The Spin-off Effects of WAAKS

While WAAKS should not be seen to represent the opinions or aspirations of every Egyptian in society, it has inadvertently fomented mini-WAAKS and injected Alexandria with a fraction more understanding of digital citizenship. Unable to obtain their rights quickly enough in the post-revolutionary period, youth have set up a great number of Facebook groups and pages to address social problems. Yet there are limits.

Sexual harassment, for example, a problem that seeks to marginalize young women in the public space, is a major epidemic in Egypt and a highly discussed topic in cyberspace. The difficulties in resolving this problem and the intense discussions that have taken place concerning it have led to the formation of anti-sexual harassment groups like Tahrir Bodyguard, *Estargel* (Behave like a Man), *Wilad El Balad* (The Country's Sons), and *Banat Masr Khat A7mar* (Egypt's Girls are a Red Line) (Samir, 2012). Legislators, politicians, and police officers do not enforce existing laws. The youth have had no choice but to channel their energy through civil society, taking inspiration from WAAKS.

Yet the discourse around sexual harassment often suffers from some of the same societal denial that distorted the life of Khaled Said and made his martyrdom conditional upon him being a saint. This form of denial about "ourselves" as a society reinforces the syndrome of victim-blaming. A woman is blamed if she is harassed; she is accused of wearing "unsuitable clothing" or choosing to go to "the wrong place at the wrong time," just as a youth who takes drugs is perceived to deserve what he gets from the police. Such attitudes are widespread across Egypt, but they are more acutely felt in Said's neighborhood where, when the name "Khaled Said" is brought up, it is met by rolling eyes. You would hear off-the-cuff remarks amongs residents like, "Khaled was not a good boy, he did drugs," and "he was a delinquent." One of Said's friends straight after his death said: "Khaled should not have run from the police!" (in any case, he did not). The implication of such remarks is that Khaled Said somehow deserved what came to him. So the question arises, "Is Said to blame for the police killing him or at the very least, the police behavior and conditions that led to his death?" (Ali, 2012a).

Conclusion

In the lead-up to the 25 January Revolution, Egyptian youth activists had been advancing a new culture of political inclusion. Yet, at the time, they had not really been looking inwards at the problems they faced as youth, or reflected on their own bias towards the middle class. As one of the authors of this article has argued elsewhere:

> questions need to be raised from the subtext of the Khaled Said construct: What about the rights of those of lower socio-economic backgrounds? Does it matter that a rural youth may not have had access to the Internet? Would a dark-skinned Nubian victim garner as much attention? Can the term "martyr" be applied to a Copt? To what extent would it have been her "fault" if it were a woman in Khaled's exact same situation? Is there even a concept of Bedouin youth in Sinai? When you add it all up, there are many "Khaled Saids" out there on standby who we may never, and we don't, hear about. Instead of utilizing Khaled Said as a signpost for the country's current disparity and looming socio-economic problems, we use him as the template of what a good martyr should be and look like.
>
> (Ali, 2012a)

The Khaled Said youth movement was undoubtedly important in advancing digitally mediated youth citizenship. WAAKS sought to use Said's death to bring national attention and outrage to the victims of the Emergency Law, and it succeeded beyond all expectations. However, the page and movement also missed an opportunity. By transforming an ordinary citizen into a heroic figure, the WAAKS page inadvertently alienated vast segments of the youth from their own realities and struggles. It neglected the everyday problems and challenges faced by Egyptian youth, as if they were somehow outside of issues of police brutality and social justice. Khaled Said's life was about so much more than his last 20 minutes of pain and agony.

In the post-revolution period young activists remain unclear about how to tackle youth problems and find a way to include more youth in the political sphere. While choosing to hold up a heroic martyr figure like Said helped to topple the regime, the morning-after effect is that people are still waiting for their problems to be addressed. Factors such as low-quality education, the search for a marital partner, working to find the very means to marry, unemployment, democracy deficits, all hampered by drug abuse and the everyday experience of sexual harassment, all form a toxic tapestry of unanswered problems.

For all their shortcomings, online youth campaigns like WAAKS have served to spread and grow youth-directed mobilization structures. Communication spaces are effectively being used by youth to craft their own form of citizenship and seek out their rights. Mini-WAAKS are still blossoming, meaning the digital mode of youth awareness and activism is very much a work in progress. It may well evolve to address and find collective ways to confront the host of problems plaguing youth such as drug abuse, depression, emigration attempts, and extremism. Even if the martyrdom of Khaled Said has turned him into an unreal youth, we must still recognize the power of the youths' symbolic ownership of Said that ensures he becomes part and parcel of the Second Republic's national identity. With time, youth will not need archetypes to galvanize them into action, but will find inspiration and answers in their own real, grounded lives.

References

Abulata, M. F., Ragui, A., Ghada, B. et al. (2010). *Survey of young people in Egypt*. Cairo: Population Council.

Aitamurto, T. & Sistek, H. (2011, September 13). *How social media is keeping the Egyptian revolution alive*. Retrieved from www.pbs.org/mediashift/2011/09/how-social-media-is-keeping-the-egyptian-revolution-alive256.html

Ali, A. (2010, July 9). Egypt's collision course with history. *Online Opinion*. Retrieved from www.online opinion.com.au/view.asp?article=10663&page=0

Ali, A. (2011, February 9). Defriending Mubarak: Egypt's social media revolution. *Online Opinion*. Retrieved from www.onlineopinion.com.au/view.asp?article=11594&page=0

Ali, A. (2012a, June, 5). *2nd year commemoration for Khaled Said 6/6/12*. Message posted to http://amroali.com/2012/06/2nd-year-commemoration-for-khaled-Said-6612/

Ali, A. (2012b, June 5). Saids of revolution: De-mythologizing Khaled Said. *Jadaliyya.* Retrieved from www.jadaliyya.com/pages/index/5845/Saids-of-revolution_de-mythologizing-khaled-Said

Ali, A. (2012c, June 13). Revolution never sleeps. *Open Democracy.* Retrieved from www.opendemocracy.net/amro-ali/revolution-never-sleeps

Assaad, R. & Barsoum, G. (2007). Youth exclusion in Egypt: In search of "second chances." *The Middle East Youth Initiative, 2*, 1–45.

Atia, M. (2008). The Arab Republic of Egypt. In *From charity to change: Trends in Arabic philanthropy.* The John D. Gerhart Center For Philanthropy and Civic Engagement. Retrieved from www.aucegypt.edu/research/gerhart/Documents/Youth%20Activism%20and%20Public%20Space%20in%20Egypt.pdf

Barsoum, G. (2010). Youth life transitions: Opportunities, capabilities and risk. *Egypt human development report 2010 youth in Egypt: Building our future.* Cairo: The American University Press in Cairo.

Dhillon, N., Dyer, P. & Yousef, T. (2009). Generation in waiting: An overview of school to work and family formation transitions. In T. Yousef (Ed.), *Generation in waiting: The unfulfilled promise of young people in the Middle East* (11–38). Washington DC: Brookings Institution Press.

El-Sharnouby, D. (2011). Youth and the 25th January Revolution in Egypt: Agents of change and its multiple meanings. (Master's thesis). Cairo: The American University in Cairo.

Facebook. (2008). *Wave Kaled.* Retrieved January 1 from www.facebook.com/kaled.wave

Facebook. (2010). *We are all Khaled Said.* Retrieved June 10, 2010 from www.facebook.com/ElShaheeed>

Handoussa, H. et al. (2010). *Egypt human development report 2010: Youth in Egypt, building our future.* Cairo: Virgin Graphics.

Herrera, L. (2006). What's new about youth? *Development & Change, 37*(6), 1425–1434.

Herrera, L. (2009). Is youth being addressed in important and distinctive ways in Middle East studies? *International Journal of Middle East Studies, 41*(3), 368–371.

Herrera, L. (2010). Young Egyptians' quest for jobs and justice. In L. Herrera & A. Bayat (Eds.), *Being young and Muslim: New cultural politics in the global south and North* (128). New York: Oxford University Press.

Herrera, L. & Bayat, A. (Eds.). (2010). *Being young and Muslim: New cultural politics in the global south and north.* New York: Oxford University Press.

Ibrahim, B. (2008). *Pathways to participation among Egyptian youth. Survey of young people in Egypt.* Unpublished Manuscript. Cairo: Arab Families Working Group.

Ibrahim, B. & Wassef, H. (2000). Caught between two worlds: Youth in Egyptian hinterland. In Roel Meijer (Ed.), *Alienation or integration of Arab youth: Between family, state and street* (161–188). London: Routledge.

Jeffrey, C. & Mcdowell, L. (2004). Youth in a comparative perspective: Global change, local lives. *Youth Society, 36*(2), 131–142.

Khalil, A. (2012). *Liberation square: Inside the Egyptian revolution and the rebirth of a nation.* Cairo: American University in Cairo Press.

Khamis, S. & Vaughn, K. (2011). We are all Khaled Said: The potentials and limitations of cyberactivism in triggering public mobilization and promoting political change. *Journal of Arab and Muslim Media Research, 4*(2), 145–163.

Lynch, M. (2012). *The Arab uprising: The unfinished revolutions of the new Middle East.* New York: Public Affairs.

McAdam, D. (2004). Revisiting the US civil rights movement: Toward a more synthetic understanding of the origins of contention. In J. Goodwin and J. M. Jasper (Eds.),

Rethinking social movements: Structure, meaning, and emotion (201–232). Maryland: Rowman & Littlefield Publishers, Inc.

Meyer, D. (2004). Protest and political opportunities. *Annual Review of Sociology*, 30, 125–145.

Radwan, A. (2007, January 27). Egypt's torture video sparks outrage. *Time*. Retrieved from www.time.com/time/world/article/0,8599,1581608,00.html

Samir, D. (2012, September 8). Fighting the good fight against sexual harassment: New, effective initiatives. *Ahram Online*. Retrieved from http://english.ahram.org.eg/NewsContent/1/64/52259/Egypt/Politics-/Fighting-the-good-fight-against-sexual-harassment-.aspx

Snow, D., Soule, S. & Kriesi, H. (2004). Mapping the terrain. In D. Snow, S. Soule, and H. Kriesi (Eds.), *The Blackwell companion to social movements* (3–16). Malden, MA, Oxford, & Carlton, Victoria: Blackwell Publishing.

Sobhy, H. (2009). Amr Khaled and young Muslim elites: Islamization and the consolidation of mainstream Muslim piety in Egypt. In D. Singerman (Ed.), *Cairo contested: Governance, urban space and global modernity* (415–454). Cairo: American University in Cairo Press.

SECTION II

Internet, Geopolitics, and Redefining the Political

7

"HUNGRY FOR FREEDOM"

Palestine Youth Activism in the Era of Social Media

Mira Nabulsi

Introduction: Palestine and a Transnational Public Sphere

"Digital activism" or "electronic resistance" are increasingly the space for trans-national and global activism for Palestine. While earlier forms of internet activism focused mainly on the dissemination of information regarding the humanitarian and political situation of Palestinians, recent patterns are showing an orientation towards online political organizing and campaigning, and also towards discussion and criticism of internal and local politics. Digital activism was especially evident after the movement of March 15, 2011 and the Boycott, Divestment and Sanctions from Israel (BDS) movement, which gave rise to a space of networking between youth in Palestine and those in the diaspora on various actions. There is now clearer evidence that a growing number of Palestinians are consciously using social media as a tool of resistance.

Many theories dealing with the public sphere assume the existence of a nation state (Bishara, 2010). In the Palestinian case identity is not based on the state or a territorial region. Rather, the shared experiences of dispossession, oppression, and resistance constitute the collective political identity (Aouragh, 2011). It becomes particularly hard to talk about a single, location-specific public sphere, especially after the 1993 Oslo Accords, which gave rise to separate authorities in the West Bank and Gaza, and no representation for those in the diaspora. Thus, issues of representation, democratization and the practice of citizenship necessitate differing frameworks because of the fragmentation of people and land, as well as the transnational aspect of the Palestinian cause and movement.

After the Palestinian legislative elections in 2006, activists had to deal with an internal division between Fateh and Hamas, the two largest political parties. With Hamas now ruling Gaza, and the Palestinian Authority led by Fateh and backed by the US and Europe ruling the West Bank, censorship became more severe, and political arrests of dissenting voices became systematic. Opposition on both sides was nearly crushed and political discussions, especially those of internal politics, ceased to be as public. The crackdown on dissent coincided with the rise of social media tools like Facebook and Twitter. Social media remained focused on challenging the Zionist narrative to the extent that discussions about internal politics were often marginalized.

The scattered Palestinian efforts online gradually solidified in the wake of the Israeli Operation "Cast Lead" in Gaza between December 2008 and January 2009. The attack was undeniably a culminating moment for Palestine activism both online and offline. With the biased coverage of the international corporate media, the strong Israeli propaganda, and the absence of international journalists—with the exception of Al Jazeera English—covering the attack from inside the Gaza Strip, Palestinians found no other space than the internet and social media to disseminate news and pictures of the atrocities committed to an international audience (Najjar, 2010).

The War on Gaza, the Goldstone Report,[1] and the "Flotillas for Gaza" all contributed to the revival of the work for Palestine and paved the way for the growing support of the Boycott, Divestment and Sanctions movement.[2] Social media was used for the dissemination of information about the circumstances in Palestine and to coordinate actions. Activists found refuge in the use of the internet, blogs, online forums, Facebook, YouTube, Twitter, and other social media platforms as their primary media and public relations tools, especially with this movement not centered in one specific location.

Social Media: A Space of Organizing for Palestinian Youth

The March 15 movement, which started organically inside Palestine and was largely inspired by the uprisings in Tunisia, Egypt, and other Arab countries, actively used social media, especially Facebook, to organize popular protests in the Palestinian territories, the Palestinian community inside Israel, and the diaspora. The movement called for the end of the division between Fateh and Hamas (Farsakh, 2012). Participants in the diaspora called for a reform of the Palestine Liberation Organization (PLO) and the election of a representative Palestinian National Council (PNC). On May 15, 2011, the date that Palestinians commemorate as *Nakba*,[3] one of the biggest marches to the Israeli borders by Palestinian refugees took place. Thousands attempted to march to the Syrian, Lebanese, Jordanian, and Gaza–Israel borders. In most of these countries, local police attempted to stop marchers, but a few managed to cross from Syria into Majdal Shams, a Syrian town north of the Israeli-occupied Golan Heights. Thirteen marchers were killed by Israeli soldiers, and one young man made his way to Yaffa, his grandparents' town (Farsakh, 2012).

The marches in 2011 were not a new form of direct action. However, the momentum was new, as was the massive dissemination of the call thanks to the

Facebook page, "The Third Palestinian Intifada." Within days of its launch, the page's fan base grew from a few hundred to thousands and then to over 170,000 fans in approximately one week. The page reached more than 350,000 fans before it was shut down by the Facebook administration on March 29, 2011. The closure of the Facebook page highlights the nature of some external factors Palestinian organizers have to deal with in their struggle, represented here in the alliances between big corporations and the strong lobby groups in the US and elsewhere in the West. In contrast to the Palestinian case, youth movements in Egypt and Tunisia received the support of Facebook during their uprisings (Giglio, 2011).

Dying to Live: From Hunger Strike to Social Media Campaign

Palestine political organizing in the digital age occurs at two levels—local/internal and global. A case study of the hunger strikes of political prisoners draws attention to some of the tactics currently used by young Palestinian activists to reach large national and international audiences, while responding also to the need for awareness and action on the ground. The hunger strike of prisoner Khader Adnan translated into one of the most successful, far-reaching, and high-profile Palestinian social media campaigns to date. It illustrates how Palestinian youth negotiate the online and offline, and the local and the global to challenge the status quo.

Khader Adnan, a 34-year-old Palestinian man from the village of Arraba, near the city of Jenin, was arrested on December 17, 2011. He began a hunger strike on the first day of his arrest and maintained it until a deal was reached on February 21, 2012 for his release in April. According to Addameer, the Prisoner Support and Human Rights Association, it was the eighth time Adnan had been arrested. He had previously spent a total of six years in Israeli prisons and had gone on earlier hunger strikes. In 2005 he had started a hunger strike that had lasted 12 days to protest his solitary confinement in KfarYuna jail (Addameer, 2012a). On January 8, 2012 Adnan was sentenced to administrative detention for four months, based on "secret information" that was only made available to the military court.[4] After multiple appeals had been lodged by his lawyer, and his health had deteriorated, the military judges rejected the appeals, calling his condition, "acceptable" to continue the sentence (Addameer, 2012a).

Despite his membership of the Islamic Jihad party, which is listed in much of the Western world as a terrorist organization, Adnan's case garnered a high degree of international attention. In a statement his lawyer released Adnan said, "I have been humiliated, beaten, and harassed by interrogators for no reason, and thus I swore to God I would fight the policy of administrative detention to which I and hundreds of my fellow prisoners fell prey" (Addameer, 2012a). Thus, Adnan went on with his strike, which he said would continue until he was released or charged. "Dying to Live" and "Hungry for Freedom" became leading slogans of solidarity actions taking place around the world to support his cause against administrative detention and bring attention to the prisoners' conditions.

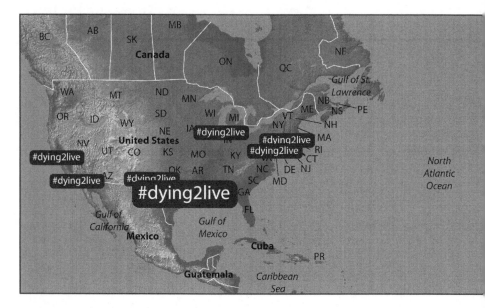

FIGURE 7.1 "Khader Adnan, dying to live." Jalal Abukhater of *Electronic Intifada,* 2012.

Online activists and bloggers picked up Khader Adnan's story after Adnan had already passed the fortieth day of his hunger strike. Until then, no single Palestinian prisoner had carried on a hunger strike for so long. Adnan would go on to beat the record reached by Irish Republican Army (IRA) members who went on hunger strikes in 1980 and 1981. Apart from a few stories on Arab or Palestine related websites and blogs, Adnan's case was publicized almost entirely through Twitter. Palestinian tweeps (Twitter users) and their allies coordinated a number of hashtags that trended globally on Twitter more than five times. It was through those repeated globally trending hashtags on Twitter that some voices in the mainstream media picked up the story. The trending hashtags include, #KhaderAdnan, #KhaderExists, #hungry4justice, #KhaderIsAlive, #Khader61days, #Respect-4Khader, #Khader62, and #HungerStrike63days.

There is no doubt that the momentum around Adnan's strike built on previous hunger strikes, the last of which ended with the Shalit deal at the end of 2011.[5] The same could be said about the online campaign. For the last few years, young Palestinian social media users have managed to make good use of the expanding network of Palestine solidarity work in the West to disseminate stories, get the attention of the mainstream international media, and make connections between Adnan's strike and political prisoners elsewhere.

Palestinian tweeps were quick to adapt new features on social media platforms and apply them to their political campaigning. For instance, just a few months before the Khader Adnan campaign, Twitter introduced the "Discover" feature.

This curates tweets from people a user might not even be following. The feature retrieves contextual information based on the user's behavior. As Jalal Abukhater, a Palestinian blogger and active Twitter user, explains in an article in the newspaper *Al-Akhbar*:

> Organizing a trending hashtag for Adnan is just like organizing a large protest on the corner of the busiest and most crowded street in the city [. . .] In a new update to Twitter.com, there is now a section named "Discover" where Twitter users can read about the top 10 most popular stories from around the globe. Each time Adnan's name trends, a story about him would remain in the "Discover" section's top 10 stories for over 6 hours after it trends.
>
> (Abukhater, 2012b)

Palestinian Twitter users and their supporters also target media personalities to report on prisoners' conditions, the illegality of administrative detention, and the hunger strikers. They used hashtags like #CoverKhader and #WaitingForKristof. The latter was directed to *New York Times* Columnist Nicholas Kristof, who wrote an Op-Ed on July 10, 2010 titled, "Waiting for Gandhi." Kristof said that if Palestinians abandoned stone-throwing and "put female pacifists in the lead," those images "would be on televisions around the world." He concluded that so far there has not been a Palestinian version of Martin Luther King, Jr. (Kristof, 2010). Tweeps responded:

@Cossa68 tweeted: So #Palestine has its #gandhi, yet we're still #waiting forkristof to #CoverKhader, not holding my breath.

@DeppenWebber tweeted: @NickKristof no longer has to wait for the Palestinian Bobby Sands. #waitingforkristof 2 #coverkhader.

@Sshusma said: We are all #WaitingForKristof but Kristof is waiting for Khader Adnan to die. @NickKristo.

@Aliabunimah of Electronic Intifada also joined, tweeting: I'm #Waiting ForKristof to say a word for Khader Adnan (charged with no crime) as he did for Shalit, an occupying soldier @NickKristof (Topsy).

In addition to answering back to the *New York Times* directly, tweeps have also addressed other mainstream media like the BBC, Sky News, Fox News, CNN, and even the US State Department, US Secretary of State Clinton, and US Ambassador to the United Nations Susan Rice (Hauser, 2012).

Online tactics to bring attention to Adnan's case were matched, although not always with the same popular rigor, by traditional offline actions. Amnesty International, Human Rights Watch, Physicians for Human Rights-Israel, and Palestinian human rights organizations like Addameer and Al-Haq provided humanitarian and legal ground for the support of Adnan and other political prisoners and urged an end to the administrative detention policy. On its website, Addameer published an activist toolkit with templates of letters people could send to their governments and to the Israeli authorities. *Samidoun*, a blog that calls itself the "Palestinian Prisoner Solidarity Network" in North America, also posted flyers, templates, social media avatars, information and fact sheets for activists to use in their actions. They also made calls and announcements for planned solidarity actions in various locations in North America.

Offline protests and online actions and petitions were largely coordinated by youth. A blog set up by Palestinian young activists managed, in a few days, to gather nearly 500 letters of support from people around the world dedicated to Adnan and his family (Posterous, 2012). Messages of solidarity continued to flow even after the deal was reached. Some messages came from prominent activist family members, like the brother and family of Irish hunger striker Francis Hughes, who passed away during the 1981 hunger strike of imprisoned IRA members. Hughes died after his fifty-ninth day of striking, while his cousin, Thomas McElwee, died after his sixty-second day. Hughes's brother expressed solidarity with all of the Palestinian prisoners and described the feelings of sympathy Irish people feel for the Palestinians under occupation (Bobby Sands Trust, n.d.). On Adnan's fifty-fourth day of the strike, a similar message was posted on YouTube from Tommy McKearney, another IRA member who went on a strike for 53 days in 1981. Supporters have also posted solidarity messages on YouTube. A US-based folk singer named David Rovics, known for his support of the Palestinian struggle, dedicated a song to Adnan and this was circulated via YouTube. In 2013 the video had over 20,800 views.

Towards the end of the second month of Adnan's hunger strike, more media started covering his story, including the *New York Times,* the *Los Angeles Times,* and CNN. *New York Times* writer Isabel Kershner covered Adnan's story with a focus on the policy of administrative detention. The article was issued in both online and print issues. She followed this article with another on news of Adnan's deal for release (Kershner, 2012a). The British media started calling Adnan, "the Palestinian Bobby Sands," or "The West Bank's Bobby Sands" (Karon, 2012a).[6] Sands's strike made him an "international cause célèbre" and got him elected as a member of the British Parliament. Adnan, however, got on the international radar long after he started his strike and after warnings that death was near (Karon, 2012a).

A digital poster of Khader Adnan was widely circulated. The poster portrays Adnan's face with a lock on his mouth symbolizing his refusal to eat and speak. The young artist behind this now famous image was Hafez Omar and he first shared the poster on his Facebook page, Hitan (Walls), at the end of January. Omar is a graphic designer from Tulkarem in the West Bank who has been quite active with youth mobilization since 2011. His work gained notoriety during the hunger strikes as well as during the Arab revolutions. The revolutionary visual portrayals he created to accompany and reflect many of the events inside Palestine and in the region helped connect Omar with many of the Arab, and particularly Egyptian, Facebook pages like "We are all Khaled Said," which have massive membership. This has indeed contributed to the widespread use of the posters that portrayed Adnan and later other strikers (Iskandar, 2012). Before long, the image was spray-painted in various streets of the West Bank and even in Israel. The image of Adnan also circulated widely on Facebook and other social media platforms as profile pictures, while protesters offline carried the picture in the numerous protests and sit-ins in Palestine and all over the world (Iskandar, 2012).

On the day Adnan was released, activists and activist journalists covered his release and arrival at his village and home, which took place around midnight. They uploaded and tweeted live pictures and personalized impressions from his family and neighbors. Adnan was received as a hero, and pictures of him being carried on other people's shoulders, giving his first speech and sitting with his two young daughters circulated globally over social media.

The Mass Strike of Political Prisoners on April, 17, 2012 (*Al Karama* Strike)

The release of Khader Adnan, as many analysts concluded, was Israel's way of avoiding an outbreak of popular unrest, which could have happened if Adnan had died during his strike, especially in light of the growing international pressure to end the Israeli policy of administrative detention. Tony Karon of *Time Magazine* wrote an article titled, "A hunger striker at death's door turns up the heat on Israel—and on the Palestinian leadership" in which he stated that the hunger strike could very well make the Palestinian leadership uncomfortable. After all, Adnan had initially been taken from his house in a Palestine Authority–controlled area where the Palestinian security apparatus works in conjunction with the Israeli one. Karon concluded that if Adnan did not end up being a Bobby Sands, he could become a Palestinian Bouazizi (referring to Mohamed Bouazizi, whose self-immolation in December 2010 set off the Tunisian uprising) (Karon, 2012a and b). The implication was that Adnan's strike could potentially lead to a popular revolt against the growingly unpopular Palestinian leadership.

On April 17, the date celebrated as Prisoners' Day to commemorate the release of the first Palestinian prisoner to ever be released in a prisoner swap in 1974, the prisoners inside Israeli jails decided to go on a mass hunger strike until their demands were met.[7] The strike built on the Adnan strike. A day before the strike even started, around 80 local and international organizations endorsed the call made by Khader Adnan to support the mass strike (Nieuwhof, 2012). Amnesty International, copying the Twitter campaigns started by Palestinian youth, called on its sections worldwide to join in a global Twitter campaign on the occasion of Prisoners' Day. It also provided suggested tweets, hashtags, and articles that tweeps could use to spread the campaign (Nieuwhof, 2012).

On the first day of the strike over 1,200 prisoners refused meals in the morning (Addameer, 2012b). Numbers increased on a daily basis and grew to include some female prisoners, prisoners held in solitary confinement, and those on administrative detention. The Israeli prison administration reportedly tried to disrupt the action by harassing prisoners and transferring some of them to other jails. Eight prisoners were already on strike when the mass strike started and two, Thaer Halahleh and Bilal Diab, were on their fifty-seventh day (Addameer, 2012b). Reports talked about over 2,000 and even 3,000 prisoners joining the strike.

The networks of communication that facilitated the coordination between prisoners in various jails remain unknown to the general public. A young member of the Popular Front for the Liberation of Palestine (PFLP) told me that actions like this mass strike could take up to a year of coordination between the various jails, and that this strike was a continuation of the strikes started in September of 2011, which had been interrupted by the Shalit prisoner swap deal. The strikers and the leading coordinating committee in the jails were predominantly factional, and strikers followed the lead of their leaders. This contrasted with Adnan's strike, which had been prompted by an individual decision.

Two online phenomena were most noticeable during the mass hunger strike: the famous brown profile picture embodying a Palestinian prisoner designed by Hafez Omar, and the @PalHunger Twitter account. @PalHunger was launched on the day the hunger strike started and featured exclusive news. The account claimed to be the only source of accurate and up-to-date news from the strike's leading committee inside the Israeli prisons. As those on the committee were primarily party members, we can assume that the people who managed the account were cadres of one of the parties or somehow connected to them, especially as the news published by @PalHunger was very much recapped in the PFLP's daily newsletter. The account was not only trying to indicate to tweeps the type of news to publish and accuracy of certain news, but it also made public calls for protest and actions in solidarity with the strikers. The account was often used to stimulate popular action and call for general strikes, or to support youths holding sit-ins and vigils near Israeli jails. Topsy, a Twitter archival and data analytics tool, indicates that the hashtag #PalHunger, which Palestinian tweeps used throughout the strike, was mentioned over 100,000 times since it was first launched in late April. The hashtag was also used by local and international organizations, including UN agencies, when issuing official statements via Twitter. For international organizations to follow the lead of Palestinian youth who first launched those hashtags is a notable phenomenon; youth activists have been able to influence, if not construct, the language used by organizations like the UN and Amnesty International. This is an indicator of who is leading the online media battle, and it shows that individual activists or grassroots collectives are able to influence international bodies in a bottom-up way that challenges the official Israeli propaganda machine.

During the strikes a picture of a faceless blindfolded prisoner dressed in brown clothes with the word *Shabas,* the Hebrew abbreviation for the Israeli Prison Service (IPS), circulated widely on social media. There are no accurate statistics of the number of people who used the picture, but some estimates gave 2 million, while others put it at up to 27 million people (Mujaz, 2013). This picture inspired multiple memes, including a bearded male prisoner, a veiled or unveiled female prisoner, and some with words like *Ma' wa Milh* (water and salt), referring to the only intake of hunger strikers. Facebook and Twitter users took snapshots of their contacts lists almost entirely covered in brown from the meme (Hamed, 2012). Soon after, activists in Egypt and Syria started using the picture in different colors to bring attention to the suffering of their political prisoners too. Omar's Facebook page with its over 30,000 fans, combined with his connections to youth groups and Facebook pages in Egypt and elsewhere, certainly helped to spread the design with such speed (Iskandar, 2012).

Omar, whose brother is himself a prisoner, said that the profile picture was pretty much inspired by the Facebook's default profile picture that everyone knows. He wanted something simple that would resonate with everyone, especially families of prisoners who feel that each of the prisoners is their son or brother; this was why the image did not represent a specific prisoner (Iskandar, 2012). He explained, "We turned Facebook into brown," before he went on to emphasize that reality and the virtual world are two parallel worlds. It is when they meet that they can achieve big things (Iskandar, 2012).

On May 15, 2012, *Nakba* day, a deal was reached with the Israeli authorities. Strikers agreed to stop their strike in return for the prison administration's commitment to respond to the prisoners' demands. Egypt and Jordan took part in mediating the deal while both Fateh and Hamas claimed victory. Despite the deal, a few prisoners continued with their strike. At first it could not be confirmed whether the prisoners Bilal Diab and Thaer Halahleh, who were on their seventy-seventh day of continuous striking, had agreed to stop their strike or not. An activist who blogs for the Electronic Intifada was the first to confirm the news after communicating with the families of the two prisoners. The two only officially accepted the deal after the IPS committed to releasing them (Abunimah, 2012). The two prisoners were the face of the mass strike and their personal stories and long continuous strikes had brought significant support.

One prisoner, however, continued his strike even after the deal was agreed on: the footballer Mahmoud Sarsak, who at the time was 25 years old. Sarsak, a member of the Palestinian national soccer team from the Gaza Strip, was arrested in July 2009 while traveling from Gaza to the West Bank for a football match. He was arrested although he had obtained permission from the Israelis to use the Erez crossing. Sarsak was kept under administrative detention under the Unlawful Combatants Law, which permits the arrest of Palestinians from Gaza for unlimited amounts of time (Addameer, 2012c). Sarsak's hunger strike continued for over three months. Following the deal that ended the mass strike, he decided to go on with his hunger strike until his release. He lost more than half his weight before the IPS finally made another deal, releasing him in July 2012. Campaigns for Sarsak were much more directed at sports and football figures and organizations than others had been. Palestinian tweeps targeted international footballers, especially those known for their sympathy with the Palestinian cause. On June 8, 2012 FIFPro, which represents professional footballers from across the world, called for his immediate release (FIFPro, 2012). This was followed by similar calls from Eric Cantona, Frédéric Kanouté, UEFA President Michel Platini, and FIFA President Sepp Blatter. Outside football, film director Ken Loach and author Noam Chomsky also urged that he be released (Hedges & Moloney, 2012; Childs, 2012; Haaretz, 2012).

Online and Offline: A Dual Role of Youth Activists

These campaigns for prisoners attest to the robust synergy between online and offline activism taking place around the Palestine struggle. The momentum and popular attention to the cause of prisoners and administrative detention increased following the mass hunger strike and the cases of Khader Adnan. Prior to the strikes, prisoners' families, especially their mothers, organized weekly and monthly protests and sit-ins in front of the Red Cross headquarters. After the campaigns, many activist youth joined the families. On May 9, 2012 many youths supported the mothers and families of prisoners by closing off the headquarters of the UN in Ramallah. Palestinian youth behind the Green Line also protested outside Israeli courts during prisoner trials and appeals, and some were arrested and assaulted.[8]

When Christiane Amanpour of CNN interviewed the Palestinian activist and journalist Abir Kopty to comment on the prisoners' hunger strike, Kopty stated that there was a huge gap between the aspirations and strategies of the Palestinian leadership, which lacks a vision for a movement, and those of the Palestinian people on the ground. The struggle, as she related, is not for solutions but for liberation and rights for the Palestinian people as a whole. On the other hand, Kopty considered the hunger strike to be yet another episode in the Palestinian struggle, which has historically used different tactics. Amanpour started her interview stating that it has been argued that if Palestinians had pursued non-violent resistance, they would have gained their rights and state long ago. Kopty responded that given that the West and the international community has been lecturing Palestinians for so long on the use of peaceful and unarmed resistance, they should support them in times like these (Amanpour, 2012). Amanpour closed her interview with what has become a common question to Palestinian activists since the start of the Arab uprisings. She said, "Many people have obviously asked, well hang on . . . why is this not happening inside the Palestinian Territories [. . .] Are you using social media? Is the Twitter, Facebook motivator not the same? . . . What is the difference?" Kopty explained that Palestinians live in an entirely different context where the fragmentation of the Palestinian people between the West Bank, Gaza, East Jerusalem, Israel, and exile has been a primary difficulty. She also emphasized the history of the Palestinian people, pointing out that throughout the last decades Palestinians have inspired other Arabs, and that the Arab uprisings had indeed given Palestinians hope and confidence in the power of the people. Social media in and of itself is not considered by her and others to be the way to bring about revolutions. However, Palestinians have been using social media extensively, mostly to voice their narrative and break out of their isolation, but it cannot necessarily be the tool to mobilize the people. She considered that a revolution will happen when people move from the online to the offline (Amanpour, 2012). Despite the inspiring successes of the Egyptian and Tunisian movements, young activists in Palestine realize that social media was not the magical spell that toppled the regimes in these countries and catalyzed mobilization in others. They call for more complex and historical analysis of the movements and struggles for dignity, freedom, and social justice in all the countries of the region.

Conclusion

The March 15 movement in Palestine, which attempted to emulate the popular mobilizations driven by youth in Tahrir Square in Egypt, as well as in other public squares, might have failed to bring Fateh and Hamas together, but it paved the way for more grassroots forms of youth mobilization that are non-partisan and growing constantly. Such mobilization takes expression in, for example, hunger strikes, support for the popular resistance in the West Bank villages against land confiscation and settlement expansion, support for prisoners and their families, boycott campaigns, refusing to normalize relations with Israeli institutions, refusing to receive visits from American and Israeli officials to Ramallah, demands for social justice and freedom of expression.

In all of the above examples, we notice the many challenges that Palestinians face. With the Palestinian leadership embarking on peace talks with Israel, and then the creation of the Palestinian Authority in the West Bank and Gaza in the early 1990s, the language of liberation and the right to return almost disappeared from the official discourse and it was replaced with a language of co-existence, post-conflict, and state building. With what many perceive to be the failure of the Palestinian leadership to achieve even a quasi self-determination in the Palestinian territories, and its transformation into an agent state serving as a proxy-occupation, while also failing to respond to the intensification of the colonial policies by Israel, the struggle became multi-faceted and distorted. Owing to this, a revolution in Palestine will have to do much more than topple a regime. It is precisely because of those reasons that any political mobilization in Palestine should work simultaneously at different levels. To summarize all those existential battles into a media or virtual war is not only naive but also counter-productive.

While activists had acted online and offline for the Palestinian cause long before the Arab uprisings, these uprisings did prompt a significant new wave of young Palestinian activity. While recognizing the failures and limitations of the Palestinian movement, we should also look into the reasons that make the use of information and communication technologies (ICT) and social media essential for a transnational Palestinian movement. Social media has become a fundamental component of youth connectedness, politicization, and participation whether inside Palestine or in the diaspora. The physical barriers and fragmentation of people and land essentially pushed more youth to reclaim the movement in which youth in their various locations are the agents of their own struggle and in which they reiterate their national identity regardless of their location. The interactivity offered by the internet challenged the restrictions on mobility and fragmentation and allowed for cross-continental discussions about political developments on the ground, the failure of the Palestinian leadership and popular actions.

It is a hard task to identify the Palestinian youth responsible for mobilization on the ground. What is clear though is that they have managed to bring in a radical discourse that is nostalgic for the earlier days of the Palestinian resistance. The variety of tactics used in the last few years have had the power to intimidate the Palestinian leadership on numerous occasions; to challenge the Israeli war propaganda; to make the Palestinian narrative known in the international media, which has been historically aligned with Zionist forces, making the Palestinian story practically indisputable; and to better coordinate transnational organizing with fellow Palestinians in the diaspora.

It is not the objective of this chapter to romanticize or idolize youth mobilization in Palestine. In fact, there are multiple reasons to not be overly optimistic, yet the baby steps taken by a small number of youth promise more creativity and larger connectivity with the rest of the Palestinian population in the diaspora. For the young organizers to be able to even compete with mass bases of existing parties, they will need to respond to the urgent need for independent, inclusive, accountable, and self-sufficient Palestinian organizing spaces where all means are employed in a comprehensive resistance and decolonization process, with a clear political vision and strategy.

Notes

1. www2.ohchr.org/english/bodies/hrcouncil/docs/12session/A-HRC-12–48.pdf
2. The global movement of Boycott, Divestment and Sanctions (BDS) against Israel came into existence following the Palestinian civil society's 2005 call for a campaign of boycotts, divestment, and sanctions against Israel until it complied with international law and gave Palestinians their rights. The campaign, which is coordinated from Palestine through the Palestinian BDS National Committee (BNC), describes itself as a "strategy that allows people of conscience to play an effective role in the Palestinian struggle for justice." See www.bdsmovement.net/
3. *Nakba* is an Arabic word that literally means "catastrophe." Palestinians and their allies use the term to refer to the founding of the State of Israel in 1948 and the expulsion of approximately 700,000–800,000 Palestinians from the land of Mandatory Palestine.
4. Administrative detention is a policy that Israel inherited from the British colonial era. Prisoners are held with no trial or charges and their detention can be renewed indefinitely on the basis of Israeli Military Order 1226. The Prisoner Support and Human Rights Association in Palestine (Addameer) has been actively working to stop this policy. See http://addameer.org/admin_detention.php
5. The last mass hunger strike was in 2011. The Gilad Shalit prisoner swap was a deal between Israel and Hamas to release over 1,000 Palestinian and Arab political prisoners from Israeli prisons in exchange for the release of Israeli soldier Gilad Shalit, who had been captured by Hamas in 2006.
6. Bobby Sands was born in 1954 in Rathcoole, a predominantly loyalist district of north Belfast. When he was 18 he joined the Irish Republican Army (IRA), and soon after he was arrested and spent three years in jail. In 1976 he was imprisoned again and was sentenced to 14 years in prison. In 1981 Sands embarked on a hunger strike that led to his death. During the strike he was elected as a Member of Parliament. After completing his sixty-fifth day of strike Sands died at the age of 27 (Bobby Sands Trust, n.d.).
7. List of demands:

    1) An end to the policy of solitary confinement and isolation which has been used to deprive Palestinian prisoners of their rights for more than a decade.
    2) To allow the families of prisoners from the Gaza Strip to visit prisoners. This right has been denied to all families for more than 6 years.
    3) An improvement in the living conditions of prisoners and an end to the "Shalit" law, which outlaws newspapers, learning materials, and many TV channels.
    4) An end to the policies of humiliation which are suffered by prisoners and their families such as strip searches, nightly raids, and collective punishment. For more info: http://samidoun.ca/site/wp-content/uploads/2012/04/April17-Strike.pdf

8. The Green Line is the agreed upon borders (not permanent borders) following the armistice signed in 1949 between the newly founded Israel and the neighboring Arab states after the 1948 "war." In this instance I am using the term to refer to the de facto border separating Palestinians inside Israel (carriers of Israeli citizenship) and Palestinians in West Bank or Gaza.

References

Abukhater, J. (2012a, February 7). Khader Adnan, dying to live. *Electronic Intifada*. Retrieved from http://electronicintifada.net/blogs/jalal-abukhater/khader-adnan-dying-live

Abukhater, J. (2012b, February 20). Hashtagging Khader Adnan: A global protest on Twitter. *Al Akhbar English*. Retrieved from http://english.al-akhbar.com/node/4365

Abunimah, A. (2012, May 14). After 77 days, Thaer Halahleh to end hunger strike as Israel agrees to release, father tells EI blogger. *Electronic Intifada*. Retrieved from http://electronicintifada.net/blogs/ali-abunimah/after-77-days-thaer-halahleh-end-hunger-strike-israel-agrees-release-father-tells

Addameer. (2012a). Prisoner profiles: Khader Adnan Mohammad Mousa. Retrieved May 12, 2013 from www.addameer.org/etemplate.php?id=428

Addameer. (2012b). Update on the Palestinian prisoners' hunger strike. Retrieved May 12, 2013 from www.addameer.org/etemplate.php?id=470

Addameer. (2012c). Prisoner profiles: Mahmoud Kamel Mohammad Sarsak. Retrieved May 12, 2013 from www.addameer.org/etemplate.php?id=487

AlSaafin, L. (2012, May 11). Why the Palestinian authority is afraid of the "intifada" in Israeli jails. *Electronic Intifada*. Retrieved from http://electronicintifada.net/blogs/linah-alsaafin/why-palestinian-authority-afraid-intifada-israeli-jails

Amnesty International. (2012). Israel must release or try Palestinian detainee on prolonged hunger strike. Retrieved May 12, 2013 from www.amnesty.org/en/news/israel-must-release-or-charge-palestinian-detainee-prolonged-hunger-strike-2012-02-06

Aouragh, M. (2011). *Palestine online: Transnationalism, the internet and the construction of identity*. London: I. B. Tauris.

Bishara, A. (2010). New media and political change in the Occupied Palestinian territories: Assembling media worlds and cultivating networks of care. *Middle East Journal of Culture and Communication*, 3(1), 63–81.

Bobby Sands Trust. (n.d). *Bobby Sands MP*. Retrieved May 12, 2013 from www.bobby-sandstrust.com/

Childs, D. (2012, June 14). Calls to strip Israel of hosting the European under-21 championships grow over detention of Palestinian footballer Mahmoud Sarsak. *The Independent*. Retrieved from www.independent.co.uk/sport/football/news-and-comment/calls-to-strip-israel-of-hosting-the-european-under21-championships-grow-over-detention-of-palestinian-footballer-mahmoud-sarsak-7851488.html

CNN. (2012, May 10). Palestinian prisoner hunger strike. Retrieved May 22, 2012 from http://edition.cnn.com/video/?/video/international/2012/05/10/amanpour-palestinian-prisoner-hunger-strike.cnn

DPA. (2012, June 14). Jailed Palestinian soccer player takes first steps toward ending hunger strike. *Haaretz*. Retrieved from www.haaretz.com/news/sports/jailed-palestinian-soccer-player-takes-first-steps-toward-ending-hunger-strike-1.436308

Eid, H. (2007). Representations of Oslo intelligentsia: A Fanonian reading of the intellectual landscape in post-Oslo Palestine. *Nebula*, 4(2), 96–106.

Falk, R., & Erakat, N. (2012, May 11). Palestinian hunger strikers: Fighting ingrained duplicity. *Jadaliyya*. Retrieved May 12, 2013 from www.jadaliyya.com/pages/index/5474/palestinian-hunger-strikers_fighting-ingrained-dup

Farsakh, L. (2012, February 21). Searching for the Arab spring in Ramallah. *Jadaliyya*. Retrieved from www.jadaliyya.com/pages/index/4438/searching-for-the-arab-spring-in-ramallah-

FIFPro. (2012). *Release Mahmoud al-Sarsak from Prison*. Retrieved May 12, 2013 from www.fifpro.org/news/news_details/1954

GazaTv News. (Producer). (2012, February 8). *Khader Adnan receives message of support from former Hunger Striker Tommy McKearney* (video file). Retrieved May 12, 2013 from www.youtube.com/watch?v=G1iwWZJPl_k

Giglio, M. (2011, Feb.25) "Middle East uprising: Facebook's secret role in Egypt." In *The Daily Beast.* Retrieved from www.thedailybeast.com/articles/2011/02/24/middle-east-uprising-facebooks-back-channel-diplomacy.html

Greenhouse, A. (2012, March 5). Social media principles behind the Khader Adnan and love under apartheid campaigns. *Electronic Intifada.* Retrieved from http://electronicintifada.net/blogs/abraham-greenhouse/social-media-principles-behind-khader-adnan-and-love-under-apartheid

Haaretz. (2012). Jailed Palestinian soccer player takes first steps toward ending hunger strike. Retrieved June 20, 2012 from www.haaretz.com/news/sports/jailed-palestinian-soccer-player-takes-first-steps-toward-ending-hunger-strike-1.436308

Hamed, A. (2012, May 15). When Facebook was painted in brown. *BBC Arabic.* Retrieved from www.bbc.co.uk/arabic/middleeast/2012/05/120515_facebook_profile_pal_prisonrersers.shtml

Hauser, J. (2012, February, 18). Twitter users turn up heat on media to #CoverKhader. Retrieved January 30, 2013 from http://storyful.com/stories/1000022194

Hedges, J. & Moloney, M. (2012, June, 12). Eric Cantona calls for release of Palestinian footballer close to death. Retrieved October 30, 2013 from www.anphoblacht.com/contents/21948

Heim, A. (2011, December 8). Why Twitter's discover feature is a game changer. *The Next Web.* Retrieved from http://thenextweb.com/twitter/2011/12/08/why-twitters-discover-feature-is-a-game-changer/

Hitan. (2012, January, 30). (Image) Retrieved May 4, 2013, from www.facebook.com/photo.php?fbid=265863370149314&set=a.144928485576137.31674.139990849403234&type=1&relevant_count=1

Iskandar, A. (2012, May 20). We are all Palestinian prisoners: Exclusive interview with artist Hafez Omar. *Jadaliyya.* Retrieved May 12, 2013 from www.jadaliyya.com/pages/index/5614/we-are-all-palestinian-prisoners_exclusive-intervi

Karon, T. (2012a, February 21). A Hunger striker at death's door turns up the heat on Israel—and on the Palestinian leadership. *Time Magazine.* Retrieved from http://world.time.com/2012/02/21/a-hunger-striker-at-deaths-door-turns-up-the-heat-on-israel-and-on-the-palestinian-leadership/

Karon, T. (2012b, March 29). A new season of Palestinian protest challenges both Israel and Abbas. *Time Magazine.* Retrieved from http://world.time.com/2012/03/29/a-new-season-of-palestinian-protest-challenges-both-israel-and-abbas/

Kershner, I. (2012a, February, 20). Hearing for Palestinian on hunger strike is set. *New York Times.* Retrieved from www.nytimes.com/2012/02/21/world/middleeast/israeli-court-speeds-hearing-for-palestinian-hunger-striker.html?_r=1&

Kershner, I. (2012b, February 21). Palestinian on hunger strike to be freed without court ruling. *New York Times.* Retrieved from www.nytimes.com/2012/02/22/world/middleeast/palestinian-on-hunger-strike-to-be-freed-without-court-ruling.html

Kristof, N. D. (2010, July 10). Waiting for Gandhi. *New York Times.* Retrieved from www.nytimes.com/2010/07/11/opinion/11kristof.html

McGuirk, L. (Producer). (2012, May 9). *Palestinian prisoner hunger strike* (television broadcast). Amanpour on CNN International. Retrieved May 12, 2013 from http://cnn.com/video/data/2.0/video/international/2012/05/10/amanpour-palestinian-prisoner-hunger-strike.cnn.html

Mujaz. (2013). *Hafeth Omar: The creator of the face that invaded Facebook in hours.* Retrieved January 13, 2013 from www.mujaz.me/socialmedia/1173/fb

Najjar, A. (2010). Othering the self: Palestinians narrating the war on Gaza in the social media. *Journal of Middle East Media,* 6(1), 1–30.

Nieuwhof, A. (2012, April 17). Amnesty joins global actions on Palestinian Prisoners' Day with Twitter campaign. *Electronic Intifada.* Retrieved from http://electronicintifada. net/blogs/adri-nieuwhof/amnesty-joins-global-actions-palestinian-prisoners-day-twitter-campaign

Nimer, A. (2012, May 9). *UN closed.* Message posted to http://arabagenda.blogspot.com/ 2012/05/un-closed.html

PalToday TV. (2012, July 21). *Hadath Wa Ab'ad: Al Hirak Al Shababi Al Falastiniy: Al Wake' wal Murtaja. Falasteen Al Yawm* (video file). Retrieved May 12, 2013 from www.youtube. com/watch?v=Fvrv433GFww&list=UU8x2fPLYmX8gH1IqsYugSpQ&index=6& feature=plcp&fb_source=message

Posterous. (2012). *Khader Adnan: Palestinian hunger striker held without charge or trial by Israel.* Retrieved January 30, 2013 from http://khaderadnan.posterous.com/?page=49

Qutami, L. (2011, October). *Arab revolutions and the Palestinian youth movement.* Paper presented to the American Studies Association Conference. Baltimore, MD.

Radford, M. (2012, May 15). Palestinian hunger strike ends on "Nakba" after viral internet campaign. *Tunisia Live.* Retrieved from www.tunisia-live.net/2012/05/15/palestinian-hunger-strike-ends-on-%E2%80%9Cnakba%E2%80%9D-after-viral-internet-campaign/

Rovics, D. (2012, February, 19). *Khader Adnan, Bobby Sands* (video file). Retrieved May 12, 2013 from www.youtube.com/watch?v=UoEPftesWyA&feature=related

Rudoren, J. (2012, May 3). Palestinians go hungry to make their voices heard. *New York Times.* Retrieved from www.nytimes.com/2012/05/04/world/middleeast/palestinian-resistance-shifts-to-hunger-strikes.html?_r=1&hp

Samidoun. (2012). *Palestinian prisoners' day: Thousands of Palestinian prisoners enter hunger strike—Global call for action.* Retrieved May 12, 2013 from http://samidoun.ca/site/wp-content/uploads/2012/04/April17-Strike.pdf

The Arabic Network for Human Rights Information. (2001). The Palestinian prisoner day: Meanings and significance. Retrieved May 12, 2013 from www.anhri.net/?p=29256

8

OPENING NETWORKS, SEALING BORDERS

Youth and Racist Discourse on the Internet

Miranda Christou and Elena Ioannidou

> Why do some people (especially some [. . .] wise people) believe that borders and nation states or even nations must be eliminated? And why is the promotion of wicked multiculturalism considered "progress"?
>
> (ELAM website, October 13, 2009)[1]

Citizenship education today is not limited to being within classroom walls: it is conducted on the internet, debated in blogs, and exchanged on social networking sites. The above excerpt is a typical entry from the right-wing website of the National People's Front, which goes by the Greek acronym, ELAM. ELAM, a self-identified nationalist political movement in Cyprus, is comprised of predominantly young people who log onto the website to deliberate on issues of national identity, border control, and immigrant jobs. In this chapter we analyze the content of ELAM's website (www.elamcy.com) to understand how their networking practices and ideological standpoints are constructed as a call for political action. We argue that the internet allows nationalist groups such as ELAM to network with other nationalist groups around the world, but at the same time it exposes contradictions in their alliances.

Citizenship, Youth, and Transnational Networks

One of the most persistent questions about the internet today is how it has reframed questions of social inequality and citizenship. In their book *Digital citizenship* (2008), Mossberger, Tolbert, and McNeal have correlated one's access to the internet with economic opportunity and political participation to analyze new forms of social inequality. By going beyond the technical aspects of the "digital divide," they suggest that access to the internet is on par with earlier notions about the importance of education as the "great equalizer": "In the information age, digital citizenship may rival formal education in its importance for economic opportunity" (Mossberger, Tolbert, & McNeal, 2008, p. 5). This means that not only access, but also technological literacy, navigation skills, and educational competencies may become major factors in determining citizens' social and political participation.

The field of education has been slow to respond to the changes of the digital age. Technology in education today is mostly circumscribed around issues of digitalizing curriculum content and using the internet as a learning tool (Anderson, 2008; Roblyer, 2003), but it has failed to address the larger political implications of young people's use of the internet as an alternative form of education. The advancement of the information age has not only influenced the work done in the classroom in terms of using technology to promote learning, but it has also fundamentally transformed the experience of defining one's self. The role of education in self-formation is now competing with the formation of a virtual self, aided by internet technologies that allow one's presence to transcend time and space (Seery, 2010). The virtual self is formed through a process in which the public and private spheres are not separate, but are in fact conflated in a "space" that is at once virtual, physical, and social.

Concepts of community, society, and citizenship are currently redefined by the increasingly central role of digital technologies in everyday life. Cognizant of larger debates about citizenship and globalization, we argue that current research on the impact of globalization has either extolled its virtues (Suárez-Orozco & Qin-Hilliard, 2004), or condemned its neoliberal character (Apple, 2000; Burbules & Torres, 2000; Carnoy, 2000; Stromquist & Monkman, 2000). This combined literature has failed to produce an understanding of *how* globalizing forces such as the internet produce subjectivities. Especially for organized youth groups, globalization has been exemplified in the form of new media usage that has radically transformed the experience of belonging and the understanding of difference, both within and beyond national borders. Our goal is to analyze how a right-wing nationalist youth group in Cyprus, ELAM, has used these new media to define its presence on the island and to connect its cause with other nationalist groups around Europe. The use of the internet has been central in providing a forum for ELAM's nationalist agenda and solidifying the group's identity.

Youth and New Media

"The new media" represents the historic convergence of computing and media technology trajectories (Manovich, 2001). This convergence resulted in the use of digital code that is both integrated and interactive (van Dijk, 2006). As the internet becomes easier to use, the "network society" (Castells, 1996) is increasingly defined by users who operate through "personalized networking" (Wellman, 2001) and redefine the meaning of community and interaction beyond face-to-face relationships. Young people have been especially adept in using these new media technologies, not only for social networking, but also for connecting on issues of political participation. While the role of educational policy and curricula in constructing national subjectivities has long been documented (Green, 1997), research on the impact of the new media in constructing ideological communities is still lacking.

Furthermore, as Bennett (2003) argues, the younger generation's disaffection with the conventional formal political process, mostly fueled by the understanding that global financial corporations are steering the power game, has facilitated the emergence of transnational activist groups. This new type of global activism transcends geographical boundaries by using web-based communication to rally around an issue or forge identity ties across national borders. Starting with the World Trade Organization (WTO) demonstrations in Seattle in 1999, and followed by those in Genoa (2001) and Cancún (2003), young people and activist organizations around the world have used the internet to connect and organize demonstrations against the increasing influence of transnational corporations in regulating the global economy to maximize their financial interests. More recently, the Arab uprisings have revealed not only the geographical expansion of digital networking, but also its revolutionary uses.

Della Porta and Tarrow (2005), who analyze the internationalization of social movements, argue that at the turn of the millennium there was a shift in the locus of political power. They observe how non-governmental organizations (NGOs) started to acquire more influence through their "complex internationalization," exemplified by the spread of informal networks across national boundaries. Indeed, the rise of what can be termed, "global activism," that is, the connection of activist networks in order to target non-state, transnational issues (i.e., corporations), has become possible with the rapid expansion of a web-based communication infrastructure (Bennett, 2003). The internet is playing a transformative role in shaping activism and citizen mobilization in what we call "transnational activism" (Chadwick, 2006; Dartnell, 2005; Pickerill, 2003).

Right-Wing Ideology on the Internet

At the same time as online networking is used for social justice causes on a global scale, the internet is also used by groups that mobilize transnationally in order to connect on a variety of issues, including racist ideology. Adams and Roscigno (2005) argue that neo-Nazi and Klan-based groups have already used internet websites as an effective forum for reinforcing collective identity based largely on the victimization of white people. In recent years, the appeal of nationalist ideology has been documented in western European countries where extreme right-wing parties have become more visible (Ignazi, 2003). This populist expansion of often blatantly racist and ethnocentric discourse has been linked to new socio-economic realities of rising unemployment and job insecurity, as well as migration policies (Dechezelles, 2008; Schuermans & De Maesschalck, 2010; Smith, 2010; Swyngedouw & Ivaldi, 2001; Zïquete, 2007).

These phenomena are also related to the visibility of white supremacist or neo-Nazi organizations that are usually devoted to proving the inferiority of those who are not white (Adams and Roscigno, 2005). In their research on white supremacist groups, Adams and Roscigno point out the three functions and processes of social movements or oppositional culture: "(1) identity building and solidarity mainte-nance, (2) providing followers and/or potential recruits with an alternative frame for interpreting grievances, and (3) promoting a sense of efficacy relative to group grievances outlined in the frame" (2005, p. 761). Although these groups are far from homogeneous, they share several characteristics, such as belief in the superi-ority of white people and recourse to religion.

Such organizations tend to be run by males and to emphasize militaristic sym-bols and imagery. Even though the relationship between gender and extreme right ideology is not always straightforward, historically white supremacy has marched hand in hand with male supremacy and fears over the changing role of women in society (Durham, 2003). According to Kimmel (2007), the involvement of young and downward mobile males with neo-Nazi groups in Sweden has more to do with establishing a masculine identity, and less with the appeal of ideological racism. Eventually, many of these young men leave such organizations and move away from the Aryan ideology.

Case Study of ELAM

ELAM, created in 2008 by "Greeks in Cyprus," identifies itself as a nationalist political movement under the ideology of Popular Nationalism, which they define as, "the political continuity of our innate patriotism that is present in every person and, as a result, in every Greek person in Cyprus." They also declare their main goal as, "working towards the survival and development of Cypriot Hellenism," and proclaim their readiness to use all forms of political struggle.[2] It is important to note here that the group uses the terms "nationalism" and "patriotism" almost interchangeably and projects a rather positive connotation of one's devotion to the nation. Whether "nationalism" or "patriotism" is the same phenomenon is still a matter of debate. Historical studies that analyze the formation of the modern nation state explain how, at its very basic level, nationalism is based on the creation of a shared narrative of common struggles and survival through time (Ander-son, 1983; Gellner, 1983; Hobsbawm & Ranger, 1983; Smith, 1998). One line of thought defines "patriotism" as state-nationalism that invokes loyalty to the state; and "nationalism," or "ethno-nationalism" as attachment to the nation (Connor, 1993, 1994; Snyder, 1976). As we explain, however, ELAM's facade of a patriotic group quickly disintegrates once their ideology digresses into blatant expressions of xenophobia and racism under the guise of civic loyalty. Our goal here is not to classify the group but to examine how language analysis can be a vehicle for understanding the nuances of ideology, whether it is labeled patriotic, nationalist, or chauvinist.

The group's Facebook page explains that its members are, "mostly young people from all social classes." Even though ELAM does not specifically identify itself as a youth group, our analysis of its activities, target audience, and online exchanges has shown that it is run by people in their 20s or early 30s and tends to attract even younger members such as high-school students. ELAM's "Youth Front" features prominently in the news announced on the group's website, and it is the driving force behind their public presence such as its organized street demonstrations. ELAM's online activity, which includes its website, Facebook page, and Facebook group, is equally dominated by young people who log on to exchange ideas about current events and respond to publications on topics of national identity and anti-immigration sentiments. More recently, the "Youth Front's" activities of delivering flyers to citizens and informing them about the economic crisis in Cyprus were presented extensively on ELAM's website.

The issue of whether a political movement is a "youth movement" is not simply a question of demographics, but points to larger theoretical debates about the definition of youth, especially in relation to the nation. Our use of "youth" in this chapter reflects the perspective that the lives of young people cannot be studied independently of how youth is constructed and debated, both in society and in academic research (see Bucholtz, 2002). Contrary to the concepts of "adolescent" and "teenager," which indicate a transitional period towards adulthood, the term youth carries broader implications, usually connected with the social and political realm. In this sense, the concept of youth goes beyond biological boundaries and signifies a generation that forms through shared experience of historical and political changes (Mannheim, 1952).

The youth of ELAM constitute what Mannheim calls a "generational unit." They do not represent a majority generational viewpoint of Greek Cypriots, but they are a vocal and important subset who articulate an extreme version of a general disaffection with the current political climate. Their main cause is to restore Greek Cypriots' Greek identity, which they believe has been adulterated by the presence of immigrants and the government's social provisions for ethnic minorities. These views are linked to a broader surge of anti-immigrant waves in both Greece and Cyprus that have only been strengthened by the current economic crisis.[3]

ELAM members became visible in 2010 when they started organizing several public events against "unemployment and illegal immigration." These events are usually military-style marches in downtown streets where members, bearing the ELAM logo and dressed totally in black, walk aligned in rows of three or four carrying Greek flags and chanting slogans. Members are mostly men, but women can also be seen in the back rows. Images of these demonstrations are regularly posted on the ELAM website, although the participants' faces are usually blurred. The media also reported an incident where ELAM members attacked a Nigerian migrant on the street following a July 20, 2010 ELAM march to commemorate the anniversary of the 1974 Turkish invasion in Cyprus. In May 2011, ELAM participated in the Cyprus parliamentary elections; they garnered 4,354 votes (1.08%), but failed to gain a parliamentary seat. Most recently, ELAM has been responding to the economic crisis in Cyprus by organizing food drives to support "only GREEKS"[4] who are in need.

For the purposes of this chapter, we focus on ELAM's positions on migration in order to understand how this youth group frames issues of citizenship rights. More specifically, we analyze their internet discursive practices as they appear on the group's official website. The collection of material is based on systematic downloading of articles, images, and videos from the ELAM website between December 2010 and June 2011. Starting from the premise that discourse is a form of social practice (Halliday, 1985; Halliday & Hasan, 1985), our goal is to understand how ideologies of citizenship rights are constructed through a clear definition and separation of "self" and "other." This language is fundamental in the process of fostering support for ELAM's cause, because it solidifies the perspective of an endangered Greek identity that has been the victim of minorities. This simple, if not simplistic, worldview of "us" versus "them" is integral to building the identity of ELAM as well as the nationalist version of Greek Cypriot identity that ELAM promotes.

Language, Ideology, and Racist Discourse

Our analysis of ELAM's language is based on the perspective that ideology permeates every aspect of language use. As Fairclough argues, "ideology is pervasively present in language [. . .] nobody who has an interest in relationships of power in modern society can afford to ignore language" (2001, pp. 2–3). Furthermore, we employ the concept of discourse in the Foucauldian sense in order to highlight the idea of discourse as a form of social practice given that the production of knowledge and truth—about the "self" and the "other"—is a form of power (Foucault, 1972). Discourse, therefore, is not simply a collection of words, it is "a way of signifying a particular domain of social practice from a particular perspective" (Fairclough, 1995, p. 14). By focusing on "the order of discourse" (Foucault, 1970) articulated by ELAM we can understand how their language becomes a form of domination in producing and reproducing definitions and representations of "others" and of themselves.

Reisigl and Wodak (2001) describe three strategies traced in racist discourse with which categories and social subjects are represented. First, they talk about "referential strategies" used to describe the way people are named and referred to semiotically; second, they refer to "predicational strategies," which illustrate the way people are described and the qualities and characteristics attributed to them; third, they mention "argumentation," focusing on the way arguments are used to support the two strategies mentioned above. Overall, it is widely agreed that in the act of naming people and creating categories using linguistic cues, social actors are

TABLE 8.1 Model of Discourse Analysis

	Self	Other
Representation (Ideational)		Referential strategies: How are people named, categories created? (nouns, adjectives)
		Predicational strategies: How are people described? (verbs)
Social enactment		Resolution: What resolutions are offered? (mottos, verbs)

created and in-group and out-group membership is established. The function of representation thus becomes an action of social enactment, merging the ideational and the interpersonal.

The model of discourse analysis we use is described in Table 8.1.

ELAM's Website

ELAM's website (www.elamcy.com) has been running since 2008. Its main function is to introduce daily updated news articles and to advertise links to the group's activities, contact information, and related internet venues. The website content is centrally controlled by the leadership of ELAM. Friends of the group comment on the articles and engage in conversation only on the Facebook pages—the website's material is one directional. The main sections of the website are: a) Press announcements; b) positions on different issues; c) articles on selected historical events; d) a section called "actions" that presents the group's electoral participation; e) a section presenting audiovisual material, and f) a section with links to other nationalist organizations in Europe.

It is also interesting to note that the aesthetics of ELAM's website seem somewhat outdated. Although every article contains links that are the main stock in trade for new media today—links for emailing, blogging, and tweeting the commentary as well as linking it to Facebook and recommending it on Google—the structure of the website (blue banner on the right side with information and links), the dominant blue color, the repetition of logos as well as the font, are reminiscent of earlier design visuals that are more than a decade old.

Apart from naming its president and its parliamentary and presidential candidates, ELAM goes to great lengths to protect the identity of active members by blurring the faces of participants in images posted on the website. Photos of events organized by ELAM show the audience from the back of the room and focus mainly on the speaker and the ELAM flags that invariably adorn the podium. The group has been regularly discussed in the media as a racist organization and several reports of skirmishes between ELAM members and minorities have surfaced in the past few years. Greek Cypriot newspapers clearly refer to ELAM as a racist, and some as a neo-Nazi, organization even though ELAM denies such accusations and maintains that it is only a popular nationalist movement.

The "Self" and the "Other": A Discourse Analysis

The various postings and articles uploaded on ELAM's website appear to be relatively homogenized in terms of format and style and constitute mainly informative texts with which ELAM seeks to express their views about contemporary social issues that concern the specific local/geographical context (e.g., migration) but also more global issues (e.g., capitalism). The group seems to be interested in connecting the current political situation in Cyprus with forces outside the island such as the European Union, NATO, or even ideologies of communism and capitalism. Furthermore, the website is not used only to lay out the group's ideology, but also as a call for action and intervention in the social context of Cyprus. The primary target audience is all the citizens of Cyprus who speak Greek, and the secondary audience all those who identify with the group's goals. Finally, texts are written in a short journalist-like style with headings and a brief description of the fact/situation. However, the text content is highly ideological, offering analysis and interpretations of different events and argumentation in favor of their values. The language used is Standard Modern Greek, and all the texts are multimodal with visual material (e.g., photographs, and sketches) and there is variation in the size and color of the fonts for emphatic purposes.

All the texts analyzed show a clear-cut distinction between self/us and other/them, adopting positive representations for the former, and negative for the latter. As noted in Table 8.2, the self includes the wider categories of "us, all of us," mentioned constantly in the majority of the postings. The selection of the personal pronoun "us" aims to stress the solidarity of the in-group and to present it as a distinct and strongly tied group. Moreover, the indefinite aspect of "people, all of us" aims to stress the openness of the group and its appeal to wider segments of the population. Nevertheless, in the other facets of the self (e.g., "Greeks," and "ELAM") the closeness of the specific community is exhibited, since people who are not Greek are excluded. Finally, all the texts analyzed here contain very few references to the term "Cypriot" or "Cyprus" since the main ideological

TABLE 8.2 Structuring of the "Self" and "Other"

Self	• Us, all of us
	• Greeks of the island
	• Nationalists
	• ELAM
	• Greek, local workers
Other	• Immigrants (illegal)
	• Other religious
	• Turkey, Turkish Cypriots
	• Government (general, leftish)
	• KISA
	• Journalists
	• Capitalists

motto of the group is that Greek Cypriots are essentially Greek. The group also refers to itself as "nationalists" and claims that its actions and ideology reflect the true meaning of being a nationalist and defending one's nation from its enemies.

In the structuring of the other we locate three different types of "others" all marked with negative connotations. On a first level the central other is the "Immigrant" who is always qualified with the adjective of "illegal." Interestingly, ELAM's descriptions and argumentations lump a variety of groups in the category of "illegal immigrants."[5] For example, political refugees are identified as "illegal immigrants."[6] On a second level, we also locate the "local other" as mainly journalists who criticize ELAM, locals who belong to antiracist organizations such as KISA,[7] and members of the left-wing government (labeled as "Stalin"-like), which was in power from February 2008 to February 2013. Finally, on a third level, the "other" is represented in wider, global categories such as Anglo-Saxon western countries, which are often labeled as the "capitalists," or traditional national "enemy" countries of the nation such as "Turkey." This multi-layered other corresponds with Fairclough's (1995) different stages of abstraction whereby a group is described on different levels: the first level involves a more immediate situational context, the second has to do with the wider context of institutional practices, and the third includes the wider frame of society and culture.

In constructing and describing the other, different lingustic means are employed. First, immigrants are described in overt negative adjectives. As Table 8.3 shows, the referential aspect for immigrants is loaded with stereotypic adjectives such as "third-world," and "underdeveloped" that are distinctively or overtly racist characterizations such as "*mavriðe'ros*" (black).[8] In terms of predication and social action, immigrants are viewed as scapegoats for a variety of social maladies such as crime and unemployment. The use of verbs in the active voice such as they "alters,"

TABLE 8.3 Portrayals of the "Other"

Adjectives	Nouns	Verbs
Third-world	Crime	Alters
Underdeveloped	Unemployment	Demolishes
Carcinoma	Insecurity	Receives
Black (*mavriðe'ros*)	Downgrading	Claim
	Problems	They arrive
	No business, take charity	They seek
	Coherence	They suck
	Benefits	They sit
	No obligations	They demand
		They receive
		They damage
		Cause problems
		They multiply

"demolishes," "suck," "damage," "cause problems" generate the image of a destructive group. Second, immigrants are accused of exploiting and taking advantage of the kindness and charity of the host country, since, ELAM claims, they do not work and they live off the benefits they receive from the state. We can locate this negative aspect from the use of verbs such as "seek," "arrive," "increase," "receive," "claim." To summarize, immigrants are depicted as the cause of various social problems and as abusers of the system in a country that was kind enough to host them.

Another linguistic technique employed to negatively portay the Immigrant-Other is the use of metaphors. Immigrants are presented with terms like "cancer," or "within-the-walls carcinoma," since they are concentrated within the old city in the capital, and "they alter our neighborhoods." In another example, the presence of immigrants is characterized as "Augeas' stables," a metaphor from the Labors of Hercules in Greek mythology.[9] In this case, the government is Augeas, who could not clean the filth from these stables, and ELAM is acquiring the role of Hercules, who managed to succeed in the difficult task.

With regard to the Local-Other portrayed in the data, we also observe negative attributes although these attributes differ from the ones of the Immigrant-Other. The Local-Other is accused mainly of three things: first, they either tolerate or enable immigrants to remain in Cyprus. This is seen in the use of adjectives such as "ignorant" and "passive," the use of nouns such as "tolerance," and verbs such as "covers" and "preserves." Second, the Local-Other is viewed as the main opponent of ELAM in terms of ideology and social goals but not in terms of cultural status. ELAM views the Local-Other as someone who is "pseudo/fake" or has been carried away on the "wrong path." Discourse markers for this difference are uses of terms such as "professional antiracists," "rapproachment followers," "open-minded" (adjectives), nouns like "luminary" and "government," and verbs

TABLE 8.4 Portrayals of the Local-Other

Adjectives	Nouns	Verbs
Passive	Luminary	Preserves
Ignorant	Plutocracy	Releases
Professional antiracists	Tolerance	Covers
Internationalist	Salaries	Restrains
Rapprochement followers	System	Triggers
Open-minded	Policies	Demolishes
Progressive	(Immigration)	Judges
	Labor (cheap)	They stop
	Government	They expect
		They condemn
		They go on TV

TABLE 8.5 ELAM's Self-Portrayal

Adjectives	Nouns	Verbs
Simple (people)	Protest, action	Protest (we)
Legal	(Nationalists, our)	Try to avoid (we)
Imperious	Despair	Want (we)
Peaceful	Decisiveness	(someone has) To clean up
Nationalist	Neighborhood (our)	Work (all day)
	Country (our) people, schools, nursing, homes	(we) Reject (violent behavior)
	Honor, duty	(we) Seek

like "covers," "judges," "restrains," "expect," "condemn." Finally, the left-wing government, which was in power between 2008 and 2013, is the main threat to the values and ideals for which ELAM stands.

Finally, ELAM has assigned itself the role of solving the country's problems, with migration seen as the main problem of the state. This means that the language ELAM uses is not merely for ideological purposes but also as a form of social enactment. The group urges its followers to act and react and become proactive in defending their nation from various "threats and dangers that surround us." The discourse techniques for offering this type of resolutions include, on the one hand, positive self-representation especially in comparison with the negative other, and, on the other hand, the use of mottos that give resolutions to the "crisis" mainly at the end of each text.

With regard to positive self-representation, the self (that is, "the Greek people, the people," and "ELAM, the nationalists") is presented as a "peaceful, legal, and imperious" movement. The choice of these positive adjectives is not accidental. ELAM was strongly condemned by antiracist organizations for resorting to violent behavior and adopting polemic values. Therefore, the group seeks to present a peaceful and legal dimension of the Self. This is evident in verbs such as "we protest," "we reject," and "we seek." According to ELAM, their main task is to protect the simple (Greek) people and to voice their worries.

Evidently, this rhetoric becomes paradoxical when we analyze their mottos used as discourse strategies for providing resolutions. Some of the most commonly used mottos of this group are war metaphors, the appeal to "blood and honor" as well as the imagery of swords and helmets. These create a semiotic virtual environment that diverges from the representation of the self as peaceful. Finally, ELAM's mottos can be categorized in two groups: immediate resolutions such as "deportation of illegal immigrants," and ideologically oriented slogans such as "Long live eternal Greece."

Networking for Nationalism

What is immediately evident in the case of ELAM is that it has systematically tried to divide the world into friends and foes by seizing every opportunity to condemn opposing groups and promote their own ideological allies. An analysis of their networking practices shows that the main ideological allies of ELAM are other nationalist groups in Europe, while their ideological enemies include mainly anti-nationalists, NATO, the European Union, and scores of other groups (such as immigrant support organizations or social justice groups) that they consider oppositional to their nationalist agenda. Furthermore, ELAM has established close relations with other organizations either through on-site visits or by showcasing events by these organizations on their website. In this way, the internet activity of ELAM is a symbolic enactment of the "self"/"other" division that uses the limitless possibility of communication and information sharing to outline an overarching world ideology. In this sense, ELAM's networking ignores national borders in order to connect with other nationalists in different nations. At the same time, however, the driving point of ELAM and all these other nationalist groups is that national borders must be reinforced in order to protect the "self" from invading "others." In this context, the immigrant is the "other" par excellence.

Our analysis of ELAM's website has shown that ELAM's divisions are not ideologically neutral since they clearly support the superiority of Greeks over other ethnic groups. As Reisigl and Wodak (2001, p. 1) argue, it is through discourse that racist opinions and beliefs are produced and reproduced and at the same time "discriminatory exclusionary practices are prepared [. . .] and legitimized." This analysis of ELAM's internet activity reflects an effort to create clear and unambiguous division between the "self" and the "other." The "self" is presented through positive language and is based on solidarity and unity. On the other hand, the "other" is not only negatively attributed but also multiple, thus unpredictable and dangerous: there are the local others, the foreign others, and the global others. The immigrant population on the island is represented by ELAM as the ultimate other, amply dehumanized and resented. The linguistic means used to construct these "others" are stereotypic adjectives, active voice verbs, and metaphors. Thus, the language used to describe immigrant populations aims at reinforcing existing political borders where ideally each territory is represented by one culture and one group of people. Eventually, the "self" is seen as the resolution to the problem.

However, these neat divisions actually fall apart when one considers the multiple positions taken by ELAM on different groups. For example, on November 25, 2009 the ELAM website posted an article titled "Persecutions of nationalists in 'democratic' Hungary." The posting described how Hungarian police raided a bar where Jobbik members were meeting and arrested some of them. Clearly intended as a form of support to Jobbik nationalists, the article argued that even though communism was abolished in Hungary certain aspects of it—obviously implying freedom of speech—remained the same. However, a few months later, on April 20, 2010 ELAM came upon an article by Jobbik that expressed support for Turkey's entry into the EU. ELAM reacted by sending a letter to all the European nationalist movements, as well as friendly Members of the European Parliament (MEPs), condemning Jobbik's inexplicable support for Turkey. The letter was also posted on Jobbik's Facebook site and this resulted in Jobbik de-friending ELAM. In its June 9, 2011 statement on the website ELAM notes that many of the Jobbik Facebook members are Turkish and underlines their argument that Jobbik is not a nationalist movement because no nationalist movement would ever support Turkey's EU entry given that Turkish people are not Europeans.

Interestingly, maintaining Turkey as the clear enemy of the "self" may be the most consistent position of ELAM. For example, on January 7, 2009 ELAM posted an article on the plight of Palestinian people, comparing the killing of Palestinian children (shown in a picture of a dead child) to Rubens's painting *The Massacre of the Innocents*. A few months later, on March 4, 2009, another article on Zionism presented historical information on the "Israeli carnivorous hyena." Just a year later, however, these positions shifted as it became evident that Turkey—the archenemy of ELAM—was trying to become a major advocate for Palestinians' rights and, at the same time, the Republic of Cyprus was collaborating closely with Israel on the exploitation of natural gas resources in the area. ELAM's postings defended Israel against Turkey (June 2, 2010), presenting Turkey's effort to support the Palestinian people as a scheme to gain geopolitical power in the region. Later on, they wrote an article in which they presented Palestinian asylum seekers in Cyprus as angry protesters who shouted death threats at asylum workers (March 5, 2011). ELAM's shifting loyalties reveal that maintaining their simple and simplistic view of the world as being divided into friends and enemies is a difficult endeavor. This is exactly what Bennett (2003, p. 153) means when he argues that "communication in diverse networks is ideologically thin" and results in several contradictions, such as bringing together groups and individuals that may not agree on all issues.

Conclusion

On April 8, 2013 the *New York Times* published an Op-Doc titled "Hail, hail, freedom in Cyprus." Created by Iva Radivojevic, a Croat-Serbian who escaped the 1990s conflict in Yugoslavia and relocated to Cyprus with her family at the age of 12, the documentary focuses on ELAM's rise as an extremist nationalist movement in Cyprus. The short five-minute segment uploaded on the newspaper's website attempts to depict ELAM's expanding appeal at a time when governmental resources are strained and locals start to view immigrants as the source of the island's economic troubles. Some of the comments on the website noted the fact that ELAM's share of the vote at the most recent parliamentary elections was only 1.08%, rendering it, therefore, a marginal and insignificant extremist group. What is interesting, however, is not the group's success rate in parliamentary elections but the ways in which their positions and ideology attract Cypriot citizens as a way of explaining societal inequalities or as a means of justifying their anxiety about the presence of "foreigners" on the island. ELAM uploaded an article commenting on the *New York Times* report, and, even though it calls it a "deceiving and slandering publication," it nevertheless notes with some pride, "It is noteworthy that the *New York Times* projects the rapid rise of Nationalism in Cyprus and the large impact of our movement, something that is meticulously avoided by the local media given that they don't present our movement nor do they devote even the smallest amount of time to us."

ELAM's preoccupation with media representations is an important clue to the group's ideological activity. The group views itself as part of a globalized movement on nationalism and it has taken painstaking efforts to connect with other nationalist organizations in Europe, thus exemplifying Wellman's (2001) "personalized networking" at the organizational level. Even though this networking falls into blatant contradictions, it nevertheless feeds the group's momentum as a participant in a larger, global wave and it is an important aspect of how the group forms its identity. Furthermore, the fact that this short video segment about a marginal group in Cyprus made it to the *New York Times* front page and then circled back to be debated on ELAM's website and Facebook page reveals the complexity of these networks as well as the capacity of new media to create novel political spaces through these communication practices (Bennett, 2003).

In the case of nationalist groups such as ELAM, the internet is used to reinforce borders and boundaries at the same time as these borders becoming irrelevant in transnational communication. ELAM's anti-immigrant rhetoric is a common threat in all of these nationalist groups that have become more visible in recent years and in some cases have resulted in the creation of right-wing political parties (Ignazi, 2003). The internet aids these groups in creating the identity of "the global nationalist," which is a concept based on the idea of restoring a version of the political world map where borders are impermeable. ELAM uses its website and other social media to provide its followers with arguments and "common sense" explanations in order to justify their grievances with immigrant populations (Adams & Roscigno, 2005). We have argued that globalizing forces such as the internet expose rifts in ideologies that might otherwise seem coherent and "reasonable." Even though the internet creates new possibilities for these groups to articulate their ideology, it also becomes a tool for deconstructing this ideology. In other words the networking of racist/nationalist groups is inherently paradoxical because racist ideology is localized and historicized; its networking exposes its tenuous presuppositions.

Notes

1. This and all translations from the website are by the authors.
2. Quotes have been taken from the ELAM website (www.elamcy.com).

3. The equivalent nationalist organization in Greece is called Golden Dawn. It has evolved into a political party and it gained substantial representation in the Greek parliament after the 2012 elections. ELAM has always been closely connected with and supported by Golden Dawn. Their views on Greek nationalism and the problems of immigration are identical.
4. Capital letters are used in all ELAM's posters and announcements.
5. The Greek language term is λαθrometa' nastes (*lathrometanastes*).
6. In the last decade, Cyprus has received large waves of asylum seekers from the Middle East (mostly Palestinians of Iraqi descent and Syrians). In 2009 Cyprus was third among EU countries in terms of its percentage of immigrant populations (Eurostat, 2013).
7. KISA is an NGO that has been active in Cyprus since 1998 and aims to be a movement for equality and antiracism.
8. It is important to note here that in the context of the Greek language and Cyprus, the characterization of someone as "black" is considered as a pure insult. The cultural context does not provide any space for deriving a positive connotation from this adjective and there is no historical/linguistic precedent for interpreting the term in an affirmative way as there is, for example, in the USA (e.g., African Americans describing themselves as "black" or using the phrase "black is beautiful").
9. Augeas is Avgias in Greek.

References

Adams, J. & Roscigno, V. J. (2005). White supremacists, oppositional culture and the World Wide Web. *Social Forces*, 84(2), 759–778.

Altheide, D. L. (2000). Identity and the definition of the situation in a mass-mediated context. *Symbolic interaction*, 23(1), 1–27.

Anderson, B. (1983). *Imagined communities: Reflections on the origin and spread of nationalism.* London: Verso.

Anderson, T. (2008). (Ed.). *The theory and practice of online learning.* Edmonton, Canada: Athabasca University Press.

Apple, M. (2000). Between neoliberalism and neoconservatism: Education and conservatism in a global context. In N. C. Burbules & C. A. Torres (Eds.), *Globalization and education: Critical perspectives* (pp. 57–77). New York: Routledge.

Banks, J. A. (Ed.). (2004). *Diversity and citizenship education: Global perspectives.* San Francisco: Jossey-Bass.

Baynham, M. (1995). *Literacy practices.* London: Longman.

Beck, U. (2000). *What is globalization?* Cambridge: Polity Press.

Bennett, W. L. (2003). Communicating global activism: Strengths and vulnerabilities of networked politics. *Information, Communication and Society*, 6(2), 143–168.

Bucholtz, M. (2002). Youth and cultural practice. *Annual Review of Anthropology*, 31, 525–552.

Burbules, N. C. & Torres, C. A. (2000). Globalization and education: An introduction. In N. C. Burbules & C. Torres (Eds.), *Globalization and education: Critical perspectives* (1–26). New York: Routledge.

Callero, L. (2003). The sociology of the self. *Annual Review of Sociology*, 29, 115–133.

Calvet, L. J. (1998). *Language wars and linguistic politics.* Oxford: Oxford University Press.

Carnoy, M. (2000). Globalization and educational reform. In N. P. Stromquist & K. Monkman (Eds.), *Globalization and education: Integration and contestation across cultures* (43–61). Maryland: Rowman & Littlefield.

Castells, M. (1996). *The rise of the network society.* Oxford: Blackwell Publishers.

Castles, S. & Davidson, A. (2000). *Citizenship and migration: Globalization and the politics of belonging.* New York: Routledge.

Cerulo, A. (1997). Identity construction: New issues, new directions. *Annual Review of Sociology,* 23, 385–409.

Chadwick, A. (2006). *Internet politics: States, citizens and new communication technologies.* Oxford: Oxford University Press

Connor, W. (1993). Beyond reason: The nature of the ethno-national bond. *Ethnic and Racial Studies,* 16, 373–389.

Connor, W. (1994) *Ethno-nationalism: The quest for understanding.* Princeton, NJ: Princeton University Press.

Dartnell, M. (2005). *Insurgency online: Web activism and global conflict.* Toronto: University of Toronto Press.

Dechezelles, S. (2008). The cultural basis of youth involvement in Italian extreme right-wing organizations. *Journal of Contemporary European Studies,* 16(3), 363–375.

Della Porta, D. & Tarrow, S. (Eds.). (2005). Transnational processes and social activism: An introduction. In *Transnational protest and global activism* (1–17). Lanham, MD: Rowman & Littlefield.

Diamandaki, K. (2003, Spring). Virtual ethnicity and digital diasporas: Identity construction in cyberspace. *Global Media Journal,* 2(2). Retrieved from http://lass.purduecal.edu/cca/gmj/sp03/graduatesp03/gmj-sp03grad-diamandaki.htm

Dobratz, B. A. (2001). The role of religion in the collective identity of the white racialist movement. *The Journal for the Scientific Study of Religion,* 40, 287–301.

Durham, M. (2003). The home and the homeland: Gender and the British extreme right. *Contemporary British History,* 17(1), 67–80.

Edwards, J. (1985). *Language, society and identity.* Oxford: Blackwell.

Eurostat. (2013). *Migration and migrant population statistics.* Retrieved May 4 from http://epp.eurostat.ec.europa.eu/statistics_explained/index.php/Migration_and_migrant_population_statistics

Fairclough, N. (1985). *Critical discourse analysis.* Harlow: Longman.

Fairclough, N. (1995). *Critical discourse analysis: The critical study of language.* London: Longman.

Fairclough, N. & Wodak, R. (1997). Critical discourse analysis. In T. van Dijk (Ed.), *Introduction to discourse analysis* (258–284). London: Sage.

Foucault, M. (1970). *The order of discourse.* Paris: Gallimard.

Foucault, M. (1972). *Power/knowledge.* New York: Pantheon Books.

Gellner, E. (1983). *Nations and nationalism.* Oxford, Blackwell.

Georgakopoulou, A. &, Goutsos, D. (2004). *Discourse studies.* Edinburgh: Edinburgh University Press.

Giddens, A. (1991). *Modernity and self identity: Self and society in the late modern age.* Stanford: Stanford University Press.

Green, A. (1997). *Education, globalization and the nation-state.* Basingstoke: Macmillan.

Halliday, M. A. K. (1978). *Language as a social semiotic.* London: Edward Arnold.

Halliday, M. A. K. (1985). *An introduction to functional grammar.* London: Edward Arnold.

Halliday, M. A. K. & Hasan, R. (1985). *Language, context and text: Aspects of language in a social semiotic perspective.* Victoria: Deakin University Press.

Halliday, M. A. & Hasan, R. (1989). *Language, context, text: Aspects of language in a social-semiotic perspective.* Oxford: Oxford University Press.

Hobsbawm, E. & Ranger, T. (Eds.). (1983). *The invention of tradition*. Cambridge: Cambridge University Press.

Ignazi, P. (2003). *Extreme right parties in Western Europe*. New York: Oxford University Press.

Kimmel, M. (2007). Racism as adolescent male rite of passage: Ex-Nazis in Scandinavia. *Journal of Contemporary Ethnography*, 36(2), 202–218.

King, R. (2000). Southern Europe and the changing global map of migration. In R. King, G. Lazaridis, & C. Tsardanidis (Eds.), *Eldorado or fortress? Migration in Southern Europe*. London: Macmillan.

Mannheim, K. (1952). The problem of generations. In P. Kecskemeti (Ed.), *Essays on the Sociology of Knowledge* (276–320). New York: Oxford University Press.

Manovich, L. (2001). *The language of new media*. Cambridge, MA: Massachusetts Institute of Technology Press.

Mead, G. H. (1934). *Mind, self and society*. Chicago: University of Chicago Press.

Meyrowitz, J. (1989). The generalized elsewhere. *Critical Studies in Mass Communication*, 6(3), 326–334.

Mossberger, K., Tolbert, C. J. & McNeal, R. S. (2008). *Digital citizenship: The internet, society, and participation*. Cambridge, MA: Massachusetts Institute of Technology Press.

Narayan, A., Purkayastha, B. & Banerjee, S. (2011). Constructing transnational and virtual ethnic identities: A study of the discourse and networks of ethnic student organisations in the USA and UK. *Journal of Intercultural Studies*, 32(5), 515–537.

New York Times. (2013). Hail, hail, freedom in Cyprus. Op-Doc by Iva Radivojevic, April 8, 2013. Retrieved on April 8, 2013 from www.nytimes.com/2013/04/09/opinion/hail-hail-freedom-in-cyprus.html?_r=0

Pickerill, J. (2003). *Cyberprotest: Environmental activism online*. Manchester: Manchester University Press.

Reisigl, M. & Wodak, R. (2001). *Discourse and discrimination: Rhetorics of racism and anti-Semitism*. London: Routledge.

Roblyer, M. D. (2003). *Integrating educational technology into teaching*. Upper Saddle River, NJ: Merrill Prentice-Hall.

Schuermans, N. & De Maesschalck, F. (2010). Fear of crime as a political weapon: Explaining the rise of extreme right politics in the Flemish countryside. *Social & Cultural Geography*, 11(3), 247–262.

Seery, A. (2010). Education, the formation of self and the world of Web 2.0. *London Review of Education*, 8(1), 63–73.

Smith, A.D. (1998). *Nationalism and modernism*. London, Routledge.

Smith, J.M. (2010). Does crime pay? Issue ownership, political opportunity and the populist right in Western Europe. *Comparative Political Studies*, 43(11), 1471–1498.

Snyder, L. L. (1976). *Varieties of nationalism: A comparative study*. Hinsdale, IL: Dryden Press.

Soysal, Y. N. (1994). *Limits of citizenship: Migrants and postnational membership in Europe*. Chicago: The University of Chicago Press.

Spolsky, B. (2004). *Language policy: Key topics in sociolinguistics*. Cambridge: Cambridge University Press.

Stromquist, N. P. & Monkman, K. (2000). Defining globalization and assessing its implications on knowledge and education. In N. P. Stromquist & K. Monkman (Eds.), *Globalization and education: Integration and contestation across cultures* (3–25). Maryland: Rowman & Littlefield.

Suárez-Orozco, M. M. (2004). Introduction. In M. M. Suárez-Orozco & D. Qin-Hilliard (Eds.), *Globalization: Culture and education in the new millenium* (1–37). Berkeley: University of California Press.

Swyngedouw, M. & Ivaldi, G. (2001). The extreme right utopia in Belgium and France: The ideology of the Flemish Vlaams blok and the French Front National. *West European Politics*, 24(3), 1–22.

Tarrow, S. (2005). *The new transnational activism*. Cambridge: Cambridge University Press.

Van Dijk, J. (2006). *The network society*. London: Sage.

Wellman, B. (2001). Physical place and cyberplace: The rise of personalized networking. *International Journal of Urban and Regionalized Research*, 25(2), 227–252.

Zïquete, J. (2007). Portugal: A new look at the extreme right. *Representation*, 43(3), 179–198.

9

COMPUTER INTIMACY

Digitally Mediated Democratization of Arab Youth Culture

Catherine Cornet

Until the 1980s, British coal miners would take a caged canary with them underground. Because the bird sings most of the time, if the oxygen level dropped or any dangerous gases were emitted, its death was an early warning system. The phrase "canary in a coal mine" refers to someone who can detect signs of trouble and danger, whose sensitivity makes them vulnerable.

Farhad Ahrarnia, "Canary in a Coal Mine" Exhibition Statement
(Rosa Issa Gallery, London, January 2012)

Since the Arab uprisings began in Tunisia in December 2010, the world has witnessed a massive "discovery" of artistic expressions of young Arabs. It was as if Arab youth had just started their cultural revolution through their graffiti, revolutionary songs, and hip-hop. In fact, this liberated and innovative turn, what I would call a digital *nahda*, or digital renaissance, started well before the "graffiti mood" associated with the uprisings, with all due respect to the revolutionary expressions. The Arab uprisings did not register a rupture, but rather a continuation of something that had been underway for more than a decade. As cultural journalist Kenza Sefrioui explains in relation to Morocco, for ten years Morocco has been witnessing an urban culture teeming with graffiti and street art. He asserts, "We've spent the last ten years singing songs of freedom" (Sefrioui, 2012, p. 1).[1] By assessing the development of different artistic patterns in the decade preceding the revolutionary moment, we can gain an understanding of how different citizenship dispositions have been coming into being.

This chapter examines the rise of digital art in Egypt, Lebanon, and Saudi Arabia that began in 1990s, but really took off between 2004 and 2005 when the digital revolution reached the Arab world (Eickelman & Anderson, 2003; Lynch, 2005). It traces the transition of the cultural scene away from clientelism and systems of patronage (Winegar, 2006). Up to the 1990s, for artists to be able to show their work, gain global recognition, and enter artists' markets, they either needed to elicit state sponsorship, be funded by foreign donors, or both. Only artists with state sponsorship could be selected in Bienniales, the main national and international showcases for visual artists. Moreover, artists needed international connections to be able to plan tours and exhibitions. From the 1990s, in parallel with the global digital revolution, this patronage system underwent a transition that resulted in a radical shift in the power relations between artists and the state. Questions considered in this chapter are: Did the digital revolution in the Arab world contribute de facto to a cultural revolution? Did the cultural revolution play a role in the "democratization" of Arab art and culture and serve as a catalyst for identity change, political awareness, and/or economic well-being?

To address these questions I review a sample of six digital artists from Egypt, Lebanon, and Saudi Arabia who work broadly in the area of "visual arts," a category that includes "popular" artistic expressions such as cartoons and web series. I also consider prominent and influential artistic works from Jordan, Morocco, Libya, and Palestine. I deliberately balance the sample between artists who declare themselves to be "political" (or *engagé*), and those who say that they are "apolitical" to be able to assess the influence of digital cultural expressions on citizenship.[2] I particularly focus on Egypt and Lebanon because of the traditionally pioneering nature of these cultural scenes, whereas Saudi Arabia is included due to the appearance of a young and vibrant artistic scene, which rose in tandem with the digital revolution. The criteria for the selection of artists for this sample are based on five variables: they are "young," between 20 and 35 years old; they put images and digital tools at the center of their work and artistic practices; they are recognized as "pioneers" in their own fields; they have significant "online" visibility and success; and they are truly independent from state or private foundation funding, even if some have received sanctuary subsidies from global internet companies (such as Google and Yahoo grants). Quite significantly, most of the artists interviewed for this research have a scientific background. They are "engineers-artists"; the computer is not just a tool for surfing the waves of modernity. Computer and digital expressions help them dig into their most intimate self. Gaber, an artist from Egypt, explained, "We are coming from a generation that finds its ways of expression through the computer. We like it. We like virtual ways. It is closer to us."

The digital medium is a very intimate one, and the computer is a tool that, just like the old diaries, is used in bed. This intimacy comes across when listening to Maya Zankoul, a young Lebanese cartoonist. She never draws on paper and actually never did. She explains, "It all started when I was drawing with Illustrator [a graphic design application] from my bed, before sleeping. The very simple lines, basic colors show my urgency to express." These young artists share what I would call "computer intimacy," a relationship between the artist and its tool that does not correct or automate an artistic process. Like the paintbrush or sketch pencil, the computer is becoming a natural part of the artistic process.

Arab Cultural Renaissance and Youth Politics

In the cultural and artistic field, to speak about "youth" and generations can be very misleading (Jacquemond, 2003). Art produced by youth is too often scrutinized as a political statement, as an artifact that is necessarily there to support a given political agenda (Lafargue de Grangeneuve, 2006, pp. 457–477). Rather than see art as a direct response to the political environment, I argue, after Rancière (2004), that art creation has in itself an important potential for dissent. It would be therefore a very dangerous exercise to look into youth art before and after the Arab uprisings through the sole lens of political activism and *engagé* art. But first we should address what we mean here by "youth" in relation to art.

I follow Bayat's definition of youth that is associated with the sociological fact of "being young." Youth are a group of people who share "a series of dispositions and ways of being, feeling, and carrying oneself (e.g., a greater tendency for experimentation, adventurism, idealism, autonomy, mobility, and change)" (Bayat & Herrera, 2011, p. 30). I hypothesize that due to a high level of visibility obtained through digital tools and platforms, these Arab artists have gained agency and been able to exert a significant influence on the cultural scene and on ways that youth citizenship is understood and expressed. Having said that, in the course of carrying out this research some interviewees jokingly refused to be quoted as being "young." For instance, Ahmed Mater, born in 1979, when asked if he considered himself to be a young artist replied, "No! I feel so old and I have so little time left for everything I need to do!" Lebanese cartoonist Maya Zankoul, born in 1986, said, "I arrived to a place of stability now. I have a company, I feel so old." To become a recognized artist, even at the very beginning of a career, requires a minimum of experience.

Youth are also more likely to be the "authors" of new artistic genres and formats for cultural expressions. In the digital age young artists have actually exploited new "platforms" of expression using new technologies available where they both work and "display" their works. Artists of the digital age possess, at the very least, a Tumblr blog (the favorite free digital artist microblogging platform subtitled "Follow the World's Creators"), a Twitter account, a Behance account (the Behance Network is an online portfolio platform for creative professionals), and YouTube and/or Vimeo channels. For example, 25-year-old Saudi artist Yousef Alshaikh writes on his blog how he divides his digital work showcase as follows: "Mixed Media, Photography, Coding & Computation, Writing, Sculpture | Motion, Type, Interactions." This mix of technical exploits and artistic expressions is one of the main strengths of this new generation of artists. Compared to their "unconnected" counterparts, the use of digital tools allows them to channel new inspirations from other fields usually not connected at all with arts (technical culture in particular). These young artists are able to enter new realms that can only be accessed through digital tools and, more importantly, with small or even no financial investments.

The CVs and gallery bios of younger artists also differ substantially from those of their counterparts of the older generation. Among the older Arab artists, you are likely to come across credentials that include bouts of study at European, American, or Russian universities, as well as studies and post-graduate studies in fine arts academies abroad. Artists of the digital age present themselves in entirely different ways. For instance, the profile of the Egyptian artist Ganzeer reads as follows, "Ganzeer uses visual arts such as graphic design, illustration, and video as means of expression and communication. Ganzeer's interests include, but are not limited to, commentary on the human condition and what's next to come."[3] The new Arab artist, young and globalized, would rather showcase his work on a fancy website than spend his time meeting New York gallery gurus.

If Arab youth have created new and extremely innovative cultural forms, it is because for the most part they are self-taught and have completely broken with traditional art education. Gaber, who describes himself as a "visual artist polluted with politics from Egypt," believes that "experimentation is the best route to learning." He says on his website, "thank God that I did not study in an Egyptian Fine Arts Academy" where, in any case, "digitally-mediated art is not taught in any of these institutions." Cyril Aris also studied engineering, and did so because, in Lebanon, art school is not considered a "career" by traditional families.

In this changing climate young Arab artists have, in the words of Pascal Amel, the editor-in-chief of the cultural magazine *Art Absolument*, "invented a new international grammar of contemporary art" that resists Arab Springs and could "put an end to contemporary art's current orientalism" (Forster, 2012, p. 1). As elaborated by Khosrokhavar (2012), during the last century Arabs "experienced at least four kinds of holistic utopia: Nationalist, pan-Arabist, Islamist, and Third-worldist" (socialist and communist). After decades of these totalizing ideologies, be they socialist ideologies or Islamic discourses on the *Umma* (community of Muslims), and martyrdom mythologies whereby personal identity could be abolished for the good of the community, the new technologies opened a path for twenty-year-olds to explore the realm of the "holy" self. Social media has been especially important in this regard. In the last decade the Arab world has been experiencing a fruitful encounter between social media and artistic expressions that fostered self-centered, artistic egotism, and the creation of a new young individual who is freer from social control. Social media has allowed young Arabs to represent themselves on their own terms, and in so doing "fight back" the "international" depictions of their "'identity and culture."

At the same time, Arab artists are less willing to act as the "bridges" between cultures. Governmental funds are still very much oriented towards the ideological exploitation of artists to show that their regimes are champions of freedom of expression, women's empowerment, and the like. Private foundations such as the Ford Foundation, Ebert Stiftung, and the grants from Google and Yahoo are less oriented towards dialogue and rather opt for the development of local scenes and art spaces (Cornet, 2010). Gulf funding, on the other hand, is not particularly interested in such topics.[4]

Instead of relying on powerful sponsors to publicize their art, young artists find their own means for marketing their work. Egyptian multimedia artist Mohamed Fahmy, a.k.a. Ganzeer, and his friend Gaber, a graphic designer, photographer, and member of the Egyptian Socialist Party since the 1990s, both use digital platforms to create and publicize their art. Their work is essentially displayed online and linked to free artistic networks like Behance. Their visibility on Facebook and Twitter is substantial.[5] They are able to mobilize important networks of artists on the ground, like the organization of the #Mad Graffiti week (January 13–25, 2011) in various cities of Egypt and the world, from Assiout to Poland. The combination of their artistic practices and online engagement has transformed them into real "citizen artists" when their fellow bloggers were coined "citizen journalists."

Similar artistic trajectories can be found among Gulf artists who display their work in internet showrooms rather than traditional galleries. The young Saudi artist Ahmed Mater is a surgeon with a deep sense of his Saudi heritage. He established himself as an artist not by following the traditional path of fine arts studies, but by innovatively mixing science and artistic expression. He has found inspiration through X-ray imaging. As he explains, "Using X-ray pictures in my daily life, looking at man in that way, makes you feel like exploring the inside. It seemed just right to me." He created his "Illumination series," inspired by Ottoman art with X-ray pictures.[6]

Remixing is another feature of the Arab artistic renaissance and a practice that connects Arab artists to global artistic circles. Young artists take control of the images of Arabs that flood the media, be they of suicide bombers, masked children throwing stones, or mourning mothers, and create their own "Arab iconography" through remixing and reusing images on their own terms. By appropriating globalized genres, young Arab artists have been breaking with past generations who remain committed to a nationalist and anti-colonial critique. Members of the younger generation are finding their own voice and striving to express themselves freely without the older cultural and political constraints. Another important feature of digital expression is that the younger generation are less "West conscious" than their predecessors. This new generation of artists is more likely to be in a struggle against the regimes of their own authoritarian states than colonial or foreign powers, be they European or American.

As an extremely innovative visual culture spreads in the region, these artists are not directly engaging in politics in the classic sense of mobilizing in the public sphere. But they are definitively developing a new cultural stratus, where freedom of expression has acquired more weight. Their political impact is difficult to ascertain since it is largely atomized. As the curators of the 2011 Venice Bienniale exhibition "The Future of a Promise" have stated with regard to young Arab artists, they are "not representative of a movement as such but they represent a 'promise' in the visual culture in an age that has become increasingly disaffected with politics as a means of social engagement" (Downey & Lazaar, 2011).

For young artists in Lebanon detachment from politics passes through the break with sectarianism. When Maya Zankoul arrived in Lebanon to go to university, she could not believe how much people in the country wanted to understand her political or religious belonging. She remarks, "I'm neutral, I do not care." Inspired by a globalized and digitally mediated scene, many young artists reject politics altogether. Maya Zankoul collaborates with other designers and art geeks through the Middle East Creative Commons conferences and Twitter groups. Facebook has completely changed her artistic practice: "I go on Facebook two or three times a day. Especially after I post a work. I wait for reactions." The isolation traditionally linked to artistic work has been replaced by the immediacy of speaking to the audience. "I always get more feedback and I love it! I love to see what people say, how they share it. To get instant feedback is very rewarding, it is encouraging, makes me willing to work harder," she explained.

New artistic forms, new codes, and reinterpretations are all key to a free, deterritorialized cultural expressions movement. The weight of the older artistic heritage, or the need for a gallery owner's recognition *in loco* or internationally, is far less important in the digital era where "unconnected" artists can rise. In addition, artists are a lot more at ease with themselves and do not need to discuss their identity or religious affiliations before exhibiting their work. Online audiences are easier to cultivate and the selection of works displayed depends on the artist herself rather than a professional curator. Young filmmakers, for instance, often bypass network television and show their works directly on YouTube.

In his recent work *The Pixealated Revolution*, the important Lebanese avant-garde theater director, Rabih Mroué, used images from social media to depict the ongoing Syrian uprising. He explained why he took images circulating on social media instead of trying to create original ones, "I'm not the one who recorded or produced them [the images]. And this came out of my belief that it's now very difficult for artists to produce images, especially with the glut of imagery in the media" (Downey, 2012, pp. 3–4). Social media contains an enormous reservoir of "raw material" coming from the Arab world that is not subject to the same censorship regime as images from official media. The appropriation of cultural expressions through social networks and the easy reproduction and sharing of material have created a good laboratory for creativity. It has above all helped to break the barriers of "high" and "low" culture, of *ibdaa'* (creativity) and the pejorative *bid'a* (innovation).

Self-Portraits, Profiles, and Citizenship

In the realm of social media, publishing one's "profile" (picture plus text) is the essential first step in taking part in the online community. For young artists this means reinventing the classical genre of "self-portrait." Since technical rules force them to "put a face," they are actually very prolific in their self-representation. Self-portraits are definitively becoming an *exercise obligé* for young artists and are tracing a way forward for a new understanding of citizenship.

Artists working with digital means are coming up with novel ways of presenting themselves as citizens. For instance, the Saudi artist Ahmed Mater's self-portrait, *The Evolution of Man*, shows a series of images that start with a fuel pump and evolve into an X-ray of a man committing suicide with a fuel pump. Mater explains the use of self-portrait here as "the only way to tell the truth. I ask myself what is our future without oil. If I don't ask myself first how can I then ask my country? It's both a way to have a more humble discourse and make it fully true." In the Saudi political context, this interrogation can be understood as an attempt to engage with the state as a full citizen, stating that one is entitled to search for a dialogue.

Together with self-teaching, the digital revolution experienced by young Arab artists is very much palpable in their approach to their works of art. They often prefer to show their work in progress by creating artistic weblogs. For instance, the young Libyan ceramist, Hadia Gana, has produced amazing animation works full of humor and poetry to document her return to Libya. Her works cannot be seen in Europe or Libya yet since she's returning to transform her home into a cultural center but they are on Vimeo. Hers is a kind of videolog that follows the Libyan events through her very personal lens. The young Saudi artist Yousef Alshaikh, who is only active online, presents many portfolios that are actually works in progress: here the accent is put on the individual work of the artist rather than on its final result.

Another example can be found with Lebanese cartoonist Maya Zankoul, whose career really took off in 2009 with her blog on WordPress. In her posts she speaks about Lebanese daily life because it is what interests her and because she believes it is important in the country, "I have no interest whatsoever in politics. How could I relate to people who take Lebanon back to the past everyday, the very people who participated in a civil war? I am more of a social person. I think of small things that can make a change. Electricity issues, a bridge that was destroyed and is not rebuilt." The individual experience is considered the only one that really counts. In one of her animation clips, "Inflation," she shows the parallel lives of an economics professor who theorizes about "Inflation" while her avatar (Zankoul has created several cartoon incarnations of herself) walks with despair through a supermarket where prices keep rising. Her art is digital but it is always very rooted in the real experience of her daily life. While playing with multiple identities, these digital artists pave the way for a new approach to citizenship, one that is more open and much less centered on the nation state.

Relationship towards the State: Censorship

State control over cultural expression was very strong in Egypt, Lebanon, and Saudi Arabia during the 2000s. In Egypt the Ministry of the Interior would censor the internet in the interest of "security" and this led to modes of self-censorship. Lebanon's freedom of expression record was also very poor as its Ministry of

Culture frequently exercised its power to censor. In Saudi Arabia strict censorship over political and religious issues is the norm. For artists who started working digitally at the beginning of 2000, the internet was the only space available in terms of both creativity and (relative) security.

Gaber explained that when he started his project "Graphics against the System" in 2006 "it was quite dangerous. The only space I had was the internet. It was actually our main space." The "GAS" project encompasses very daring political statements and strong language: a highly unflattering portrait of Mubarak has a caption that reads, "27 years of bullshit! Enough." Another one bears the title, *Egypt is tired, Down with Mubarak*, while a collage showing Bush Junior reads, "We make peace, piece of shit." All posters were made downloadable, available to be printed, put up the streets, or distributed. Two years later the independent space Townhouse Gallery (funded by American and European private foundations) in Cairo asked Gaber to exhibit in the venue, but he refused because, "standing around looking cool at my exhibition is not my style." But even more importantly, he viewed this gallery as belonging to the system of power and contrary to the spirit of his work.

Tunisian artist Nadia Kaabi-Linke, the Ibraaz prize winner in 2011, talked about the censorship regime under the former president Ben Ali as something that was "very positive for creation, to have to do things indirectly" (Davis, 2011, pp. 1–2). This same provocative thinking crosses Mroué's narrative when he draws a parallel between the aesthetics of the avant-garde filmmaking movement Dogma 95 and the way in which young Syrians are actually filming and posting their revolution. His work implied that the aesthetics of Danish Dogma 95 could be seen to be somewhat similar to those employed, consciously or not, by the protesters in the Syrian revolution (Downey, 2012, pp. 3–4).

Digital Artists: Linking Global, Regional, and National Belongings

Social networks are often coined as "Western" or "globalized" cultural expressions. Some globalization theories state that Western cultures have invaded all other cultural areas (Fraser, 2005), which leads to creating a whole set of discourses around "genuine, traditional" cultural productions (Ramadan, 2004; Winegar, 2006). I would argue that the innovative and digitally mediated cultural expressions of young Arab artists actually illustrate the importance of our living in a multi-centered world. Asia, Africa, and the Middle East have become locations where artists use new media to develop new cultural genres (Matar, 2007). Long before the Arab uprisings, the Arab artists used new tools and platforms to narrate history while it happened. They founded many collaborative websites that involved literary writers and visual artists.

In Gaza Palestinians are the most eager to use Skype for conferences and concerts and to use websites to speak to the diaspora and the world. They encourage writers, artists, or ordinary people, young and old, to contribute to the writing of contemporary Palestinian history. The website Hakayat Gaza (Narrating Gaza) for instance, deals directly and indirectly with the brutal aggression inflicted by Israel on Gaza in the winter of 2008 and its aftermath. The website promotes self-narration as being fundamental to creating one's space on the globalized scene and it states that it "allows [people] to tell the story while it happens, giving voice to young artists who are the most secluded in the world." The same principle applies to the Lebanese blog *Hakaya* (Narrated stories). It started as "Muzna's Stories" during the Israeli assault on Lebanon in the summer of 2006 and it was a space to "share how we were living through that assault and the marks it was making on our lives." The site features literary short stories of war and love.

The internet revival of pan-Arabism is all the more powerful where humor is concerned. As underlined by Bayat in "Islamism and the politics of fun," it represents an important element of youth non-movements (Bayat, 2009). In this context, digital creation and social networks can be considered as a non-formal political education tool. They channel, through satire, real political debates that youth might not have considered if presented in another form.

The Jordanian cartoon platform Kharabeesh is a case in point. It produces its high-level cartoons for the internet, its political satire having never found space on television. The Kharabeesh creators went from the street to a digital platform directly, without passing through another medium. Prolific cartoonist Omar Abd-ullat explains, "I tried to get my work into newspapers, but quickly realized there were restrictions on freedom of expression. I found my outlet on the internet, where I could publish my work without [any] hassle. My team grew and eventually became a corporation. I hope the Arab world continues to like and engage with our work."

Wael Attili, CEO of Kharabeesh, explains that the idea of Kharabeesh was born in 2007 when short-movie sharing sites such as YouTube became popular, offering more freedom to create and share: "We felt there was a lack of original Arab content that was tailored to today's youth who did not follow mainstream media." What I would call a new form of pan-Arabism is quite clear in the marketing prospect of Attili: "When we tackle a political issue, we noticed that it speaks to the whole region, while for social and cultural issues we need to knock at each door on each street." The common political satire is very palpable on Arab youth and after the revolutions this new front of pan-Arab humor just exploded: "We were able to feel the pulse of the Arab street," said Attili. "Now we started to speak to a wider audience and we started to become more like pan-Arab."

Their parodies "Mubarak is high" and "Gaddafi speech in Libya" both registered more than 1,475,513 views on YouTube (April 8, 2013). The lack of Arabic content on the internet has created a niche and windows of opportunity for young creative entrepreneurs like Attili. Gaber and Ganzeer, for their part, have received a Google grant to develop a new Arabic font that works better in digital format. The website Shashafont (http://shashafont.com), which displays their work step by step, is definitely an attempt to reconstruct a pan-Arab cultural identity in the digital world. Cyril Aris and Mounia Akl received a grant from Yahoo under the Arab web series grant scheme. The search for Arabic content by big internet search engines or news aggregators has had a highly important impact on the young digital scene.

Songs, jokes, and satire, comedic sketches, plays, and poetry all provide opportunities for discussion and debate about national identity, as has been underlined by recent works on popular culture (Armbrurst, 2000; Fahmy, 2011). While the international press and scholars were focusing on "citizen journalism," the cultural responses of the former type have been largely ignored (Gonzalez-Quijano, 2009). This is partly due to the porous divide between the two. At a national level, young Arab artists have managed in a number of cases to break through the usual market blockage by selling content that they had first created as amateurs and disseminated through digital devices and social networks.

Thanks to her online graphic diary, young Lebanese comic designer Maya Zankoul was asked to publish two volumes of the comic book *Amalgam*. After their publication in May 2011, she actually closed the blog that made her famous, but continued the "e-self-marketing" through different platforms. In the "Where to find me," she explains: "In my design studio, most probably working like a madwoman! At pro.mayazankoul.com; On the Zankoulizer, where you can create your own avatar:zankoulizer.me; In my 2 comic books! (that you can find at Virgin Megastore & Librairie Antoine in Lebanon); on my Facebook page and Twitter page where I'll be updating you with all events/exhibitions/projects, etc." The desperate figure of the *artiste maudit* is strongly rejected. "I am so against the artist type that nobody understands [. . .] I believe art is a profession, it is my job, not a hobby." She has become a young entrepreneur thanks to her digital activities. She turned 26 years old one day before our interview but feels she is not a "young artist" anymore: "I have a company, I published two books, I have people working for me, I feel I have loads of experience now."

Cyril Aris and Mounia Akl with their "Orange Dog Productions" experienced a similar success story when they made the leap from YouTube to the Lebanese Broadcasting Corporation (LBC). It all started when Cyril and Mounia posted their first short film on their respective Facebook walls. The success of *Beirut I love you—I love you not* is totally web-based. It went viral and got 100,000 views overnight. Cyril recounted, "Then LBC called us. They had watched us on YouTube and wanted us to make a web-based series to be broadcast in primetime before the evening news." It was then developed as a web series for the LBC website. The production of this series could not have happened if it were not digitally mediated and initially broadcast on YouTube, where it struck a chord with young viewers.

Arab youths are also just starting to extend their "democratization" to the art market. Through digitally mediated tools, young artists have invented new ways of presenting themselves. They are well aware of the "marketing tools" that the social networks represent in order to network with the people who count (private gallery owners, editors, art critics, and journalists) and have become in that sense their "own promoters," thus skipping intermediaries. This is all the more important considering that figures in the art market from the Middle East and North Africa are on the rise. Collectors are increasing rapidly. The Ayyam Gallery in Dubai has even created the annual Ayyam auctions, which, according to its website, are "custom-made for new and young collectors freshly introduced to the auction experience as well as veteran buyers looking to discover that next new star." This explosion of interest in Middle East art could well be a "market bubble" and further analysis should be undertaken to assess its impact. Young artists from the region face a lot of regional determinism. Alaa Al-Shroogi, Director of the Cuadro Fine Art Gallery in Dubai, asks, "Is an artist's work still relevant if it does not depict calligraphy, veils, or fallen dictators?" (2011).

Ahmed Mater is very conscious of the danger of commercialization in the region since it could kill the young and burgeoning scene. He says, "The market of the Gulf is very rich but not yet artistically oriented. If the phenomenon is not counter-balanced, young artists will soon have no other option but to create paintings that match the colors of the cushions and the living room." However, with social media and digital showcases, artists may have a better chance of living from their art. Mater continues, "I've been contacted more than once by collectors through my Facebook page and this allows me to earn a living from my art."

Conclusion

Like canaries in a coal mine, young Arab artists of the past ten years years have been paving the way for a more conscious and intimate use of social media and internet tools. Long before the revolutions and upheavals that shook the Middle East from 2010, a cultural revolution had actually taken place in the world of technically savvy artists. This shy cultural renaissance, which had started a decade earlier, challenged the state monopoly on the definition of the national culture. It also helped break the boundaries between artists living similar experiences in different Arab states and gave birth to a "newborn pan-Arabism" in the artistic world. A young generation of artists was born who were much more independent financially and mentally from the old colonial and oriental assumptions still visible to this day in the commercial and state-sponsored spheres. While they were freeing themselves from the expectations placed on them, whether by the older generation of Arab nationalists or Western audiences with an orientalist bent, they also engendered innovative cultural expressions using computer-mediated tools in the most intimate way.

Creating a complete rupture with their predecessors, these technically savvy artists have also managed to create a high level of visibility for themselves, thanks to their digital tools. They have created their own platforms to display their works rather than interact with the state to ask for visibility. These Arab artists have been able to exert a significant influence on the cultural scene and on ways that youth citizenship is understood and expressed. Finally, through new digital tools and an increased digital intimacy, art practice, production, and consumption have witnessed a real "democratization," passing from closed spaces to an enlarged youth public sphere. This opening of the sphere should have a long-lasting impact on state–society relationships vis-à-vis youth citizenship.

Notes

1. Similarly, William Wells, the director of the Cairo-based independent Townhouse Gallery, stressed how established Egyptian artists had focused on political issues long before the 25 January Revolution. He pointed to the works of Hala Elkoussy, a 2010 Abraaj Capital Art Prize winner, and Lara Baladi. They were both among the many artists who protested in Tahrir Square against Mubarak's rule (Harris, 2011, pp. 1–3).
2. The in-depth interviews were conducted in 2012 through Skype (one- to three-hour conversations) and were semi-structured, taking as a starting point questions linked to the artists' expressions and trajectories. Unless otherwise indicated, the direct quotations from the artists are from these interviews conducted by the author.
3. See ganzeer.blogspot.com.
4. The biggest global internet companies have all created special funds for digital savvy artists and political activists. See www.google.com/grants.
5. Ganzeer has 19,919 followers and Gaber has 34,955 as of February 26, 2013.
6. To view Mater's work, see http://ahmedmater.com/artwork/illuminations/dyptichs/illumination-ottoman-waqf/.

References

Al-Shroogi, A. (2011, November 1). With the benefit of hindsight, what role does new media play in artistic practices, activism, and as an agent for social change in the Middle East and North Africa Today? In *Ibraaz*. Retrieved from www.ibraaz.org/platforms/4/responses/63

Armbrurst, W. (Ed.). (2000). *Mass mediations: New approaches to popular culture in the Middle East and beyond.* Berkeley: University of California Press.

Auge, M. (1992). *Non-lieux, introduction à une anthropologie de la surmodernité.* Paris: Le Seuil.

Balza, F. (2011, October). L'art aux origines des révoltes arabes. *Qantara*. Retrieved from www.imarabe.org/magazine-qantara/qantara-numero-81

Bayat, A. (2007). Islamism and the politics of fun. *Public Culture*, 19(3), 433–459.

Bayat, A. (2009). *How ordinary people changed the Middle East.* Stanford: Stanford University Press.

Bayat, A. (2011). *Muslim youth and the claim of youthfulness.* Oxford: Oxford University Press.

Bayat, A. & Herrera, L. (2010). Being young and Muslim in neoliberal times. In L. Herrera & A. Bayat (Eds.), *Being young and Muslim: New cultural politics in the global south and north* (3–24). New York: Oxford University Press.

Cornet, C. (2010). *Foundations and change in the Mena region.* Budapest: European Cultural Foundation.

Cummings, M. (2003). *Cultural diplomacy and the United States government: A survey.* Washington DC: Center for Arts and Culture.

Dakhila, J. (2006). *Créations artistiques contemporaines en pays d'Islam: des arts en tension.* Paris: Kimé.

Davis, B. (2011, April 22). It is life that inspires me: A Q&A with Tunisian political artist Nadia Kaabi-Linke. *Art info*, p. 7.

Donohue, J. (2006). Arab literature on internet. In C. V. Yves Gonzalez-Quijano (Ed.), *La société de l'information au Proche-Orient* (201–211). Beirut: Presses de l'Université Saint-Joseph.

Downey, A. (2011). *Restaging the (objective) violence of images: Reza Aramesh.* Retrieved May 8, 2013 from www.ibraaz.org/interviews/5

Downey, A. (2012). *Lost in narration.* Retrieved May 8, 2013 from www.ibraaz.org/interviews/11

Downey, A. & Lazaar, L. (2011). *The future of a promise.* Ibraaz Publishing.

Eickelman, D. & Anderson, J. (Eds.). (2003). *New media in the Muslim world: The emerging public sphere,* 2nd edition. Bloomington and Indianapolis: Indiana University Press.

Fahmy, Z. (2011). *Ordinary Egyptians: Creating the modern nation through popular culture.* Stanford: Stanford University Press.

Falk, R. (1997). Resisting "globalisation-from-above" through "globalisation-from-below." *New Political Economy*, 2(1), 1469–9923.

Farjam, L. (2009). *Unveiled: New art from the Middle East.* London: Booth Clibborn Editions.

Forster, S. (2001). Les artistes arabes agencent l'art contemporain. *RFI.* Retrieved November 1, 2011 from www.rfi.fr/afrique/20111026-artistes-arabes-agencent-art-xxie-siecle

Fraser, M. (2005). *Weapons of mass distraction: Soft power and American empire.* New York: St. Martin's Press.

Goffman, E. (1959). *Presentation of self in everyday life.* New York: Doubleday Anchor Books.

Gonzalez-Quijano, Y. (2007). Nouvelles technologies et processus démocratiques dans le monde arabe. In D. B. A. Hammoudi (Ed.), *La démocratie est-elle soluble dans l'islam?* Paris: CNRS.

Gonzalez-Quijano, Y. (2009). Communautés virtuelles de la Toile arabe: Une nouvelle "fabrique du social." In Y. Gonzalez-Quijano (Ed.), *Les Arabes parlent aux Arabes. La révolution de l'information dans le monde arable* (272). Paris: Sindbad.

Gonzalez-Quijano, Y. (2011, April 18). *Don't be evil ! Révolutions virtuelles sur un Net pas très net.* Message posted to http://cpa.hypotheses.org/2626

Harris, G. (2011, June 17–19). The ripple effect of the Arab Spring. *The Art Newspaper*, p. 7.

Herrera, L. & Bayat, A. (2010). *Being young and Muslim: New cultural politics in the global south and north.* New York: Oxford University Press.

Jacquemond, R. (2003). *Entre scribes et écrivains. Le champ littéraire dans l'Égypte contemporaine.* Arles: Sindbad-Actes Sud.

Kahf, U. (2007). Arabic hip hop: Claims of authenticity and identity of a new genre. *Journal of Popular Music Studies*, 19, 359–385.

Kernane, H. & Schoepf, L. (2011). L'art arabe contemporain. *Arabies*, Autumn, 60–63.

Khosrokhavar, F. (2012). *The new Arab revolutions that shook the world.* London: Paradigm Publishers.

Lafargue de Grangeneuve, L. (2006). L'ambivalence des usages politiques de l'art. *Revue Française de Science Politique*, 56, 457–477.

Leary, M. (1995). *Self-presentation: Impression management and interpersonal behavior.* Madison, WI: Brown & Benchmark Publishers.

Levine, M. (2008). Heavy metal Muslims: The rise of a post-Islamist public sphere. *Contemporary Islam*, 2(3), 229–249.

Lynch, M. (2005). *Voices of the new Arab public: Iraq, al-Jazeera, and Middle East politics today.* New York: Columbia University Press.

Matar, D. (2007). Crafting the Arab media for peacebuilding: Donors, dialogue and disasters. In N. Sakr (Ed.), *Arab media and political renewal: Community legitimacy and public life* (118–134). London: I. B. Tauris.

Mitchell, T. (Ed.). (2001). *Global noise: Rap and hip hop outside of the USA.* Middletown: Wesleyan University Press.

Ramadan, D. (2004). Regional emissaries: Geographical platforms and the challenges of marginalisation. *Paper presented at Proceedings of Apexart Conference 3.* Honolulu, Hawaii: Apexart.

Rancière, J. (2004). *The politics of aesthetics: The distribution of the sensible.* G. Rockhill (Trans. and introd.). London and New York: Continuum.

Scheid, K. (2007). The agency of art and the study of Arab modernity. *The MIT Electronic Journal For Middle Eastern Studies Spring,* 7, 6–23.

Sefrioui, K. (2012). *Tant de chaines à briser.* Retrieved May 8, 2013 from www.babelmed.net/Pais/M%C3%A9diterran%C3%A9e/tant_de.php?c=7186&m=34&l=fr

Shabout, N. (2007). *Modern Arab art: Formation of Arab aesthetics.* Florida: University of Florida Press.

Shabout, N. (2009). *New vision: Arab art in the twenty-first century.* New York: Transglobe Publishing Ltd and Thames & Hudson.

Shannon, J. (2006). *Among the jasmine trees: Music and modernity in contemporary Syria.* Middletown: Wesleyan University Press.

Stein, R. L. & Swedenburg, T. (Eds.). (2005). *Palestine, Israel, and the politics of popular culture.* Durham: Duke University Press.

Winegar, J. (2006). *Creative reckonings: The politics of art and culture in contemporary Egypt.* Stanford: Stanford University Press.

10

"WE ARE NOT ALL MALALA"

Children and Citizenship in the Age of Internet and Drones

Fauzia Rahman

Blogs, Burqas, and the BBC

> I want to tell my story, but it will also be the story of 61 million children who can't get education. [. . .] I want it to be part of the campaign to give every boy and girl the right to go to school. It is their basic right.
>
> (*I am Malala*, a memoir by Malala Yousafzai, 2013)[1]

Malala Yousafzai's career as a child activist is intricately intertwined with geo-politics, development, and corresponding notions of citizenship in the internet age. Her rise to international fame as the poster child for Muslim girls' education began in her hometown of Mingora, in the northwest of Pakistan. Mingora is located in the region that has been most severely hit by the US drone war. A recent study conducted by the Bureau of Investigative Journalism estimates that since 2004, Pakistan has had 365 drone strikes and they have killed between 2,536 and 3,577 people, including 411 to 884 civilians, with much of the death and destruction occurring in nearby Waziristan and the Federally Administered Tribal Areas (FATA) (Stanford Law School & New York University School of Law, 2012). It is no coincidence that since the drones started falling in 2004 the region has served as a prime Taliban recruiting ground. Since 2009 the Taliban have controlled Mingora.

In 2009 BBC Urdu service reporter Abdul Hai Kakar contacted Ziauddin Yousafzai, a school principal in a private girls' secondary school, looking for some-one to blog about life under the Taliban. When not a single girl volunteered, Ziauddin hesitantly volunteered his daughter Malala, who was just 11 years old at the time. She started blogging for the BBC's Urdu site under the agreement that she would remain anonymous. Kakar chose her penname, Gulmakai, the heroine of Pashtun folk stories. Kakar stated: "I wanted to give an indigenous, symbolic attachment to Swat so that the people could own it journalistically" (Bezhan, 2012).

From January to March 2009, Malala had regular phone conversations with Kakar, who turned their calls into her blog posts. During these calls, which lasted about 30 minutes, Malala would talk about life under the Taliban. Kakar would transcribe and edit the conversations and post them onto the BBC website under the title, "Diary of a Pakistani schoolgirl." The blog dealt in detail with things such as the closing of girls' schools in the region, and Malala's great passion for education. When her blog became more popular, it was translated and posted on the BBC English website, giving it a much larger global audience. Soon after the Pakistani army pushed the Taliban out of the region, her father revealed her true identity. At that point, Malala's career as an activist began to take off and garner the attention of major media outlets.

In 2009 *New York Times* journalist Adam B. Ellick filmed a documentary highlighting Malala's campaign for girls' education called "Class dismissed: Malala's story." In November 2011 CNN's Reza Sayah interviewed Malala. She was also becoming a rising celebrity in Pakistan, where she appeared on almost every national talk show in the country. People's fascination with her seemed to revolve around the fact that she was a young girl, Muslim, Pakistani, one of the "powerless" of society and she had been given voice through the means of blogging. The message around her was always, imagine, if a girl like Malala can be given a voice and stand up to the structures of oppression around her, then what's not to say that a new wired generation of girls can rise out of their current contexts of patriarchy, repression, cultural backwardness, and poverty, and claim their rights not only as Pakistani citizens, but also global citizens for the twenty-first century?

The story of Malala has allowed what we can call "foreign policy internet optimists" to point to the emancipatory power of internet connectivity in geopolitically volatile regions like Pakistan (Clinton, 2010; MacKinnon, 2012; Schmidt & Cohen, 2010). The rise and spread of new information and communication technologies has led to new policies and understandings about digital activism and their relation to a more robust and engaged civil society. For many the story of Malala is a prime example of the "power" and "promise" of the internet and it reinforces ideas, as articulated in the US State Department's Internet Freedom policy, that an "open internet will lead to stronger, more prosperous countries" (Clinton, 2011). These analysts suggest that young people can overcome the immense obstacles they face through empowering means such as blogging and online organizing.

Malala and her campaign for girls' education were framed as the greatest and most effective weapon against the Taliban, and a potential turning point in the "war on terror." However, in the midst of the celebratory reporting, Malala's story took on a potentially tragic, and certainly more complicated turn. On October 9, 2012 Taliban-led thugs shot the Pakistani teen activist. This act of violence, which could have cost Malala her life, brought home the point that online activism and blogging for foreign media outlets can carry heavy risks.

When news broke of the shooting of young Malala, the world responded instantaneously through Twitter, Facebook, blogs, YouTube, webpages, radio, television, and newspapers. People around the world expressed awe at the courage of a young girl who had been willing to stand up to the Taliban for the cause of girls' education. Her story became an inspiring tale. Parents from the US and UK narrated the story of Malala to their children, governments rallied around her cause, and non-governmental organizations re-vamped their efforts around girls' education. Malala seemed to be responsible for this whirlwind of events as slogans such as, "I am Malala," and "We are all Malala," began to surface on Facebook pages, blogs, campaigns for girls' education, and songs. The Taliban had met its match: a 14-year-old girl born and raised in Taliban-held territory was fighting back, and the world was on her side. Malala succeeded where all else—development, drones, and diplomacy—had failed, and she was seen as mobilizing Pakistani citizens against the Taliban in a moment of national unity. Fareed Zakariya vocalized this sentiment best when he exclaimed:

> Malala exposed the lie of Islamic extremists and they were willing to kill her for it. [. . .] Her courage in taking on the Taliban has inspired moderate Pakistanis. Pakistan may blame the West but the enemy lies within and it took a 14-year-old girl to bring that to people's attention. We wish her a speedy recovery so that she can be back in the fight for her country and her religion.
>
> (CNN, 2012b)

There is no doubt that Malala is an extraordinary person who has shown enormous courage and strength, and that there is a crisis in girls' education in Pakistan. According to figures released by UNESCO, primary-school enrolment for girls stands at 60% compared to 84% for boys. Only 32% of females enrol in secondary school (UNESCO, 2012). However, what is at issue here is the way in which Malala's story has been framed in the Western media. Malala's story has been used to show the promises of the digital age while ignoring its "dark side" (Morozov, 2010). The case of Pakistan, perhaps more than any other country, serves as a cogent reminder that the digital age has given birth to both the internet *and* drones. The two phenomena comingle in the lives of children and youth in ways both positive and devastating.

In the remainder of this chapter I trace how Malala Yousafzai has become a global icon for girls' education and in so doing raise questions about youth, citizenship, and internet freedom in a "virtual Pakistan." I argue that Malala's campaign serves the needs of Western power and development, but fails to address the physical and material realities of girls' lives in the Swat Valley. Among the questions under investigation are: How has internet connectivity in a remote region like the Swat Valley actually changed the lives of young girls? What are the risks associated with connectivity and what are the promises? How can a better understanding of the digital age actually aid in advancing girls' education?

Good Muslims, Bad Muslims, and the War on Terror

After Malala was brutally shot by Taliban-led thugs on October 9, 2012, her image went viral. Malala's image was plastered on Facebook pages, online news sources, television screens, and Twitter accounts. Her injured body evoked feelings of sympathy, anger, and confusion. Various Western media outlets began to construct a narrative embedded within the "War on Terror" framework. Headlines like, "Will Malala unite us against terror?" appeared on popular news websites like *The Daily Beast*. Senator Diane Feinstein wrote in *The Huffington Post*: "The barbaric attack on this brave girl should be condemned by the civilized world" (Feinstein, 2012). Social activist Saman Jafery told CNN, "If the Taliban is a mindset, then Malala is a mindset too. It's a mindset of educated and empowered women" (Sayah & Mullen, 2012). To use the language of Mahmood Mamdani, the media was constructing an image of Malala as being the "good Muslim" in contrast to, not only the Taliban, but any group that did not support US involvement in Pakistan as being the "bad Muslim" (2004). Battle lines were being drawn and citizens from Pakistan and countries around the globe were being asked to choose one of two sides: the side of Malala or that of the Taliban? These were the only options available.

Pakistan was the United States' key ally in Central Asia during the Cold War. The CIA used Pakistan as a training ground for the fighters in the US-funded Afghan *jihad* against the Soviet Union. The effect on Pakistan was devastating. Opium production increased so that the profits could be used to fund the war and this led to an increase in local consumption (Mamdani, 2002). The Taliban rose as a movement from this period in this context; they were the children that were born out of this war, coming of age in refugee camps along the Pakistan–Afghan border. The CIA did not directly create the Taliban, but they did create the Mujahedeen (fighters in the *jihad*) and, during the Cold War, embraced both Osama Bin Laden and the Taliban as alternatives to secular nationalists who stood opposed to US power and threatened their interests in the region.

Following the September 11, 2001 attacks on the US, the former president of Pakistan, Pervez Musharraf, aligned with the US against the Taliban government in Afghanistan after being given an ultimatum by the former US president, George W. Bush. Musharraf agreed to give the US the use of three airbases for Operation Enduring Freedom. As American forces pushed out the Taliban in Afghanistan, they began to re-group in neighboring Pakistan. It was said that many retreated into the mountains and the tribal areas, but their growing presence was felt throughout Pakistan. The Swat Valley in the Khyber Pakhtunkhwa province would in later years become a Taliban stronghold.

The Swat Valley used to be referred to as the "Switzerland" of Pakistan and was a prize tourist destination for Pakistanis. The formerly princely state only became part of Pakistan in 1969. Between 1949 and 1969 the last ruler of Swat, Miangul Jahan Zeb, built many schools in the valley. Prior to 2001, there were 1,576 schools in Swat and a literacy rate of 46%, which was much higher than the national average (Khan, 2011). The residents of Swat were widely considered to be the most liberal in the nation. Following the US-led invasion of Afghanistan in 2002, a wave of anti-Americanism swept the region and led to an alliance of Islamist political parties, the Muttahida Majlis-e-Amal, which won all the seats in the national and provincial elections (N. Yousafzai, 2013). In 2004 the US introduced another weapon to its "War on Terror": unmanned drones. As civilian casualties rose, local anger and frustration grew and the Taliban gained a stronghold in the region. It was in this context in 2006 that the radical cleric, Maulana Fazlullah, nicknamed "Radio Mullah," started an illegal local FM channel in the Swat Valley.

Even though Fazlullah condemned most communication-based electronics as "major sources of sin," his sermons were delivered via radio. Radio Mullah was said to have ruled the airwaves and was responsible for radicalizing minds and enlisting new recruits to the Taliban. Radio signals were relayed from mobile transmitters mounted on motorcycles and trucks. During nightly broadcasts Fazlullah routinely identified residents by name for taking part in any number of transgressions, and violators were often condemned to death, often by beheadings. In 2007 Fazlullah became the leader of the local branch of the Taliban and began to patrol the streets of the main urban areas, telling barbers and owners of CD shops to shut their "un-Islamic" businesses. He had the support of more than 4,500 armed militants. By late October, Fazlullah had established Islamic courts enforcing Shariah law in 59 villages of the Swat Valley. The courts functioned as "parallel governments" within the region, an indication of the growing power of the Taliban.

The Taliban targeted tribal elders, many of whom were local feudal landlords and operated large agricultural estates. When the Taliban first came to power, locals say that they used a strongly socialist rhetoric to enlist the support of poor villagers, telling them that once the old landowners were killed or driven off, their land would be equitably distributed among those who had nothing. But when the time of Taliban rule came, they broke all promises.

In 2008, amidst local frustrations and mounting pressure from the US, the Pakistani army began to engage in an operation to take back control of the area. This resulted in an escalation in suicide attacks, rocket attacks, individual attacks, men being hanged for opposing the Taliban, journalists being killed for not covering them in a favorable light, and policemen being killed for attempting to maintain order. The Taliban enforced a complete ban on female education in the Swat Valley in 2009. Fazlullah preached that immorality and decadence in Swat was a consequence of women's education. Over the airwaves he explained that the only way to eliminate this immodesty was for females to be barred from leaving their homes and especially from going to school. Some 400 private schools that enrolled 40,000 girls were shut down (N. Yousafzai, 2013). At least ten girls' schools that tried to open after the January 15, 2009 deadline, which had been set by the Fazlullah-led Taliban, were blown up by militants in the town of Mingora, the headquarters of the Swat Valley and Malala's hometown. More than 170 schools were bombed or torched, along with other government-owned buildings. After a long, bloody battle the army secured the valley in 2010 and the US rewarded Pakistan with the Kerry–Lugar Bill, which tripled non-military aid to Pakistan to $1.5 billion per annum, and pledged its long-term commitment to its key ally against extremism (N. Yousafzai, 2013). As the people of Swat began to piece their lives together they were hit by another calamity.

The devastating floods of July 2010 were recorded as the worst in the country's history. The disaster claimed 3,000 lives and wiped out whole villages in the northwest region, including the Swat Valley. As aid and relief were slow to come, locals criticized the government for its lack of assistance in the Khyber Pakhtunkhwa province. In an attempt to fill this void, Islamist militants took the lead in distributing emergency aid throughout the region. The US viewed this as a setback in the "War on Terror" and began to compete to deliver aid. They feared the Taliban would once again take hold of the Swat Valley (CBS News, 2010).

Youth and Citizenship in "Virtual Pakistan"

As we begin to understand Malala's Swat, the risks of a virtual Pakistan become more pronounced and complicated than those allowed by the concept of Internet Freedom. The "War on Terror" became a living reality for young Pakistani citizens. The US feared the radicalization of this new generation that was coming of age in a country with high rates of unemployment, poverty, sexism, militarism, and violence. Children and youth were recognized as important investments since they were the members of society who could change the anti-American tide in the country. The US State Department, private companies (like Google, Nokia, and MobiLink), intergovernmental organizations (UNESCO, and the UN), and non-governmental organizations supported projects to promote youth citizenship as they aided in the construction of a new "virtual Pakistan." Youth initiatives that centered on the use of new digital technologies as a tool for "empowerment" and "agency" were created throughout the provinces. Many of these youth programs represented the "soft power" side of the US "War on Terror."

Pakistan has a population of over 190 million, and 67% are under the age of 30 (Population Reference Bureau, 2013). The internet penetration rate in the country is 15%, meaning 85% of the population is not wired (Internet World Stats, 2013). Regardless, the communications landscape has been changing rapidly in the last decade and efforts to bridge the digital divide are ongoing. With the explosion of mobile phone use and the spread of broadband internet in Pakistan also increasing, access to information and communication technologies (ICTs) is on the rise. As a consequence, there are larger numbers of citizen journalists and cyberactivists.

Accompanying this rise in connectivity has been the growing popularity of various social networks. Over 8,007,460 Pakistanis use top social networks, favorite among them are Facebook (53%), YouTube (25%), and Google+ (14%). Facebook has witnessed the most notable rise in users. According to a report in 2012, 1,379, 360 new users in Pakistan joined Facebook in the six-month period from June to December 2012. This means that every 12 seconds a new user signed up for the service (Socialbakers, 2012).

To be sure, connectivity and social media allow citizens to communicate in a virtual space that provides a new platform for civic engagement. However, the risks and challenges of "Virtual Pakistan" cannot be forgotten. Physical reality cannot be separated from the virtual, a fact that becomes glaringly evident when we consider virtual warfare, a point to which we will now turn.

"Drones Kill so Malala can Live"

Unmanned US drones are a recent form of virtual warfare that have become all too familiar in Pakistan. Drone strikes began in 2004 under the Bush administration and are carried out in the Federally Administered Tribal Areas of Waziristan. As US soldiers command these technologies from afar, the physical repercussions are all too real for Pakistani civilians whose lives have been taken or severely altered by the ongoing strikes. Drones are said to target militants, but local reports reveal that civilian casualties are common.

Many supporters of the drone war argue that it has benevolent goals, that the drones ensure the safety of young citizens like Malala. For instance, the American journalist Nicholas Kristof wrote in the *New York Times*: "The greatest risk for violent extremists in Pakistan isn't American drones. It's educated girls" (Kristof, 2012). Kristof is asking his readers to forget about drones and focus on girls' education. The hardships, losses of life, land, and livelihood Pakistani citizens are incurring as a result of the continued drone strikes are seen as irrelevant. The casting of Malala by Kristof and others as a heroine serves the purpose of those interested in revitalizing Western-led development projects and legitimizing foreign policy in the region, but neglects the everyday realities of a community that is suffering from the direct and indirect consequences of drone strikes.

Alongside drone strikes, the US is concerned about the radicalization of new generations of Pakistanis, particularly in the northwest region. What has been overlooked is how the ongoing strikes are increasing anti-Western sentiments, and leading to new and ever more extreme forms of radicalization. However, the State Department continues to argue that changing the mindset of the population can be achieved not by stopping military intervention, but by increasing internet connectivity and promoting a policy of Internet Freedom.

Hillary Clinton, in her capacity as Secretary of State, launched the State Department's Internet Freedom policy in 2009 as part of the 21st Century Statecraft initiative (State Department, 2009a). This concept is connected to "promoting democracy" in regions of the world that appear most averse to Western intervention. Partnerships between the State Department and private companies like Google have taken a front seat in framing the debate on Internet Freedom. At the center of this policy is an understanding that youth in developing nations will be the driving force behind such initiatives. Hillary Clinton, in a speech given just before the launching of the 21st Century Statecraft initiative, highlighted the role of young citizens in this new form of public diplomacy: "The biggest challenges we face today will be solved by the 60% of the world's population under the age of 30. Young people like you are using their talents and ingenuity to fashion their own forms of service and diplomacy" (State Department, 2009a).

Through 21st Century Statecraft, the State Department is investing in young tech-savvy citizens to promote the growth of civil society groups. An example of this work is the Civil Society 2.0 initiative. The vision for this initiative is to build the "technical capacity of civil society organizations to accomplish their missions through the use of connection technologies" (State Department, 2012a). In order to accomplish this vision, the State Department hosts Youth TechCamps around the world with the hopes of encouraging citizen journalism and online youth activism.

In September of 2012 the State Department hosted a Youth TechCamp in Islamabad, Pakistan in which 40 young Pakistanis from different regions of the nation participated. The participants were alumni of the US-sponsored Kennedy–Lugar Youth Exchange and Study Program, through which Pakistani high-school students spend one academic year living and studying in the US. The theme of the camp was "Empowering Youth for Social Change." In an online news brief the US Embassy in Islamabad reported, "Youth TechCamp Pakistan was the third such TechCamp held, following similar programs in Washington and Bangladesh" (State Department, 2012a). They went on to say that the main goal of the camp was to increase digital literacy and to encourage young people to engage in and contribute to the digital networks and technologies of today's interconnected world. The camp consisted of three full days of training with top local technology experts specializing in civic journalism and social activism. On completion of the camp the State Department issued an online media note that applauded the success of Youth TechCamp Pakistan. "Youth TechCamp Pakistan enabled these future leaders to learn how they can leverage connection technologies to make a positive impact in their communities and around the world" (State Department, 2012a).

These initiatives created by the State Department reveal a new foreign policy agenda that is embedded in the idea of the emancipatory power of the Internet. This agenda aims to create youth activists like Malala Yousafzai and partner with them. On April 5, 2013 Hillary Clinton was the keynote speaker at the Women in the World Conference, where she quoted Malala as saying: "If this new generation is not given pens they will be given guns." Clinton went on to say that Malala was indeed a "threat," but a threat that had been underestimated by the Taliban. They had attempted to silence her and her cause, "but instead they inspired millions of Pakistanis to say enough is enough" (Women in the World, 2013).

Who is Malala? . . . "We all are Malala"

> A teenage girl speaking out for girls' education is just about the most terrifying thing in the world for the Taliban. She is not some Western NGO activist who just parachuted into Pashtun country to hand out ESL textbooks. She is far more dangerous than that: a local, living advocate of progress, education, and enlightenment. If people like Yousafzai were to multiply, the Taliban would have no future.
>
> (Dobson, 2012)

As Malala's story began to spread through tweets, Facebook statuses, blogs, and online news sources, Clinton's words seemed to ring true. She not only inspired millions of Pakistanis, but the entire world was mesmerized. Everyone wanted to know: who is Malala? How could a global audience understand a Pakistani girl from the Swat Valley? The narrative constructed by Western media sources is one that laid the foundation for her transformation into a global icon. Celebrities like Angelina Jolie and Madonna began to display unique acts of solidarity and, in the case of Jolie, financially support Malala's global campaign.

Angelina Jolie penned an essay in *The Daily Beast* that was reported in almost every major news outlet in the US titled: "We all are Malala." The essay was a reflection on the incident and she explains how she discussed the situation with her own children.

> Malala's story stayed with them throughout the day, and that night they were full of questions. We learned about Malala together, watching her interviews and reading her diaries. Malala was just 11 years old when she began blogging for the BBC. She wrote of life under the Taliban, of trading in her school uniform for colorless plain clothes, of hiding books under her shawl, and eventually having to stop going to school entirely. [. . .] Our 8-year-old suggested that the world build a statue for Malala, and fittingly create a reading nook near it. Our 6-year-old asked the practical question of whether Malala had any pets, and if so, who would take care of them? She also asked about Malala's parents and if they were crying.
>
> (Jolie, 2012)

In the essay Jolie exclaims that the issue of girls' education cannot be forgotten and the story of Malala serves as a reminder and a source of motivation for all. Jolie sees the incident as marking the beginning of a necessary revolution in girls' education and she believes that global solidarity with Malala is the first step. Malala's story inspired Jolie, along with *Daily Beast* editor Tina Brown, to lend their support to the Women in the World Foundation's campaign to raise money for girls fighting for education in Pakistan and Afghanistan. Jolie's own Education Partnership for Children of Conflict donated the first $50,000 to the fundraiser. Jolie noted that campaigns around the nation were erected, and chants of "We all are Malala" began to resonate throughout Pakistan and the world.

Jolie's essay takes Malala out of the Swat Valley and allows a global audience a glimpse into the life of a young Muslim girl fighting for girls' education. She is seen as being "empowered," "enlightened," and, most importantly, connected. The message the media gave was loud and clear: more Malalas are necessary to win this war of oppression and terror. Malala was understood as the oppressed Muslim girl who was able to speak back and organize a campaign for girls' education. The internet gave her that opportunity, and as a citizen journalist she was able to challenge the Taliban and what they stand for. Before the shooting, in an interview with CNN's Reza Sayah, she uses her Muslim identity to speak back to the Taliban about girls' education. In the interview she asks, "Where in the Qur'an does it say that a girl cannot get an education?" (CNNa, 2012). Both before and after the shooting, her Muslim identity is highlighted as making her both vulnerable and the perfect enemy for the Taliban.

As pop artists took on Malala's cause, she became even more vulnerable and exposed, a person in no-(wo)man's land. Madonna, during one of her concerts, performed a striptease for an audience in Los Angeles. After taking off her costume, she revealed the name MALALA written in big black letters across her back, between her bra strap and thong. The crowd broke out in applause, but reactions within Pakistan were not as enthusiastic. The Taliban picked up on the video as soon as it was posted. The shooting had provoked an unprecedentedly fierce backlash against the Pakistani Taliban and "now Madonna's performance allowed the militants to recast Malala as a symbol of Western immodesty and immorality" (S. Yousafzai, 2012a). Many of the Taliban say that Malala's Western supporters only prove that she was a bad person and that if she were a "good" Muslim such immoral people would not raise their voices for her. Perhaps Madonna's intentions were sincere, but local reactions reveal there is a larger context from which Malala cannot be separated.

We are not all Malala . . .

Malala was airlifted to a hospital in the UK for special treatment. Famous journalists, celebrities, and high-ranking government officials took up her cause. She received visits from Pakistani army generals, President Zardari, and numerous politicians. The girls of Mingora in Swat began to ask "What about us?" Several other young girls were with Malala on the bus when she was attacked. The Taliban did not target them, but some suffered injuries. One young girl in particular, Kainat, was transferred to a Peshawar hospital where she required additional treatment. In an interview with Al Jazeera, Kainat and her father revealed the lack of assistance they received from hospital staff: "We received no support at the hospital. We had to buy all of the medicines ourselves. So much so that we even had to buy the thread for her stitches," her father said. "Even the syringe" (Hashim, 2012a).

Despite promises from the federal government that the other two girls injured in the attacks would be taken care of and treated at the best hospitals, no one from the federal government contacted the families. Kainat's father did point out that several local political leaders had visited and helped with sums of money in their individual capacities. The reality was that Kainat was not Malala, and perhaps no one felt that more than Kainat and her other classmate injured that same day.

These girls are all too familiar with the atrocities of war. Numerous children have been victims of suicide bombings and found themselves in search of protection and proper healthcare. Uncounted children's lives have been taken and disrupted by ongoing drone strikes. Where was the international outcry and condemnation for their losses? As Kainat and other young girls in Swat continue with their studies, they live in fear of Taliban threats. Those like Kainat understand that the Taliban did not randomly target Malala. The Taliban made it clear that they did not attack Malala because she promoted girls' education, but because she audaciously formed an alliance with the "enemies from the West," a West that has set out to introduce immorality and exert their power in the guise of education. The people of Swat recognized that Malala was an example for all to show that those who side with the so-called "enemies" will be punished.

The Taliban were successful in instilling fear in the hearts of young girls. Nevertheless, even within the local community, Malala's campaign for girls' education continued to be force-fed to young girls and boys in the region. Malala's campaign has been branded as a local grassroots initiative, not a Western-led development initiative. In the ensuing months, a series of protests revealed the growing disconnect between Malala and the girls of Swat Valley. One incident in particular was reported in *The Express Tribune,* a Pakistani online media source. A girls' college near Malala's hometown was renamed in her honor, setting off protests from the student body. The students refused to attend classes until the name was changed and the sign was taken down. The pictures of Malala in the school were defaced and one girl told reporters that this was their school and Malala was in the UK, so why should she represent their college. She also added that if the signs were not taken down, they would also become targets of the Taliban, putting their lives in jeopardy. They approached the principal and finally the students' demands were met. *The Express Tribune* reported a few days later that Malala had come to know of the incident and had supported the girls' position, requesting the college to respect the girls' demands. Although these acts of local protest have been glossed over, slogans like "We All Are Malala" and the global solidarity campaigns that have been promoted by journalists, celebrities, and US government officials are being challenged locally, and rightfully so. The voices coming from the Swat Valley are not chants of "We all are Malala" but cries of, "We are not all Malala."

"I am Malala": A Campaign for Girls' Education

There is no doubt that Malala's story is one of courage and great resolve. It is also undeniable that campaigns for girls' education are much needed in a country where gender disparity in education is a major issue. Having said that, Malala's transformation into a global icon by mainstream media, social media, celebrities, government, and development agencies is problematic and highly deceptive. In order to improve girls' education, there is a need first to understand its implications in geopolitics, history, development, and corresponding notions of foreign policy and citizenship in the internet age. Girls' education, and children's lives more generally, cannot be separated from the realities of life on the ground. Young people in the region remain the victims of an intractable struggle between the United States, the Pakistani army, and the Taliban. This generation knows all too well the realities, horrors, and struggles of war and conflict.

Youth in Pakistan are indeed growing up in a digital age, but their "virtual Pakistan" is one that consists of all the possibilities of internet connectivity *and* all the horrors of the drones. If we are to continue girls' education initiatives in the region, and these are much needed, it is crucial to recognize the complex and sensitive issues that shape their communities. Local realities will not improve as youth become more connected, but when they receive a real education about the causes of their oppression. Malala's case forces us to rethink ideas of Internet Freedom, online citizenship, and girls' education in the digital age.

Note

1. This is an excerpt from Malala's memoir "I Am Malala" released in 2013. She signed a contract for two million pounds sterling and will be published globally by Little, Brown Book Group and Weidenfeld & Nicholson in the UK and Commonwealth. http://tribune.com.pk/story/527772/malala-seals-2m-deal-for-memoir/

References

Bezhan, F. (2012). *Malala Yousafzai: The "voice of Swat Valley."* Retrieved May 1, 2013 from www.theatlantic.com/international/archive/2012/10/malala-yousafzai-the-voice-of-swat-valley/263590/

British Council. (2009). *Pakistan the next generation report.* London: British Council.

CBS News. (2010, May 1). Pakistan floods swamp war-ravaged Swat Valley. Retrieved from www.cbsnews.com/2100–202_162–6735391.html

Clinton, H. (2010, January 10). Internet Freedom. *Foreign Policy.* Retrieved from www.foreignpolicy.com/articles/2010/01/21/internet_freedom?print=yes&hidecomments=yes&page=full

Clinton, H. (2011, January 21). Clinton unveils U.S. policy on Internet Freedom. Retrieved from www.voltairenet.org/article168204.html

CNN. (2012a, October 10). In 2011, CNN's Reza Sayah talked to Malala Yousafzai. Retrieved from www.youtube.com/watch?v=_8TBa278v1Y

CNN. (2012b, October 24). Fareed Zakaria GPS-Malala's story. Retrieved from www.youtube.com/watch?v=L_3Wk9R0-gg

Daily Beast Videos. (2013, April 5). Hillary: Malala was a "threat". Retrieved from http://news.yahoo.com/video/hillary-malala-threat-153656368.html

Daily Times. (2013). *WEF's global information technology report 2013 Pakistan's ICT ranking downgraded to 105th.* Retrieved March 31, 2013 www.dailytimes.com.pk/default.asp? page=2013%5C04%5C11%5Cstory_11–4-2013_pg5_9

Dobson, W. (2012). Why the Taliban fears teenage girls. Retrieved March 1, 2013 from www.slate.com/blogs/xx_factor/2012/10/10/taliban_shoots_14_year_old_girl_here_s_why_malala_yousafzia_scares_them.html

Express Tribune. (2012a). Students protest against naming of Shaidu Sharif college after Malala. Retrieved March1, 2013 from http://tribune.com.pk/story/478808/students-protest-against-naming-of-saidu-sharif-college-after-malala/

Express Tribune. (2012b). Taliban says its attack on Malala justified. Retrieved February 13, 2013 from http://tribune.com.pk/story/452331/taliban-says-its-attack-on-malala-justified/

Express Tribune. (2013). *Malala seals 2m deal for memoir.* Retrieved March 28, 2013 from http://tribune.com.pk/story/527772/malala-seals-2m-deal-for-memoir/

Feinstein, D. (2012). *Malala tragedy reveals plight of AfPak girls.* Retrieved February 5, 2013 from www.huffingtonpost.com/sen-dianne-feinstein/malala-tragedy-reveals-pl_b_1974662.html

Hashim, A. (2012a). Swat valley on edge after Malala shooting. Retrieved May 2, 2013 from www.aljazeera.com/indepth/features/2012/10/2012101416273881308.html

Hashim, A. (2012b). Reporter's notebook: Inside the Swat Valley. Retrieved April 1, 2013 from www.aljazeera.com/indepth/spotlight/2012review/2012/12/201212289161528556.html

Internet World Stats. (2013). Internet users in Asia. Retrieved April 31, 2013 from www.internetworldstats.com/asia.htm#pk

Jolie, A. (2012). We all are Malala. Retrieved March 1, 2013 from www.thedailybeast.com/articles/2012/10/16/angelina-jolie-we-all-are-malala.html

Khan, R. S. (2011, May 10). *Swat Valley NGO finds a solution to the assault on education.* Message posted to www.guardian.co.uk/global-development/poverty-matters/2011/may/10/swat-ngo-solution-to-assault-on-education

Kristof, N. (2012). Her "Crime" was loving schools. Retrieved March 12, 2013 from www.nytimes.com/2012/10/11/opinion/kristof-her-crime-was-loving-schools.html

MacKinnon, R. (2012). *Consent of the networked: The worldwide struggle for freedom.* New York: Basic Books.

Mamdani, M. (2002). Good Muslim, bad Muslim: A political perspective on culture and terrorism. *American Anthropologist*, 104(3), 766–775.

Mamdani, M. (2004) *Good Muslim, bad Muslim.* New York: Pantheon Books.

Morozov, E. (2010) *The net delusion: The dark side of internet freedom.* New York: Public Affairs.

New York Times. (2009). Class dismissed: Malala's story. Retrieved from www.nytimes.com/video/world/asia/100000001835296/class-dismissed.html

Population Reference Bureau (PRB). (2013). *The world's youth: Data sheets.* Retrieved May 19, 2013 from www.prb.org/pdf13/youth-data-sheet-2013.pdf

Sayah, R. & Mullen, J. (2012). Attack on pakistani schoolgirl galvanizes anti-Taliban feeling. Retrieved May 1, 2013 from www.cnn.com/2012/10/16/world/asia/pakistan-activist-reaction/index.html?hpt=hp_t3

Schmidt, E. & Cohen, J. (2010, October 16). The digital disruption: Connectivity and the diffusion of power. *Foreign Affairs.* Retrieved from www.foreignaffairs.com/articles/66781/eric-schmidt-and-jared-cohen/the-digital-disruptionTop of Form

Shirky, C. (2011). *Cognitive surplus.* New York: Penguin Press.

Socialbakers. (2012). Pakistan Facebook statistics. Retrieved May 1, 2013 from www.socialbakers.com/facebook-statistics/pakistan

Stanford Law School & New York University School of Law. (2012). *Living under drones: Death, injury, and trauma to civilians from US drone practices in Pakistan.*

State Department. (2009a). 21st Century Statecraft. Retrieved May 1, 2013 from www.state.gov/statecraft/overview/index.htm

State Department. (2009b). Remarks at the New York University Commencement Ceremony. Retrieved May 2, 2013 from www.state.gov/secretary/rm/2009a/05/123431.htm

State Department. (2012a). U.S. Department of State hosts youth TechCamp in Pakistan: Empowering youth for social change. Retrieved May 2, 2013 from www.state.gov/r/pa/prs/ps/2012/09/198475.htm

State Department. (2012b). Youth TechCamp in Pakistan boosts civic journalism. Retrieved May 19 from http://iipdigital.usembassy.gov/st/english/inbrief/2012/09/20120930136857.html#ixzz2RA6KwZer

UNESCO. (2012). *Education for all global monitoring report: Youth and skills putting education to work.* Paris: UNESCO.

Women in the World. (2013, February 4). Malala speaks! Retrieved from www.thedailybeast.com/articles/2013/02/04/malala-fund-raises-150–000-for-girls-education.html

Yousafzai, M. (2009). Diary of a Pakistani schoolgirl. Retrieved October 25, 2012 from http://news.bbc.co.uk/2/hi/south_asia/7834402.stm

Yousafzai, N. (2013). Crimes behind the curfew: The tragic stories of Swat under the Taliban and the military. Message posted to http://pashtunwomenvp.com/index.php/2013–01–28–03–21–27/political/178-crimes-behind-the-curfew-the-tragic-stories-of-swat-under-the-taliban-and-the-military

Yousafzai, S. (2012a). Malala: With friends like Madonna. Retrieved October 22, 2012 from www.thedailybeast.com/articles/2012/10/22/malala-with-friends-like-madonna.html

Yousafzai, S. (2012b). Pakistani Taliban declare war on media. Retrieved Jan 31, 2013 from www.thedailybeast.com/articles/2012/10/16/pakistani-taliban-declare-war-on-media.html

11

THE POWER OF ONLINE NETWORKS

Citizenship among Muslim Brotherhood Cyber Youth

Rehab Sakr

Introduction: The Birth of a Youth News Network[1]

In October 2010, shortly before the Egyptian legislative elections of November 2010, a group of young cyber citizens established a page on Facebook called "Rassd Network News" to monitor the elections. The page goes by the abbreviation R.N.N., or simply "Rassd," which means "monitoring." The page was created to provide a platform to document the anticipated election fraud and to take these infringements to the courts after the elections. The founders of the page introduced themselves as "Egyptian youth who have a desire to present the real practices of the regime during the elections through an alternative media channel since the official media is completely dominated by the political regime." The slogan of this supposed citizen-driven news network was "Rassd: A media created by the audience." The page called on all its Facebook fans to monitor the elections in their regions and districts and to send pictures and video shots that documented election irregularities to the page's email account to be published on the page's virtual wall.

During the first and the second rounds of the elections, the page published hundreds of pictures and videos of electoral fraud from all over Egypt of violations against both voters and candidates. The page had a very simple structure that consisted of a section for videos, another for photos, and a news stream. All the materials were presented objectively, with no specific commentary from the administrators (admins), who appeared as neutral, objective, and non-partisan election monitors. Many internet-based outlets shared the materials from Rassd, which gained the reputation of being a reputable election monitoring site. In a short period of time the fans of the page increased dramatically. Just one month after its launch, the page gained roughly 100,000 fans. After the elections, in which the ruling National Democratic Party (NDP) claimed that they won nearly 99% of the parliament seats, the page changed its focus. The page started to cover news of the Tunisian uprising, which began at the same time, in December 2010.

In addition to aggregating information and news, the page was a space where people could talk, exchange opinions, and try to crystallize views about the political situation. Through the page, members could also participate in public opinion polls regarding the policies of the page and ways to carry out offline events and actions. These modes of participation gave members the illusion that it was their page, that they could decide on its policies, that the admins were just like them. It seemed that Rassd was a totally non-partisan platform that operated as a neutral space for the youth of the internet to debate democracy and coordinate pro-democracy activism.

When the page changed its orientation in light of the Tunisian uprising, the voice of the admins became more active and directive. The admins started to use the much-visited virtual wall of Rassd to post questions like: "Can Egyptians have their own Tunisian-style revolution?", "How can they do it?", "How would you feel if you woke up and did not find the Mubarak regime?" Such questions triggered lively discussions. For some these propositions about preparing for a Mubarak end game appeared to be a mere fantasy, but for others they were the start of a hope, a dream that might be achieved. A group of especially active members on the page began suggesting that the fans start to prepare for anti-Mubarak mobilizations since that time was bound to come sooner or later.

Throughout the elections in 2010, during the critical coverage of Tunisia, and then during the 25 January Egyptian Revolution, when the page gained nearly 1 million fans in a very short time, the Rassd admins remained anonymous. It was not until mid-2011, well after the fall of President Mubarak, that it became clear that the admins of the page were closely associated with the Muslim Brotherhood movement, either as active members or with frozen memberships.[2]

The information about Rassd's identity emerged through different means. Some of the page's admins resigned and published on their personal Facebook pages that they were no longer admins in Rassd. One example is Anas Hassan. Hassan is a young Muslim Brotherhood member, a fact he himself revealed openly on his Facebook page. Another early piece of evidence came from Wael Ghonim's memoir about his role in the revolution, *Revolution 2.0* (2012). Ghonim was one of the admins of the "We are all Khaled Said" (Kulina Khaled Said) Facebook page that issued the call for the 25 January Revolution. He writes about how he coordinated with Amr Al-Qazaz from Rassd, a Muslim Brotherhood activist, to mobilize and prepare for the 25 January Revolution.

Knowing that the Rassd admins were from the Muslim Brotherhood does not necessarily mean the page was created as a Muslim Brotherhood page. Rather, the page was a trial for these young people to prove their independence away from the group and to give a deeper meaning to the term "citizenship." Through the page they showed that they not only belonged to the Muslim Brotherhood, but were also part of the larger society. They were exerting initiative and independence from a group that, from its inception, had frowned upon breaking ranks.

The Muslim Brotherhood was founded in 1928 by Hassan al-Banna to fight against British colonization and, more importantly, to lay the groundwork needed to reestablish the Islamic Caliphate state, which had come to an end in 1924 (al-Banna, 2006). From its creation until 2011, the Muslim Brotherhood had been operating as an opposition group. Although it had had the chance to have its own newspaper and magazine during the 1940s, the movement was banned in the 1950s and 1960s during the rule of President Gamal Abdel Nasser.

In the 1970s and early 1980s the group had permission to work as a social, but not political, group. It took advantage of this status to build a huge network of social services directed to the poor in urban slums and in the countryside. However, it was not allowed to have its own media channels. From the mid-1980s, the Muslim Brotherhood was banned again. The Brotherhood elders, in fear that the movement could be dissolved, ran the group through an even more rigid, top-down organizational structure. The elders expected the rank and file, especially the younger members, to blindly obey their orders. Younger members were not even allowed to have contact with the higher-ranked members, let alone voice opinions about policies within the group.

When the group of younger Muslim Brotherhood members established Rassd, they were in fact asserting some independence and demonstrating that they could successfully run a media channel away from the supervision of Brotherhood elders. These young members wanted to send a message to the Muslim Brotherhood leadership that they could run their own successful project, and that they should be involved in decision-making. In other words, they took it into their own hands to try to democratize the organization.

The Power of Networking and the Weakness of Hierarchical Models

Theories of democracy have been concerned with the creation of spaces where citizens can meet, discuss, and develop ideas and solutions to address community problems. As Saco observes, "The theories of democracy assume a form of government at least *of* the People (if not also *for* and *by* them) and that has entailed imaginative projections of the spaces through which people collectively engage in their democratic practices" (2002, p. 35). Similar ideas have been posited by other scholars, most notably Jürgen Habermas, whose theories about the public sphere address how the formation of active social networks can help to empower citizens to participate actively in public affairs (1989). In the early 1990s when the internet was envisioned to serve mainly commercial purposes, scholars such as Rash (1997) and Dyson (1998) saw it as a new space for empowering citizens and for creating new democratic practices, especially for under-represented and marginalized groups. Young citizens living in oppressive regimes and under authoritarian structures constitute an under-represented group. Through means of the internet and other communications, possibilities arose for them to cultivate good communication among themselves and even build networks trans-nationally (Ferdinand 2000; Mossberger, Tolbert, & McNeal, 2008).

For Toffler and Toffler (1995) and Castells, the main logic inherent in the internet is that it allows for networking in the information age (Castells, 2001, 2010). They argue that the building of networking structures is a very old practice. However, in the digital age structures take on new features related to information networking. Unlike traditional networking, information networking allows for a higher degree of coordination of tasks, and for better management of complex situations among its nodes. Information networking, therefore, is more flexible and adaptable to different conditions.

From the late 1990s, youth from different parts of the world began using the internet in different activities and soon discovered its empowering capabilities. Digital technologies have the ability to destroy hierarchies, or at least weaken them. Moreover, decentralized virtual networks that lack an individual leader at the top have the potential to shift power towards more disempowered individuals. These digitally enabled networks can initiate specific actions and political activities (Germany, 2006; Jordan, 2003; Matthew, 1997; Oates and Owen, 2006). The "anti-hierarchy" is one of the sources of the power of online social networks, since cyberspace is a more egalitarian space where otherwise disempowered people can find a place where they can act and move (Jordan, 2003; Miller, 1995).

Another way power operates with online social networks is that it allows for anonymity. Through the creation of online avatars, people can bypass differences based on ideology, ideas, and identity. In this model of social networking, people who belong to different ideological frames can work together for a specific project or joint action. People who come together online may not know about each other's backgrounds, but they still share a common objective. In addition, in virtual spaces people can deal with taboos and discover their abilities away from social control and supervision. Social pressure in the physical world can impede individuals and groups from expressing themselves freely. By shielding themselves behind anonymity, people can deal with issues they may have difficulty confronting with their real identities (Jordan, 2003; Saco, 2002).

Most literature from the early 2000s onwards about social media views them as spaces for supporting democratic practices (Gross & Acquisti, 2005). For example, authors have pointed out that social media provides the space for an alternative press (Khamis & Vaughn, 2011) where individuals can work as citizen journalists who participate in the practice of documenting and sharing news instead of just passively receiving it (Rosen, 2008). There has been much attention to the ways in which the younger generations use Facebook groups for civic engagement, organization, and mobilization (Mascaro & Goggins, 2011) in ways that create powerful youth networks (Metzgar & Maruggi, 2009). Still others have pointed to the ways in which social media is class blind and, barring access issues, does not discriminate along lines of income or social class. Anyone with access to the internet can express their opinions freely and build communities online.

It is true that social media can be a factor in youth empowerment and can allow for a redistribution of power in favor of marginalized groups, but this is not the whole story. Social media can also mirror offline power struggles raging between society and state, the political opposition and the ruling regime, and the older and younger generations. In fact, networking structures do not cancel out hierarchical structures. As we will see with the further case study of Rassd and the Muslim Brotherhood, the two structures—horizontal networks and vertical hierarchies—can work in a parallel way online.

Muslim Brotherhood Youth: From Blogging to Social Media

The online presence of the Muslim Brotherhood youth began in the mid-2000s through a network of bloggers who can be categorized into three generations (Alanani, 2008). The first generation emerged in 2005 during the legislative elections. These blogs for the most part focused on election monitoring news. The second wave of blogging began in 2007, a year of heightened conflict between the Muslim Brotherhood and the government. A number of Muslim Brotherhood leaders, including one of its most important figures, Khairat al-Shater, were facing military trials. These bloggers reported on the trial, human rights abuses, and news of the prisoners in Arabic and English.

From about 2009, a group of auto-critics emerged who advocated for greater democratization and transparency of the Brotherhood. The majority of these young Muslim Brotherhood bloggers were male, but there were some important female voices too, and for the most part they did not know each other offline. Nevertheless, they formed a strong networked community and many eventually became acquainted with each other in person during offline demonstrations and meetings. These bloggers started by writing about questionable political strategies of the Brotherhood leadership, such as the way they entered into alliances with the Mubarak government during the elections of 2005. These youth also complained about the group's rigid hierarchical structure, which does not allow the younger generation to have any role in the decision-making process. They came up with their own platform for reform of the movement that included: (1) that the leadership make information available and easy to access; (2) that all members be held accountable for their actions, regardless of position and rank; (3) that the group stop operating with such a high degree of secrecy and make information about the rules, laws, and leaders of the group available to all members; (4) and that the group reform along gender lines and allow women to stand for office in the movement.

By 2010 with the widescale adaptation of social media, many Muslim Brotherhood youth switched from blogging to "Facebooking." Social media has several advantages over blogging. The user can easily circulate photos and videos through tagging others. Social media, organized on a horizontal 2.0 system, also provides opportunities for building much larger networks in very short periods. As the young tech-savvy Muslim Brotherhood activists moved to Facebook, their influence spread in fast and furious ways.

Building a Virtual Empire

The online presence of the movement began in the late 1990s, starting with its official Arabic and English websites. These were the group's only *official* media channels where it published statements and the speeches of the movement's top-ranking leader, the *murshid* (General Guide). Other popular websites loosely affiliated with or sympathetic to the Muslim Brotherhood position, such as the Islam advice website, islamonline.net, were also somehow part of the Brotherhood presence online.[3] In the 2000s, with the mounting ubiquity of the internet among youth, the group was aware that it needed to grow its online audience. The group worked on developing a network of websites for different purposes that was mainly directed at university students and intellectuals.

The older generation in the Brotherhood, wanting to supervise the discussions and activities of the group's youth on social media, launched an alternative to Facebook by the name of Ikhwanbook. This Facebook-style social media site was created as a space for Muslim Brotherhood members to interact. The group stated that Ikhwanbook offered a higher level of privacy than Facebook as on Facebook strangers can see the pictures or videos of members. At the same time, the group claimed that Ikhwanbook was a good opportunity for Muslims to establish their own networks, rather than using a "Western, or Israeli-biased website like Facebook" (Anonymous source, personal communication, April 12, 2011).

In 2010 the group also launched Ikhwanwiki, the Muslim Brotherhood's virtual encyclopaedia, Ikhwan Twitter, and Ikhwantube, the Muslim Brotherhood's platform for videos. These platforms serve as a valuable resource insofar as they house thousands of documents, books not published because of censorship and political constraints, speeches, statements, and videos. Having said that, these projects differ in significant ways from the original ones on which they are based, Wikipedia and YouTube, insofar as they severely restricted capabilities for user-generated content.

The Brotherhood's attempt to conquer virtual spaces reveals a few important points. First, the official Brotherhood initiatives online were mere imitations, but with severe restrictions to users, on already established and successful projects such as Facebook and YouTube. The group never created unique projects and technical innovations that were organic to an Islamic environment. Second, the group copies the design and appearance of the famous websites, but does not adopt the core principles behind them about user-generated content. For example, anyone with an account can upload a YouTube video as long as they abide by the basic rules set by the site (videos should not incite violence, violate a group's rights, and so on). In contrast, with Ikhwantube, participants are not allowed to upload any video; they can only receive media produced by the movement. The same thing can be said about Ikhwanwiki. In contrast to Wikipedia, which operates on a principle of crowdsourcing, visitors to Ikhwanwiki cannot produce or edit entries, they can simply consume the prepackaged knowledge formally produced by the group. For these reasons, we cannot call these Muslim Brotherhood platforms "social media." Rather, they are websites that serve as archives of the group's materials and official thought.

After the 25 January Revolution, it became clear that social media can play a major role in organizing and mobilizing audiences. At the same time, the social media of the Muslim Brotherhood failed to attract a considerable audience, which led to their abandoning Ikhwanbook and Ikhwan Twitter. A young ex-member of the Brotherhood, Amar, explained to the author that the reason behind the failure of the group's social media websites was that "they were supervised and monitored by the group. All our accounts were under the supervision of the Muslim Brotherhood electronic committees. Many of us got messages telling us to delete or change the style of our writings and some of our posts were deleted." Since the Muslim Brotherhood wanted to have a presence and influence on social media, it took an alternative path: it opted to control successful pages on Facebook and use them in the service of the group.

Social Media and the Egyptian Revolution

Shortly before January 25, 2011 there were some successful pages on Facebook that attracted hundreds of thousands of youths. One of these pages was "We are all Khaled Said." It was established after the young man Khaled Said was killed in the street by two policemen, and the page turned into a youth movement and anti-torture campaign that eventually set the date for the 25 January Revolution (see Chapter 6). Another important page was "6th of April," established in 2006. The movement took its name from the strike of April 6, which was organized and mobilized on Facebook. The admins who coordinated the strike, Israa Abdel Fatah and Ahmed Maher, decided to establish a movement online, something that they could not do offline due to political restrictions. Their Facebook page and youth movement have been an important entity to recruit new members and organize events and demonstrations. Prior to the revolution all these pages operated anonymously, something that youth members generally accepted. The main demand of the Egyptian youth at that time was *change*; however, the direction and the type of that change were not clear. One youth explained during an interview with the author: "We were born during the Mubarak presidency, and we were afraid to die while he was still the president. I myself wanted to see any change, even if it would be worse."

We can generally observe an overlap between the admins and fans of "Rassd," "We are all Khaled Said," and "6th of April" even if they represent different campaigns, namely election monitoring, anti-torture, and labor respectively. The pages also differ organizationally. "Rassd" operates as a professional news media network,

"We are all Khaled Said" as a campaign and political forum, whereas "6th of April" is the platform for an organized youth movement. Late in 2010 Rassd, in co-ordination with the pages "We are all Khaled Said" and "6th of April," called for a demonstration online to reject the results of the legislative elections. The relationship between the admins of the three pages was not clear that time. However, it was customary from the late 1990s for youth to work in coalition frameworks offline and online.

After the fall of Mubarak in 2011, many Muslim Brotherhood members claimed that Wael Ghonim, who was revealed as one of the two main admins of the "We are all Khaled Said" Facebook page, had had close ties with the Muslim Brotherhood when he had been a student at university, although he does not appear to have been a formal member of the group. He was also instrumental in establishing one of the biggest Islamic websites: www.islamway.com. The second admin on the page, Abdelrahman Mansour, is an ex-Muslim Brotherhood member. When the identities of these admins became known, it became clearer that the admins of the main political opposition groups were linked through ties around the Brotherhood.

From Online to Offline

Even though Rassd was established by Muslim Brotherhood youth to escape from the hierarchical structure of the group, the admins exerted hierarchy and control over the fans of their page. Prior to the 25 January Revolution, when the page still operated as an anonymous youth-run news site, the admins exhibited behavior that was less than democratic. The page prevented fans from publishing directly on the page's wall, and all material had to be filtered through the admin. The admin would also ban or block fans who used strong language or whose opinions diverged too far from the group. In their *unconscious* search for an anti-hierarchical model, many fans of the page took matters into their own hands and organized themselves away from the heavy-handed control of the page admins.

Members of main youth pages started to get to know each other by exchanging messages on Facebook, and then private emails, and mobile numbers. Conversations they started online often led to offline meetings at coffee shops or parks. Soon, these meetings became bigger as participants spread the idea among their own social networks. As different networks of people from online met offline, their discussions became more heated and more serious. These meetings created trust and later helped for more effective mobilization. For these young people, what began online with activism and network building could easily be transferred to the streets. Their online activism, in other words, was a good experience that eased them into activism offline. The more they connected, online and offline, the more these increasingly politicized youth recognized that they were a potentially powerful force. They got the feeling that the regime could not harm them, or stop them. According to a young woman:

What was done on the internet could easily be done in the streets. We gained a lot of experience on Facebook and nothing bad happened to us. I remember the first time I became a member of this page, and started to participate in discussions, I used a fake name. But after a while I started to log in with my real name. Democracy is something to be learned.

(Personal communication, August 19, 2011)

It is widely believed that the "We are all Khaled Said" page published the first call for the revolution to take place on 25 January, which was "Police Day." By choosing this date they wanted to show that they rejected police practices and the November parliamentary election results. Within less than a day the other pages, Rassd and the "6th of April," joined the call and took part in coordinating the offline actions. Even though the Muslim Brotherhood officially announced that it would not participate in the demonstrations, Rassd was actively mobilizing for it. The Muslim Brotherhood youth, with over 15 years of blogging and joining coalition politics, had formed its own "youth collective consciousness" (El-Taraboulsi et al., 2011). They considered themselves to be different from the older generations, who had not faced the same economic, political, or social challenges and did not experience society in the same way. Sameh, a young programmer and Muslim Brotherhood member, explained:

Our generation is different. After my father graduated from university the state offered him a job. Everything was easier. Before the revolution I felt like a young Egyptian who was oppressed and needed to do something about that, more than [I felt like] a young Muslim Brotherhood member who should obey the decisions of his leadership.

(Personal communication, May 23, 2011)

The internet and social media helped in building such youth consciousness, but youth crises of poverty and injustice were even more powerful contributing factors. It is for this reason that when the internet was cut (for four days) during the 18 days of the revolution, from January 25 to February 11, 2011, people were still pouring into Tahrir Square (El-Taraboulsi, 2011).

From January 25, Rassd succeeded in reporting on news of the Egyptian revolution from all regions of the country. The page received copious pictures and videos from "citizen journalists." By the site giving credit to the mainly young volunteer journalists for their contributions, others were encouraged to send in their materials. The visitors and contributors to the page had a general perception of it as a neutral space with anonymous admins who were not affiliated with any particular group or orientation. Many supporters of the page and the revolution wanted to maintain a non-partisan stance and not support one group over another. As one activist, Salma Ali, states: "We trust depoliticized pages because we feel that they were established in the public interest, not to help the interests of a specific party or group."

Soon after Mubarak stepped down on February 11, 2011, a revolution started in Libya on February 17, 2011. Rassd contacted some of the Libyan revolutionaries; it shared the experience of R.N.N. with them and helped them to establish the Facebook page B.R.Q. (from the Arabic word for "lightning") to cover the Libyan revolution. Later on, because of the destruction of the communication infrastructure in Libya, some Egyptians took the responsibility of running B.R.Q. from Egypt. Admins from Syria, Morocco, and Yemen joined B.R.Q., which was declared a page for all revolutionaries in the Arab world. A similar story happened with the Syrian revolution. Some Syrian revolutionaries, under the tutelage of R.N.N., established the Sham News Network (S.N.N.) and this became one of the most active and important news sources for the Syrian revolution. The experience also extended to Turkey, as Turkish youth cooperated with the admins from Egypt's R.N.N. to establish a Turkish version of it. In this way Turkey, Syria, Libya, Egypt, and Yemen were interlinked on social media to cover the revolutions in the region.

By the end of 2011, it became clear that Rassd was a clear-cut Muslim Brotherhood page. In the clashes between the Egyptian youth and the temporary caretaker government, the Supreme Council of Armed Forces (SCAF) in November 2011, the page termed the youth "thugs" and called for the parliamentary elections to be hurried through. In other words, it was directly voicing the formal line of the Muslim Brotherhood. From that time forward the page did not even disguise that it was a mouthpiece for the Brotherhood not only in Egypt but in the other countries where it had helped to establish similar social media news networks. It supported the Muslim Brotherhood in the elections that took place in Tunisia and Libya.

By the end of 2011, the director of Rassd, Amr Farag, had become the person responsible for the "electronic media" section in the Freedom and Justice party, the political wing of the Muslim Brotherhood. It is clear that the Rassd admins had reached a compromise with the Muslim Brotherhood for mutual benefit; the Muslim Brotherhood benefitted from the popularity of Rassd and the Rassd gained from the expected domination of the group in the political arena in Egypt.

Conclusions: Social Media as a New Space for Democracy?

> The Internet is the fabric of our lives. If information technology is the present-day equivalent of electricity in the industrial era, in our age the Internet could be likened to both the electrical grid and the electric engine because of its ability to distribute the power of information throughout the entire realm of human activity. [. . .] The Internet is the technological basis for the organizational form of the Information Age: the network.
>
> (Castells, 2001, p. 1)

Castells argues that the internet's horizontal network structure is the main organizational form in the information age, but I believe that it can also be used for building hierarchical structures. Similar to in the offline world, hierarchical structures online can also be characterized by strong supervision and by flow of orders, not information, from top to bottom. While ideological divisions are eliminated in online networking structures, they appear strongly in online hierarchical ones.

The experience of Rassd on Facebook illustrates not only the generational conflict within the Muslim Brotherhood, but also ways that online networks can be co-opted to serve traditional hierarchical patriarchal power structures. The Brotherhood youth briefly succeeded through blogging and social media to build their own networks. However, the success of Rassd and other Facebook pages in mobilizing for the revolution made the elders of the Brotherhood keen to control Facebook, especially after it became clear that Ikhwanbook was a failed experiment.

A medical doctor and member of the Muslim Brotherhood provided details of how Rassd was co-opted by the Brotherhood leadership (personal communication, May 17, 2011). He recounted:

> After the 25 January revolution, and after the clear success of R.N.N. and its role in the revolution, Khairat al-Shater [the vice-leader] called the admins for a meeting. He offered them some privileges, mainly the chance to rise in the hierarchical structure of the Brotherhood.[4] The one condition was that Rassd should be under the supervision of the Muslim Brotherhood. The admins stared at him in astonishment and replied: "You know we succeeded because we were away from you. If the page falls under your supervision, it will fail. The Brotherhood does not want to understand that we are in a different age. If you [ruling elders] continue living and behaving as if we were still in the 1960s, the group will dissolve in a few years' time."

Tempted by promises of rising through the Brotherhood ranks, and with visions of a Brotherhood-led government, the admins accepted the deal. From September 2011, the Rassd admins took direct orders from Khairat al-Shater. The page launched a website and hired tens of correspondents, paid directly by the Muslim Brotherhood, to cover news in Egypt and in other Muslim majority countries. Rassd, which began as an independent youth initiative and successful network, developed into a top-down mouthpiece of the Brotherhood and became part of its media empire.

The fact that the Muslim Brotherhood transferred its hierarchical model to Rassd does not mean that the group can conquer the internet, or that hierarchies will supersede horizontal networks. The networking model online remains powerful. The initial networks born out of Rassd continue to work independently of Rassd and the Brotherhood. Online social networking communities are highly viral and networks are born of other networks (Rosendorf, 2006). Another point we need to remember is that networks have the ability to work independently and freely from their initiators. Rassd worked as a tool to connect individuals with common interests at a specific moment. When the time was right, the individuals devised their own ways to connect and organize themselves away from the page. When it became known that Rassd was a Muslim Brotherhood page, it lost its credibility and many networks separated from it. In November 2012 many anti-Brotherhood pages whose admins were early fans of Rassd called on their own fans to "unlike" the page and to block or report it as a way of punishing the page admins for their affiliation with the Muslim Brotherhood. One of the anti-Brotherhood pages put up a post that circulated among independent networks and that crystalized the state of the larger struggle: "The war between the 'Brotherhood state' and the 'Egyptian state' is not only offline but also online."

Notes

1. The author obtained the material for this study through participation observation in many Facebook pages and from interviews with members in the Muslim Brotherhood. Upon their request, some of these interviewees are anonymous.
2. Frozen memberships occurred when some members from the younger generation of the Muslim Brotherhood were at loggerheads with the leadership, who insisted on blind obedience. The leaders would not concede any of the demands of the youth for reform, more freedoms, and the ability to take initiative. These younger members, instead of resigning from the group, decided to freeze their memberships, meaning that they were still counted in the group in organizational terms, but they did not participate in activities.
3. The website was launched in 1998 in Arabic and English versions from Egypt to deal with Islamic problems and Muslim minorities in the West and to present Islam to non-Muslims. It was financed by Qatar, but the administration was in Egypt, and the responsible person was Sheikh YusefAlqaradawy, one of the religious leaders of the Muslim Brotherhood. In 2008, the financing organization in Qatar decided to expel the editors and the managers because of a clash over the editorial policy and the topics of the website. At the same time, its Egyptian editors launched another website under the name www.onislam.com.
4. Escalating a member in the group means to give him a higher administrative position. The escalating within the group has no clear standards or conditions and one of the complaints of the Muslim Brotherhood youth is that the sons of the group's leaders are being escalated faster than those who are from non-Muslim brotherhood families, even if the formers are less active.

References

Alanani, K. (2008). *The Muslim Brotherhood youth search for a new path*. Retrieved April, 12, 2010 from www.ikhwanweb.com/uploads/trans/7BXPNZWKTKANMDG.pdf
al-Banna, H. (2006). *The messages*. Cairo: Al-Shrook Publications.
Beckett, C. (2008): *Super media: Saving journalism so it can save the world*. Oxford: Blackwell Publishing.
Castells, M. (2001). *The internet galaxy: Reflections on internet, business and society*. Oxford: Oxford University Press.
Castells, M. (2010). *The rise of network society*. Oxford: Wiley Blackwell.
Dyson, E. (1998). *Release 2.1: A design for living in the digital age*. London: Penguin.
El-Taraboulsi, S. et al. (2011). *Youth activism and public space in Egypt*. Cairo: The American University in Cairo Press & Innovations in Civic Participations Publications.

Fauad, W. (2009). Facebook and the Arab youth: Social activism or cultural liberation? In M. Elmenshawy (Ed.), *New chapter of political Islam* (91–100). Washington DC: World Security Institute.

Ferdinand, P. (Ed.). (2000). *The internet, democracy and democratization.* London: Frank Cass Publishers Ltd.

Germany, J. (Ed.). (2006). *Person-to-person-to-person: Harnessing the political power of online social networks and user generated content.* Washington DC: G. W.'s Institute for Politics, Democracy & the Internet.

Gross, A. & Acquisti, A. (2005, November 7). Information revelation and privacy in online social networks: Case study of Facebook. Paper presented to ACM Workshop on Privacy in the Electronic Society (WPES), Alexandria, Virginia.

Habermas, J. (1989). *The structural transformation of the public sphere: An inquiry into a category of bourgeois society.* T. Burger & F. Lawrence (Trans.). Cambridge, MA: Massachusetts Institute of Technology Press.

Jordan, T. (2003). *Cyberpower: The culture and politics of cyberspace and the Internet.* London & New York: Routledge.

Khamis, S. & Vaughn, K. (2011). *Cyberactivism in the Egyptian revolution: How civic engagement and citizen journalism tilted the balance.* Retrieved June 13, 2012 from www.arabmedia-society.com/?article=769

Mascaro, C. & Goggins, S. P. (2011). *Brewing up citizen engagement: The coffee party on Facebook.* Brisbane: QUT.

Matthew, T. J. (1997). Power shift: The rise of global civil society. *Foreign Affairs*, 76(1), 50–66.

Metzgar, E. & Maruggi, A. (2009). *Social media and the 2008 U.S. presidential election.* Massachusetts: Society for New Communications Research.

Miller, L. (1995). Women and children first: Gender and the settling of the electronic frontier. In I. Boal & J. Brook (Eds.), *Resisting the virtual life: The culture and politics of information* (49–57). San Francisco: City Lights Books.

Mossberger, K., Tolbert, C. J. & McNeal, R. S. (2008). *Digital citizenship: The internet, society and participation.* Cambridge, MA: Massachusetts Institute of Technology Press.

Oates, S. & Owen, D. (2006). *The internet and politics: Citizens, voters and activists.* London & New York: Routledge.

Rash, W. (1997). *Politics on the nets: Wiring the political process.* New York: W. H. Freeman.

Rosen, J. (2008). *Citizen media.* Retrieved March 12, 2013 from www.youtube.com/watch?v=WtYVclYXtF4

Rosendorf, C. (2006). Building networks of informed online adults. In J. Germany (Ed.), *Person-to-person-to-person: Harnessing the political power of online social networks and user generated content* (33–36). Washington DC: G. W.'s Institute for Politics, Democracy & the Internet.

Saco, D. (2002). *Cybering democracy: Public space and the internet.* Minneapolis: University of Minnesota Press.

Toffler, A. & Toffler, H. (1995). *Creating a new civilization: The politics of the third wave.* Atlanta GA: Turner Publications.

12

DIGITAL TECHNOLOGY AS SURVEILLANCE

The Green Movement in Iran[1]

Narges Bajoghli

From the advent of Iran's Green Movement in 2009 to the Arab revolts that began with Tunisia in December 2010, a wealth of debates and discussions have ensued about the role of social media as an effective organizing tool in these movements.[2] Though the first flush of overwrought enthusiasm is long past, there is consensus that Facebook, Twitter, and other Web 2.0 applications, particularly on handheld devices, have been effective organizing tools against the slower moving security apparatuses of authoritarian states. The new technology has also helped social movements to tell their story to the outside world, unhindered by official news blackouts, unbothered by state censors, and unfiltered by the traditional Western media.

But, what happens when digital means of communication and coordination are no longer an option for activists or they are, at least, a very dangerous option? The state of activism in Iran, nearly four years after the largest protests since the 1979 Revolution, offers a cautionary tale for partisans of social media's emancipatory promise. The internet, in fact, has become the site of a protracted cat-and-mouse game as the state attempts to reassert its control after the 2009 presidential elections, which large segments of the population believe to have been rigged by the state for the incumbent Mahmoud Ahmadinejad. The very qualities that make new media so attractive to people seeking change from below also make them an ideal means of surveillance and manipulation from above.

What are the methodological implications for social scientists doing research on mobile and digital technologies when the plug can be pulled on them so quickly? There is increasing attention in the anthropology of media and communications studies on "the digital." Questions of how to study "the digital" (Boellstroff, 2010; Boellstorff, Nardi, Pearce, & Taylor, 2012; Coleman, 2010; Miller & Slater, 2001), what constitutes the field of study and the users of digital technology, attention to the infrastructure of creating "the digital" (Larkin, 2008), and how people interact with the mediality of the new and ever-evolving technologies, are questions that scholars contend with. Building on these works, in this chapter I consider the example of Iran in order to raise questions of control, resistance, and cyber warfare.

The question of the danger of new media, or even the *absence* of new media, is one that resonates with the experience of living in post-2009 Tehran, the focus of this chapter. This struggle over digital technology is a locale for developing notions of what the future of the Islamic Republic should look like. Given high external pressures from the United States, Israel, and exiled opposition groups, as well as constant pressure from internal opposition movements (the student movement, women's movement, labor movement, teachers, movement) that challenge the Islamic Republic, a prime question for the Iranian state is who should be allowed to have access to technology and information. As online interactions are increasingly pulled offline in Iran, I argue that it is even more imperative that we do ethnographic, offline work as social scientists when studying online activity.

This chapter draws upon my ethnographic work in Iran over the past eight years. I left Iran for New York in August 2009, after having lived there for a total of five years, and I return regularly for extended periods of time. This chapter focuses on how protesters in Tehran used new media on the ground following the 2009 presidential elections, and what has happened since that time.

Media in Iran

The Iranian case offers a tremendous amount to social scientific understandings of media due to the rich media landscape in the country, and in the Iranian diaspora. In spite of the authoritarian nature of the Islamic Republic and its attempts to control media production since 1979, the Iranian case complicates notions of state-centered media, and "resistance" media, and it sheds light on the new field of cyber warfare, which remains understudied.

In the case of the Iranian revolution, from the 1979 generation to the present, different media forms have been critical indicators of generational sensibilities, from graffiti, posters, faxes, and other "small media" that characterized the early days, to work in feature film, television, and social media identified with the contemporary moment. Scholars have studied the "small media" practices of the 1979 revolutionary moment (Sreberny-Mohammadi & Mohammadi, 1994), arguing that the dissemination of cassettes with Ayatollah Khomeini's sermons, and the photocopying of open letters and leaflets from different opposition groups, produced a coherent and viable "imagined community." This "small media" was in contrast to the "big" state-owned mass media of the Shah of Iran, Mohammad Reza Pahlavi, who ruled with an iron fist over Iran from 1941 until his overthrow in 1979.

Today, despite state controls on media technologies, Iran is also home to a thriving blog culture. Young Iranians and the clerical elite alike are both conversant in digital technologies (Alavi 2006; Kamalipour, 2010; Sreberny & Khiabany, 2010).

Persian is among the most widely used languages on the internet. As Annabelle Sreberny & Gholam Khiabany explore in *Blogistan* (2010), blogging in Iran and by Iranians in the diaspora is a dynamic field of inquiry and one that defies stereotypes. Middle-class urbanized youth blog, but so do members of the clergy, the paramilitary Basij, and the Revolutionary Guards (RG); men blog, but so do large numbers of women, from all ethnic and socio-economic backgrounds. As Sreberny and Khiabany highlight, although the internet remains a relatively expensive commodity in Iran (especially high-speed internet), it has flourished at an exponential rate in the past few years.

Despite the high levels of bloggers in Iran, states and corporations have inverted the initial "emancipatory" promise of the internet for surveillance purposes. Rebecca MacKinnon advances the term "networked authoritarianism" in her book *Consent of the networked* (2012) to refer to states like China and Iran, in which state intelligence agencies no longer need to rely on informants, but employ software and hardware to give them information on citizens.[3] MacKinnon notes: "A networked authoritarian regime benefits from the lively online discussion of many social issues and even policy problems. The government follows online chatter, which alerts officials to potential unrest, better enabling authorities to address issues and problems before they get out of control" (p. 34). In the Iranian case, questions about the role of the state in limiting internet access, the creation of a "National Intranet" in order to restrict the flow of information,[4] and the latest development of cyber warfare, discussed further below, all still need to be explored.

The Seeds of the Green Movement

The Green Movement did not emerge out of thin air. Although many groups and individuals who participated in the 1979 Revolution were sidelined after the establishment of the Islamic Republic and heavily persecuted, a growing number of social movements began to reemerge after the end of the Iran–Iraq War (1980–1988). The Green Movement (green is in reference to the green campaign color of Mir-Hossein Mousavi; green is also the color of Islam), an amalgamation of various strands of society, owes its genesis to the groundwork laid in the previous 20 years. Specifically, the Green Movement came about through the work of the women's movement, the student movement (Rivetti & Cavatorta, 2012), the labor movement, and the reform movement. Each of these movements played a large role in galvanizing their members into action and in disseminating information to their networks in the aftermath of the elections. Given that nearly 70% of Iran's population of 75 million is under the age of 35, the student movements of the past decade have played a large role in mobilizing, and, in some cases, radicalizing, young people. The violent crackdown by state forces on students in the University of Tehran in July 1999 continues to play a large role in social memory, as does the subsequent suppression of student protests. The strong and enduring women's rights movements showed their impact on the Green Movement by the fact that women dominated the protests in numbers and were at the head of many of the charges against the pro-state Basij militia who attacked protesters. The labor movement, especially the bus drivers' union and the teachers' union, played a substantial role in the aftermath of the elections. The networks built in civil society organizations during the presidency of Mohammad Khatami (1997–2005) were influential in spreading news of the protests, and the plethora of journalists from banned newspapers (Yaghmaian, 2002) played a large role during the evolution of the Green Movement in getting news out of the country. Added to this were small pockets of disaffected reformist politicians and reformist Revolutionary Guards and Basij, who supported the Green Movement (personal interviews). All of these informal channels fed the Green Movement, and, in turn, helped spread engagement to other sectors of society.[5] As Kevan Harris (2012) notes:

> Individuals printed out pictures of dead or wounded participants of earlier protests and held them aloft during marches. Since most protesters were not Internet users, they had not heard of these casualties. Individuals then used their cellphones and cameras to take pictures of the printed photos in order to show them to relatives and coworkers who had not attended the rallies. People took pictures of pictures, of crowds, of themselves in crowds, and of other people taking pictures. This was not a postmodern exercise but a highly emotional interaction ritual that drew in participants and convinced them to convince others to join.
>
> (p. 441)

The participants in the demonstrations throughout the first year of the Green Movement included a cross-generational segment of the population, some of whom were more comfortable with digital technologies than others. Thus, the reliance on offline contacts and offline news outlets (especially satellite television stations) cannot be understated. Although satellite dishes are formally illegal in Iran, it is believed that upwards of 60% of families all over the country watch satellite television (Wojcieszak, Smith, & Enayat, 2012). In the Iranian satellite sphere over 20 stations are broadcast in Persian to Iran from the United States alone (Naficy, 1993), while others are broadcast from Europe. For news, people relied on satellite television. BBC Persian, which had started broadcasting not long before the elections, became a lifeline, as did Voice of America's Persian service. It is important to note that protests occurred not just in Tehran, but in Isfahan, Tabriz, Mashad, Gorgan, Qazvin, Babol, Ahvaz, and Zanjan. Nonetheless, the post-election suppression and the clampdown on technology was focused on Tehran.

The Post-Election Protests

The four candidates of the 2009 presidential elections in Iran were the incumbent president Mahmoud Ahmadinejad, former prime minister (1980s) Mir-Hossein

Mousavi, former chairman of the parliament Mehdi Karrubi, and former chief commander of the Revolutionary Guards Mohsen Rezaei. In the aftermath of the June 12, 2009 presidential elections, hundreds of thousands, some claim millions, poured onto the streets of Tehran and other main cities of the country to protest the announcement of Ahmadinejad's victory with 65% of the vote.

After one week of non-violent protests, the state deployed anti-riot police and Basij militia to attack protesters.[6] Throughout the summer of 2009, scores of protesters, student leaders, reformist politicians, women's rights activists, journalists, and artists were rounded up and imprisoned. Though estimates vary on the exact number of those imprisoned for partaking in the Green Movement, the BBC reported that 170 people were arrested after the first two days of protests in June. Another 200 students were arrested in the raid on the University of Tehran dormitories on June 15, and 100 students were arrested on June 16 at Shiraz University. During June 2009 alone, *The Guardian* estimated that 500 people were arrested.

The Green Movement created the largest demonstrations in the history of the Islamic Republic, and the state responded by imprisoning former ministers and vice presidents, in addition to activists and lay people participating in the demonstrations. According to opposition accounts, 107 individuals were killed between the aftermath of the June 2009 elections and March 2010. These deaths include those on the streets during the protests, as well as those in prisons and in the hospital. This number is significantly lower than the number of dead in the Egyptian uprising of 2011, but as news of the torture and killings in the prisons and streets began to leak out, the anger grew, and the heavy-handed suppression eventually quelled the Green Movement for the moment.

The predominant feature of the Green Movement, beyond being the largest protests since the 1979 Iranian Revolution, was the way its birth and development were captured and spread across the world via social media. Unlike the 25 January Revolution in Egypt in 2011, foreign and domestic media were not allowed to cover the events, and foreign journalists had their permits and visas revoked shortly after the protests started. The few foreign correspondents allowed to stay were kept under close scrutiny by the Ministry of Culture. In one lunch I had with a European journalist in July 2009, government minders kept watch over us from at least two different tables in the restaurant.

Thus, it was ordinary citizens, relying on their camera phones and their Facebook and YouTube accounts, who had to get the news out to the world. The Burma protests of 2007 had raised awareness on this scale through social media, a process that is captured in the film *Burma VJ: Reporting from a closed country* (Østergaard et al., 2008). The spread of news about the Burmese and Iranian protests movements signaled the start of a new era of "citizen journalism." As the excitement about new media technologies and the ways they allow citizens to bypass state-controlled media caught people's imagination, corporations and states began to develop means to control and monitor these very same channels. The use of new media technology has been very important in maintaining certain social movements in Iran and in developing others, but it has become an increasingly limited tool since the start of the Green Movement.

Digital Technology in Iran: Passing the Word

Cell phone technology has spread like wildfire over the last half-decade in Iran. In 2004 it cost around $1,000 to buy a SIM card, but today SIM cards are available for $5 and the latest cell phones are on sale countrywide, albeit at highly inflated prices due to the sanctions.[7] During the Green Movement protests, Iranians could not connect to the web from their cell phones, because the 3G network was only introduced in Iran in January 2012. In 2009 cell phones, whether "smart" or not, had four main uses: Phone calls, texting, capturing photographic or video images, and using Bluetooth. Bluetooth, an application that facilitates communication between electronic devices over short distances, allowed the Green Movement (Greens) to share footage with each other in the streets and then upload the images to a computer at home. Many of the well-known protest videos that were seen on YouTube abroad circulated inside Iran via Bluetooth on mobile phones, since Iranians' access to YouTube was irregular, at best, due to internet filters.

The Western press began to erroneously call the Green Movement Iran's "Twitter Revolution." Contrary to reports, Twitter was not in wide use in Iran among the protesters. According to consulting firm Sysomos (Evans, 2009), the number of Twitter accounts that had been created inside Iran as of mid-May 2009 was 8,600. After the June election, this number jumped to 19,000, an improbable leap given that internet speeds and mobile technology were brought down during that very same period. Some journalists did use Twitter, and Iranians from the diaspora who were in Iran during that summer also tweeted. It is most likely that the increase in numbers was due to coordinated efforts by activists outside the country and Iranians in the diaspora to change their Twitter setting location to Iran in order to protect online activists in the country from the state crackdown on digital media users.

In mid-June 2009, the first week of the massive post-election protests, Tehran residents passed the word about gatherings to strangers on the streets, in shops, and in taxis, as well as to friends and acquaintances via cell phones. The state, however, owned the companies that provided all cell phone and internet service in the country at the time. By the end of the month, officials there had blocked SMS service and slowed down internet speeds, compelling protesters to rely on offline contacts. One node of information was the highly organized campaign of Mir-Hossein Mousavi, who had been a favorite to unseat Ahmadinejad but finished a distant second to the incumbent in the official results. At afternoon protests, Mousavi volunteers held up signs that read, "Tomorrow, 4p.m., Revolution Square," announcing the time and place of the next day's demonstration in broad daylight. The next morning, alarming rumors would spread: The police had cordoned off the demonstration site's perimeter; security forces had been given the green light to fire on the crowd; Mousavi had disowned the event; and so on. People looking to protest nevertheless showed up near the designated spot in the afternoon, pretending that they were out shopping or on their way home. As the crowds swelled, they joined together and walked to the rally point.

By July 2009, security forces had begun to assault protesters in the streets without restraint. Iranians anxious about loved ones' safety had to rely solely on person-to-person contacts for reassurance, since the telecommunications company had shut down SMS service. The protests did not stop, however: Since most of them took place around 4p.m., there was time during the day to relay news of changed locations in various old-fashioned ways—landlines or word of mouth. For news, people relied on satellite television, BBC Persian, and Voice of America's Persian service. For those who had the patience to deal with the slowed internet speeds, or who went to internet cafés, Facebook became a hub of information sharing. However, as Sreberny and Khiabany note in *Blogistan* (2010):

> There is little evidence that Twitter and Facebook or YouTube played a major role in organizing demonstrations. They did became [*sic*] channels through which messages could be sent to international media organisations that had little access and first-hand information about what was happening in Iran. These sites also attracted messages and actions of international solidarity as well as mobilising the Iranian diaspora.
>
> (p. 175)

Scare Tactics

For all its autocratic tendencies, the Islamic Republic is not a police state that induces dread like the Shah's regime did before 1979 or like Asad's Syria. Before the advent of the Green Movement, Iranians were not afraid to voice discontent with the government to strangers in shops or taxis. However, that all changed in the summer of 2009. The crackdown on communications spread something close to paranoia in society.

Security forces picked up people in the streets and scrutinized the text messages and address books saved on their cell phones. Interrogators presented arrested students with printed-out transcripts of their cell phone conversations, saying they were evidence of plotting against the state. Most alarming of all were news reports days after the protests started in June 2009 that Nokia Siemens Networks had provided Iran with equipment that allowed the state-controlled telecom company to monitor its customers' calls (Fildes, 2009). There were also stories to the effect that Nokia Siemens had provided internet censorship tools to the Iranian government (Rhoads & Chao, 2009). These tales reverberate in Tehran to this day.

People began to suspect that the government could listen to them via any cell phone, even one that was not in use. Two friends sitting down to talk would first put their cell phones away in their pockets or purses. As the rumors of surveillance grew, Tehranis would turn off their phones, remove the batteries and SIM card, and place everything on top of the table in plain view. This happened in larger groups at coffeehouses or restaurants, and at family gatherings or parties in private homes. Only then would conversations continue.

For the first time, I witnessed paranoia and fear like I never had before in my past 10 years in Iran. Meeting with friends in coffee shops or in homes or even in cars, we turned off our cell phones and took the batteries out. For the first time, we looked around as we spoke about all that was going on. For the first time, we lowered our voices in public when criticizing all the arrests. For the first time, my friends dared not call one another on our cell phones, especially those who had been interrogated and detained.

Whether any of these rumors were true was beside the point. Daily news of interrogations, mass arrests, and torture, rape, and death in prison, the sight of riot police deployed continuously in every major square (a novelty for post-revolution generations), the sound of security men on motorcycles, batons and guns in hand, roaring down main thoroughfares, all made it very difficult to take a deep breath and question the credibility of the talk of pervasive surveillance. The anxiety came to overwhelm the comfort protesters took in the fact that the world was witness to what was unfolding in Iran via social media.

Adaptation

It is true that mobile and digital technology gave a strong sense of comfort to people during the protests. At least the world was bearing witness to what was unfolding in Iran thanks to circulated images on YouTube, Twitter, and Facebook, but, at the same time, there was a very real anxiety that new media technology helped foster due to how easily it could serve as a surveillance tool. As trepidation grew in tandem with the state's crackdown, people assiduously sought advice on protecting their identities online. Iranians in the diaspora emailed primers on safe internet usage to friends and relatives back home. Iranian American computer engineers in Silicon Valley recommended that all messages be sent as attachments rather than in the body of emails, so as to get around surveillance programs that flag email accounts by searching for words judged sensitive by the state. Other advisers cautioned that conversations on Skype were insecure (most Iranians, as a result, prefer the comparable service ooVoo), or that Yahoo! was less safe for email correspondence than Gmail. The list went on and on.

Facebook became another site of secret police scrutiny. As arrests mounted, many Iranians changed their last names on their Facebook pages to "Irani" in order to conceal their identity. Iranians in the diaspora began to do the same, out of solidarity, and in reaction to rumors that the authorities were searching Facebook for the names of anyone entering the country. (To this day, inbound travelers will deactivate their accounts or adopt "Irani" or another pseudonym.) No one knew what the government's internet surveillance capabilities were, so everyone was taking wild guesses. However, with the advent of Iran's cyber army, discussed below, student activists on Facebook have reported receiving messages from users in Iran warning them that they should watch what they post on Facebook as they are being watched.[8]

Eventually, custom internet safety courses developed abroad. Users in Iran can sign up via email at a myriad of sites that offer training free of charge. They receive instructions in how to secure their personal computers as well as how to browse the internet without fear of being monitored. Advice includes: never use Internet Explorer; the safest way to surf the net is Google Chrome; and Macs are safer than PCs. Computer engineers in the diaspora have been very active in providing these tools to their compatriots in Iran, as have non-Iranian internet activists such as Austin Heap, a software developer based in San Francisco. The US government also remains very keen on providing open access technology to opposition activists in Iran, as well as Syria and other countries around the Middle East.

As the Iranian government has become more adept at blocking access to websites a plethora of ways to circumvent the restrictions have emerged. One tool that became highly valuable in Iran was the virtual private network, or VPN, which afforded access to virtually any website, since the actual connection was from a location outside the country. Prior to 2010, Iranians in the diaspora would supply their family and friends back home with usernames and passwords so as to connect to the internet via a university or company abroad. From 2010 to mid-January 2012, Iranians could buy access to their own VPN for $8–10 per month. This service has now been rendered ineffectual, however. State interference has slowed the VPNs so dramatically that they can no longer call up unfiltered websites for the user. From late December 2011 to late February 2012, moreover, the general speed of the internet in Tehran was reduced to near dial-up levels. It is important to note that the slow speeds mostly affect the capital. Even in Karaj, a sprawling city 45 minutes away, the internet is accessible at high speeds. Residents of other big cities also have little trouble. The capital, however, is the prize in the regime's game.

Internet cafés, prior to the summer of 2009, were a fairly safe haven, a place one could go to surf the web without running up against filters, as the staff kept the computer settings up to date and downloaded "filter breaker" programs. The cafés were quickly targeted in the aftermath of the election, however. Many were shut down that summer, and others had to abide by strict new regulations and endure the constant scrutiny of intelligence services. My Facebook account, for instance, was hacked minutes after I left an internet café in the winter of 2011. Today, internet cafés are required to record the national identification card number of each and every patron.

Who's in Charge?

In much the same way that hardline factions in the Islamic Republic cracked down on newspapers and print media during the presidency of Mohammad

Khatami (1997–2005), these same factions began to develop ways of policing new media following the advent of the Green Movement. In September 2009 Etemad-e Mobin, a consortium reported to have extensive links to the Revolutionary Guards, bought a 51% share in Iran's telecommunications company, minutes after it was privatized.[9] The Guards' various fronts and "charitable foundations" already control vast swaths of the construction, oil, and gas, and import–export businesses in Iran, as well as substantial parts of the black market. The telecom deal has deepened the Guards' near monopoly while giving it access to every text message and phone conversation in the country.

The state is already using this power to enhance its control over the flow of information and remind everyone who is in charge. The Ministry of Islamic Guidance, which doles out work permits to reporters and news photographers, now sends morning text messages to inform journalists if they can report on the day's events. When an Iranian nuclear scientist was killed in January 2012, for instance, journalists received a message to say that they did not have permission to work that day.

Complicating matters further is the new "National Internet," or *Internet Melli,* that is underway. The Islamic Republic has reportedly been working on this project since 2005. In August 2011 the minister of communication and information technology, Reza Taqipour Anvari, said a "clean internet" would be launched nationwide in early 2012. Many Iranians believe, however, that this "clean internet" will be an intranet, a closed loop that severely limits Iranians' access to the outside world, in much the same way that systems in Cuba and North Korea do. Rumors abound as to what this "National Internet" will actually entail, and until it is launched there is no way of knowing for certain. Officials, however, say the rationale for the National Internet system is to improve the nation's cyber security, warding off such threats as the Stuxnet worm that attacked the computer networks supporting Iran's nuclear program in 2010, infecting around 30,000 Iranian IP addresses (mostly in government). Determined not to be thus humiliated again, Iran has made its efforts to boost cyber security very public. Since 2009 instances of cyber warfare have increased between Iran, Israel, and the United States. Cyber warfare, which includes "actions by a nation-state to penetrate another nation's computers or networks for the purposes of causing damage or disruption" (Clarke and Knake, 2010), can also be used for espionage. Scholars have written about the work of celebrated hacktivists such as Anonymous (Coleman, 2011), yet we still have limited knowledge of the increasing field of cyber warfare, especially that between states. This area deserves further attention due to the increased reports of cyber warfare between the United States, Israel, and Iran, as well as reports of the creation of an Iranian cyber army as part of the paramilitary Basij organization.

On April 23, 2012 the United States enforced new sanctions on any parties in Syria and Iran that operate information technology repression tools. Though some Iranian activists welcome this move, many also see the irony in these sanctions, as

Iranians remember the news from 2009 that it was the Nokia Siemens Networks that provided this technology to the Iranian state.

More importantly for the Iran case is the fact that foreign governments, such as that of the United States, use the internet to gather data from Iran for their own intelligence purposes. The CIA's Open Source Center reviews millions of tweets, Facebook updates, and internet activity from around the world to build intelligence of what is going on "on the ground." Established in response to a recommendation from the 9/11 Commission, the center's main focus is to collect information from "the Internet, databases, press, radio, television, video, geospatial data, photos, and commercial imagery" (CIA, 2005). However, the center began focusing on social media after watching the Green Movement in Iran in 2009 (Dozier, 2011).

Given the plethora of blogs and news magazines online in Persian, Google announced the launch of their Persian translation tool just six days after the start of the Green Movement protests. On June 18, 2009 Google released this statement:

> Today, we added Persian (Farsi) to Google Translate. This means you can now translate any text from Persian into English and from English into Persian—whether it's a news story, a website, a blog, an email, a tweet or a Facebook message. The service is available free at http://translate.google. com. We feel that launching Persian is particularly important now, given ongoing events in Iran. Like YouTube and other services, Google Translate is one more tool that Persian speakers can use to communicate directly to the world, and vice versa—increasing everyone's access to information.[10]

Further campaigns, whether from the US government or large corporations, began to offer services that would allow Iranian internet users to break through the extensive online censorship system.[11] Some of these same corporations were also involved in helping the Iranian state increase its surveillance. Programmers from all over the world created filter-busters that were posted on Facebook and subsequently emailed by Iranians in the diaspora to friends and family in Iran. The *Los Angeles Times* (2009) reported that Twitter received an urgent message from Secretary of State Hillary Clinton (via one of her staffers, Jared Cohen) to postpone a site maintenance that they had planned, which would result in their site going down for a few hours, until after the protests in Iran had calmed (*BIOSS*, 2009). As the cat-and-mouse game between Iranian government authorities and Green Movement supporters continues, geopolitical considerations, especially from the US, are never far from the picture.

As for the Green Movement, its spiritual leaders Mir-Hossein Mousavi and Mehdi Karroubi were placed under house arrest in 2011. In February 2012, as the one-year anniversary of their confinement approached, activists circulated flyers and posted to opposition websites calling for a new round of protests. Then, for four days in the middle of the month, there was an internet outage in the entire country. The semi-official Mehr news agency said that more than 30 million people were affected. The planned mass rallies did not materialize. Though I do not mean to imply a causal relationship between internet outages and the absence of mass rallies, I do think the Iranian case shows us that with the internet and text message outages, the Islamic Republic communicates to the public that it is alert and that it will respond to any mass display of protest. The Islamic Republic preemptively shuts down the internet and text message capabilities as a warning to any would-be protesters.

Conclusion

Social media and other Web 2.0 applications facilitate organizing for activists around the world. Despite their usefulness for organizing, such tools are also employed by states for surveillance, and not just in places like Iran. This multisited struggle over rights to the internet, from the state, citizens in Iran, the diaspora, internet/computer engineers both abroad and at home, and foreign states, has led to a constant cat-and-mouse game of access, denial, and invasion (as the Stuxnet worm attack revealed). As the atmosphere of surveillance has increased in Iran post-2009, it is imperative for social scientists to look at the social life of online activism, offline. In the realm of media and internet studies, the Iranian case allows us to think through issues of what it means to want to remain invisible on the internet—whether in blogs, or social networking sites, or even on sites such as Skype, ooVoo, and others. What does invisibility in new media mean in an authoritative state? What does it mean to pull the plug on these online communities? Crucial to the discussions of social media in movements around the Middle East and the world is the issue of surveillance. The very mediality of the digital not only makes it an effective organizing tool, but also an ideal locale for surveillance and control.

Notes

1. Parts of this chapter first appeared in Narges Bajoghli, "Iranian Cyber-Struggles," *Middle East Report Online*, May 3, 2012.
2. Though as Adi Kuntsman and Rebecca Stein note, social media have been an important part of the landscape in the Middle East since before these movements as well: www.merip.org/mero/interventions/another-war-zone
3. Yet, cyber surveillance is not limited to states like Iran or China. In 2011, United Kingdom Prime Minister David Cameron made remarks about the need for the British government to expand its monitoring power over the British public's access to mobile services and social networks; in San Francisco, authorities shut down wireless service at several subway stations to prevent planned protests against the shooting of a knife-wielding man by a Bay Area Rapid Transit (BART) police officer; in early 2012, United States Homeland Security officials arrested two young Brits when they landed in Los Angeles International Airport because one of them had tweeted: "Free this week, for

quick gossip/prep before I go and destroy America." The two were held for 12 hours and then deported from the United States.

4. The "National Intranet" is different from the Cuban and North Korean experiences, in that the leaders of those countries limited the internet from the outset, whereas in Iran citizens had access to the internet, but now the state is taking steps to limit that access through the creation of an intranet, sometimes referred to as a "Halal-Web."

5. The post-election protests also had a lot to do with the way the 2009 presidential elections were organized: live debates between the candidates were broadcasts for the first time, increasing the level of competition and street taunting between supporters of the different candidates. Mir-Hossein Mousavi's campaign was also highly organized and used new media in effective ways in the lead-up to the elections. For an in-depth analysis of the preelection atmosphere, see Kevan Harris (2012).

6. Ayatollah Khomeini launched the Basij as a new division of the Revolutionary Guards in 1980, just one year after the Iranian Revolution, and facing the onset of the disastrous Iran–Iraq War. Initially a volunteer paramilitary group in the service of the war effort, hundreds of thousands of men and women received training in the use of weapons in mosques and schools, and by the late 1980s, some three million volunteers had been inducted. Today, long after the Iran–Iraq War ended in 1988, the Basij remain one of the most important sites of state power and citizen participation in the Islamic Republic. Structurally, the Basij is the Revolutionary Guards' (RG) primary apparatus for organizing and controlling the Iranian population through neighborhood branches (Golkar, 2012). In turn, the Basij are active in universities, offices, and factories throughout the country. Since their establishment in 1980, the organization has collaborated with various police enforcement agencies in an effort to exert moral control over society. This has included law enforcement (at times specifically targeting dissidents), the organization of public religious ceremonies, emergency management, providing social services throughout the country.

7. The iPhone 4S, for instance, cost roughly $1,600 USD in January 2012 and this price has only increased since the sanctions have severely devalued Iran's currency.

8. Based on personal interviews conducted by the researcher.

9. That December, the head of the consortium, Majid Soleimanipour, and his wife, were found dead in their Tehran home, reportedly of gas inhalation from a leaky pipe.

10. http://googleblog.blogspot.com/2009/06/google-translates-persian.html

11. See for example Censorship Research Center (retrieved, January 5, 2013): www.haystacknetwork.com

References

Alavi, N. (2006). *We are Iran: The Persian blogs*. Richmond BC: Raincoast Books.

Bajoghli, N. (2012, May 3). Iranian cyber-struggles. *Middle East Report Online*. Retrieved from www.merip.org/mero/interventions/another-war-zone

BIOSS. (2009). Hillary Clinton defends Twitter–Iran position. Retrieved May 19, 2013 from www.billingworld.com/news/2009/06/hillary-clinton-defends-twitter-iran-position.aspx

Boellstorff, T. (2008). *Coming of age in Second Life: An anthropologist explores the virtually human*. New Jersey: Princeton University Press.

Boellstorff, T. (2010). *Coming of age in Second Life: An anthropologist explores the virtually human*. Princeton: Princeton University Press.

Boellstorff, T., Nardi, B., Pearce, C. & Taylor, T. L. (2012). *Ethnography and virtual worlds: A handbook of method*. Princeton: Princeton University Press.

Cellan-Jones, R. (2009, June 22). Hi-tech helps Iranian monitoring. *BBC News*. Retrieved from http://news.bbc.co.uk/2/hi/technology/8112550.stm

CIA. (2005, November 8). Official press release. Retrieved from www.cia.gov/news-information/press-releases-statements/press-release-archive-2005/pr11082005.html

Clarke, R. & Knake, R. (2010). *Cyber war: The next threat to national security and what to do about it*. New York: Ecco.

Coleman, E. G. (2010). Ethnographic approaches to digital media. *Annual Review of Anthropology*, 39, 487–505.

Coleman, E. G. (2011). Hacker politics and publics. *Public Culture*, 23(3), 511–516.

Coleman, E. G. (2012). *Coding freedom: The ethics and aesthetics of hacking*. New Jersey: Princeton University Press.

Dozier, K. (2011). CIA open source center follows foreign Twitter, Facebook accounts. Retrieved May 19, 2013 from www.huffingtonpost.com/2011/11/04/cia-open-source-center_n_1075827.html

Evans, M. (2009, June). A look at Twitter in Iran. Retrieved October 27, 2013 from http://blog.sysomos.com/2009/06/21/a-look-at-twitter-in-iran/

Ferran, L. (2012, January 30). Pair detained in Twitter homeland thread mix-up. *ABC News*. Retrieved from http://abcnews.go.com/Blotter/pair-held-twitter-homeland-threat-mix-reports/story?id=15472918#.T6KvojJYvqs

Fildes, J. (2009, February). MEPs condemn Nokia Siemens "surveillance tech" in Iran. *BBC News*. Retrieved October 27, 2013 from http://news.bbc.co.uk/2/hi/8511035.stm

Golkar, S. (2010). The ideological-political training of Iran's Basij. *Middle East Brief*, 44. Massachusetts: Brandeis University, Crown Center for Middle East Studies.

Golkar, S. (2011). Politics of piety: The Basij and moral control of Iranian society. *The Journal of the Middle East and Africa*, 2(2), 207–219.

Harris, K. (2012). The brokered exuberance of the middle class: An ethnographic analysis of Iran's 2009 Green Movement. *Mobilization: An International Quarterly*, 17(4), 435–455.

Kamalipour, Y. R. (2010). *Media, power, and politics in the digital age: The 2009 presidential election uprising in Iran*. Lanham, Maryland: Rowman & Littlefield Publishers.

Larkin, B. (2008). *Signal and noise: Media, infrastructure, and urban culture in Nigeria*. Durham: Duke University Press Books.

Los Angeles Times. (2009, June 17). Hillary Clinton defends Twitter efforts for Iran.

MacKinnon, R. (2012). *Consent of the networked: The world-wide struggle for internet freedom*. New York: Basic Books.

Miller, D. & Slater, D. (2001). *The internet: An ethnographic approach*. Oxford: Berg Publishers.

Naficy, H. (1993). *The making of exile cultures: Iranian television in Los Angeles*. Minneapolis: University of Minnesota Press.

Østergaard, A., Krogsgaard, J., Lense-Møller, L., Plum, S., Billeskov, J. J., Papapetros, T., Malmqvist, C., Oscilloscope Laboratories (Firm). (2008). *Burma VJ: Reporting from a closed country*. New York: Distributed by Oscilloscope Laboratories.

Rhoads, C. & Chao, L. (2009, June 22). Iran's web spying aided by Western technology. *Wall Street Journal*. Retrieved May 13, 2013 from http://online.wsj.com/article/SB124562668777335653.html

Rivetti, P. & Cavatorta, F. (2012). Iranian student activism between authoritarianism and democratization: Patterns of conflict and cooperation between the office for the strengthening of unity and the regime. *Democratization*, 20(2), 1–22.

Sreberny, A. & Khiabany, G. (2010). *Blogistan: The internet and politics in Iran.* London: I. B. Tauris.

Sreberny-Mohammadi, A. & Mohammadi, A. (1994). *Small media, big revolution.* Minneapolis: University of Minnesota Press.

Wojcieszak, M., Smith, B. & Enayat, M. (2012). *Finding a way: How Iranians reach for news and information. The Iran Media Program's 2011–2012 report on media consumption in Iran.* Philadelphia, PA: Annenberg School for Communication, University of Pennsylvania.

Yaghmaian, B. (2002). *Social change in Iran: An eyewitness account of dissent, defiance, and new movements for rights.* New York: SUNY Press.

LIST OF CONTRIBUTORS

Amro Ali is a PhD scholar at the Department of Government and International Relations, University of Sydney. His research focus is on new spaces of politics in the Egyptian city of Alexandria. He is a graduate of the Australian National University with a Master of Arts in Middle Eastern and Central Asian Studies (with Honors), and a Master of Diplomacy. His writings can be found at www. amroali.com.

Narges Bajoghli is a PhD candidate in Anthropology at New York University. Narges's research focuses on media, revolution, and war, specifically in Iran.

Charis Boutieri is Lecturer in the Social Anthropology of the Middle East at King's College London. Her research so far has delved into the cultural politics of Moroccan public education from independence onwards as these underpin a contemporary experience of learning and the various self-fashioning projects of young Moroccans. She is currently working on a manuscript based on her dissertation entitled, *Learning in Babel: The politics of knowledge and language in Morocco.* She has published in the *International Journal of Middle East Studies* and *Anthropology & Education Quarterly.* She holds a doctorate in Socio-Cultural Anthropology from Princeton University.

Catherine Cornet is a PhD candidate at the University of Rome II and at the École des Hautes Études en Sciences Sociales in Paris. She holds a Master's Degree in Middle Eastern Politics from the School of Oriental and African Studies in London, a diploma in Études Politiques from the Institut d'Études Politiques of Aix-en-Provence and a Maîtrise of Comparative Literature from the University of Provence. For 10 years she has been active in the cultural field as a project manager of various Euro-Mediterranean projects. Her field of research concerns the development of innovative cultural expressions in the Middle East, the links between social networks and creativity, and the role of private foundations in the region.

Miranda Christou (Ed.D. Doctorate in Education, Harvard University, 2002) is an Assistant Professor in Sociology of Education at the University of Cyprus. Her research has explored the role of educational systems in shaping questions of history and collective memory, the pedagogical function of the media in representations of human pain and suffering, and the cultural implications of globalized educational systems.

Chiara Diana is currently a PhD candidate finalizing her thesis dissertation in the social history of Egypt at IREMAM/Aix Marseille University. She obtained a Master's degree in Arab and Middle East Studies from the University of Paris III: Sorbonne Nouvelle. Her major areas of research include education policies and globalization, early-childhood education systems, childhood and youth citizenship and social media in the Middle East.

Dina El-Sharnouby obtained her MA in Sociology/Anthropology from the American University in Cairo. Her main research areas relate to youth groups and movements around the Egyptian revolution. She will start her PhD at the Berlin Graduate School Muslim Cultures and Societies in 2013.

Linda Herrera is a social anthropologist with regional specialization in the Middle East and North Africa. For 17 years she lived in Egypt, where she was involved in research and work in critical ethnography of schooling, the cultural politics of youth, the Islamization of education, and the politics of international development. She held a position as Senior Lecturer of International Development Studies at the International Institute of Social Studies, Erasmus University Rotterdam (2005–2010), and is currently Associate Professor in the Department of Education Policy, Organization and Leadership at the University of Illinois at Urbana-Champaign. Her publications include the forthcoming, *Revolution in the age of social media* (Verso), and the co-edited volumes, *Cultures of Arab schooling: Critical ethnographies from Egypt* and *Being young and Muslim: New cultural politics in the global south and north*. She holds a PhD from Columbia University.

Elena Ioannidou is a Lecturer in Literacy and Applied Linguistics/Sociolinguistics at the University of Cyprus. Her research focuses on issues of language and identity, discourse analysis, multiliteracies, linguistic variation, and language policy. She received her PhD from the University of Southampton in 2003.

Demet Lüküslü is Associate Professor of Sociology at Yeditepe University, Istanbul. She completed her MA and PhD at the École des Hautes Études en Sciences

Sociales in Paris. For her MA and PhD dissertations she conducted research on youth in Turkey. A revised edition of her PhD dissertation was published in Turkish by İletişim Yayınları in 2009: *Türkiye'de Gençlik Miti. 1980 Sonrası Türkiye Gençliği* (The myth of youth in Turkey: The post-1980 youth in Turkey). Her areas of interest include sociology of youth, cultural identity, new social movements, sociology of everyday life, and cultural studies.

Mira Nabulsi holds an MA degree in Peace, Conflict, and Development Studies, and is currently completing a graduate degree in Communication Studies at San Francisco State University. Her research interests include the investigation of communication in social movements, specifically that of Information and Communication Technology (ICT) among Palestinian youth organizing inside Palestine and in the diaspora.

Fauzia Rahman is a doctoral student in the Global Studies in Education program with an Interdisciplinary minor in Gender Relations and International Development at the University of Illinois, Urbana-Champaign. Her research focuses on girls' education, development, geopolitics, and citizenship in northwest Pakistan. She received both her BA in South Asian and Middle Eastern Studies, and MA in Education Policy Studies from the University of Illinois, Urbana-Champaign. In fall of 2013, she will be conducting ethnographic research in the Khyber Pakhtunkhwa province of Pakistan.

Rehab Sakr is an instructor in the Faculty of Economics and Political Science at Cairo University. She received her PhD in Middle Eastern Politics and Technological Studies from Albert Ludwig Universität Freiburg in 2013. Her research interests are technology and politics, social movements, Islamist movements, and Middle Eastern studies.

INDEX